KENNETH
CLATTERBAUGH

THE
CAUSATION
DEBATE
IN MODERN
PHILOSOPHY
1637–1739

ROUTLEDGE
New York London

Published in 1999 by
Routledge
29 West 35th Street
New York, New York 10001

Published in Great Britain by
Routledge
11 New Fetter Lane
London EC4P 4EE

Copyright © 1999 by Routledge

Printed in the United States of America on acid free paper.
Text Design by Debora Hilu

Library of Congress Cataloging-in-Publication Data

Clatterbaugh, Kenneth C.
   The causation dabate in modern philosophy, 1637–1739 / Kenneth
Clatterbaugh.
      p.   cm.
   Includes bibliographycal references and index.
   ISNB 0-415-91476-0 (hardcover). — ISBN 0-415-91477-9 (pbk.)
   1. Causation.   I. Title.
BD541.C47   1999
122'.09'032—dc21   98-17267
                                                                CIP

CONTENTS

ACKNOWLEDGMENTS

Primarily, I wish to thank those students and scholars of modern philosophy who through their careful scholarship have uncovered the details of this debate. There are too many to mention by name. Certainly, Margaret Wilson deserves special thanks; repeatedly, she has called our attention to the importance of the causation debate in modern philosophy, and without the excellence of her scholarship, books like this one would be impossible. Wesley Salmon first taught me some of the complexity of thinking about causation. Other scholars, who have made so many major contributions, are cited in the text. My thanks to my students Nick Serafimidis, Marc Bobro, and Jack Harris for their contributions as students, scholars, and researchers. And, finally, thanks to Roger Woolhouse, Daniel Garber, Eileen O'Neill, Robert Sleigh, Jr., and Steven Nadler for their inspirational scholarship.

EDITIONS AND ABBREVIATIONS

Aristotle
B   Jonathan Barnes, ed. 1984. *The Complete Works of Aristotle,* 2 vols. Princeton: Princeton University Press. Cited by page.

Saint Thomas Aquinas
ACP Anton C. Pegis, trans. and ed. 1945. *The Basic Writing of Saint Thomas Aquinas,* 2 vols. New York: Random House. Cited by volume and page.

Descartes
CSM John Cottingham, Robert Stoothoff, Dugald Murdoch andAnthony Kenny, trans. and eds. 1985©1992. *The "Philosophical Writings of Descartes",* 3 vols. Cambridge: Cambridge University Press. Cited by volume and page.

O   Paul J Olscamp, trans. 1965. *Discourse on Method, Optics, Geometry, and Meteorology.* Indianapolis and New York: Bobbs©Merrill.

Gassendi
G   Craig B. Brush, trans. and ed. 1972. *The Selected Works "of Pierre Gassendi.* New York: Johnson Reprint

Hobbes
MO Sir William Molesworth, ed. 1839. *The English Works of "Thomas Hobbes of Malmesbury",* 11 vols. London: Bohn. Cited by volume and page

CU   E. M. Curley, ed. 1994. *Thomas Hobbes: Leviathan.* Indianapolis/Cambridge: Hackett..

C   Mary Whiton Calkins. ed. 1948. *The Metaphysical System of Hobbes in Twelve Chapters from* **Elements of Philosophy concerning Body** *Together with Briefer Extracts from Human Nature and Levoathon. La Salle, Ill.:* Open Court

Le Grand

LG   Anthony Le Grand 1694. *An Entire Body of Philosophy, according to the Principles of the Famous Renate de Cartes in Three Books: I. The Institution, II. The History of Nature, III. The Dissertation of the Want of Sense and Knowledge*. London: Samuel Roycroft. Cited by book, part, chapter, and page.

Malebranche

D   Willis Doney, trans. 1980. *Nicolas Malebranche: Entretiens sur la Metaphysique* (Dialogues on Metaphysics). New York: Abaris.

LO   Thomas M. Lennon and Paul J. Olscamp, trans. 1980. *Malebranche: The Search after Truth/Elucidations of the Search after Truth*, Columbus: Ohio State University Press.

R   Patrick Riley, trans. 1992. *Treatise on Nature and Grace*. Oxford: Clarendon.

Spinoza

EMC E. M. Curley, trans. and ed. 1985. *The Collected Works of Spinoza*, vol. 1. Princeton, Princeton University Press.

E   R. H. M. Elwes, trans. 1883. *The Chief Works of Spinoza*, 2 vols. London: Bell (reprinted 1951. New York: Dover).

Leibniz

AG   Roger Ariew and Daniel Garber, trans. and eds. 1989. *G. W. Leibniz: Philosophical Essays*, Indianapolis and Cambridge: Hackett.

LL   Leroy L. Loemker, trans. and ed. 1969. *Leibniz:'Philosophical Papers and Letters*, 2nd ed. Dordtecht™Holland: Reidel.

RB   Peter Remnant and Jonathan Bennett, trans. and eds. 1981. *G. W. Leibniz: New Essays on Human Understanding*. Cambridge: Cambridge University Press.

FH   Austin Farrer, ed., and E. M. Huggard, trans. 1990. *Theodicy: Essays on the Goodness of God and Freedom of Man and the Origin of Evil*. La Salle, Ill.: Open Court.

Rohault

RS   John and Samuel Clarke, ed. and trans. 1723. *Rohault's System of Natural Philosophy, with S. Clarke's notes* (reprinted 1969. New York: Johnson Reprint). Cited by part, chapter, page.

Boyle

S   M. A. Stewart, ed. 1979. *Selected Philosophical Papers of Robert Boyle.* Manchester and New York: Manchester University Press and Barnes & Noble.

Newton

MC   Andrew Motte, trans. 1729 and Florian Cajori, ed. 1934. *Issac Newton: Mathematical Principles of Natural Philosophy.* Berkeley and London: University ofCalifornia Press and Cambridge University Press.

TH   H. S. Thayer, ed. 1953. *Newton's Philosophy of Nature: Selections from his Writings.* New York: Hafner.

Locke

N   Peter H. Nidditch, ed. 1975. *John Locke: An Essay concerning Human Understanding.* Oxford: Clendon.

Berkeley

LJ   A. A. Luce and T. E. Jessop, eds. 1948. *The Works of George Berkeley Bishop of Cloyne.* London: Nelson. Cited by volume and page.

DJ   Douglas M. Jesseph, ed. and trans. 1992. *George Berkeley, De Motu, and The Analyst.* Dordrecht, Boston, and London: Kluwer.

Hume

EHU L. A. Selby-Bigg, ed. 1902. *David Hume: An Enquiry concerning Human Understanding,* 3d ed. rev. by P. H. Nidditch. Oxford: Clarendon.

T   L. A. Selby-Bigge, ed. 1888. *David Hume: A Treatise of 'Human Nature,* 2d ed rev. by P. H. Nidditch. Oxford: Clarendon.

1.
The Debate

There is no question, which on account of its importance, as well as diffi-culty, has caus'd more disputes both among ancient and modern philoso-phers, than this concerning the efficacy of causes, or that quality which made them be followed by their effects. (T, 156)

Abstract?
– ₰

Treatments of causality in seventeenth-century philosophy present the interpreter with a peculiar problem. On the one hand, the notion of causality is central to the period's major positions and disputes in metaphysics and epistemology. On the other hand, few of the most prominent figures of the period enter into detailed or precise accounts of the relation of causal depen-dence or causal connection. (Wilson 1991, 133)

THE PROJECT

In our contemporary world, scientists seek causes; philosophers talk about causation. Scientists use causes to explain phenomena, whereas philoso-phers try to understand the nature of causation. At the same time contempo-rary philosophers, too, use causation to answer a variety of questions in phi-losophy of science, epistemology, philosophy of language, and ethics. For example, many philosophers understand scientific explanations as causal accounts of why changes occur, and they interpret natural laws as expressing causal relationships. The meaning of names, descriptions, and even the possi-bility of knowledge may depend upon how the world is causally structured. What things can do causally is sometimes treated as an indispensable part of collecting them into categories or natural kinds. And, finally, contemporary

Epistemology? JTB?

philosophers of ethics hold that knowing what is causally possible is crucial to deciding what we ought to do since we are not bound to do what we cannot (causally) do.

As Wilson notes in the above passage, the concept of causation is also central to the writings of seventeenth- and eighteenth-century philosophers (the modern period). Yet the emphasis in modern philosophy courses tends to be epistemological: beginning with the *Meditations*, the question that unfolds is how the rationalists and empiricists respond to the skeptical challenge. However, the nature of causation immediately intrudes itself into these epistemological discussions. Descartes, in the *Meditations*, begins his quest for knowledge beyond himself with a causal proof for the existence of God, a proof that makes key assumptions about the nature of causation. And Spinoza, in one of the first axioms of the *Ethics*, makes knowledge of something dependent on knowledge of its cause (EMC, 410). Beyond these immediate epistemological concerns, modern philosophers continue to worry about the nature of causation and to use the causal connection to solve a variety of philosophical puzzles.

Perhaps, in appreciation of the philosophical centrality of causation in this period, there is now a growing body of secondary literature about causation in the modern period. This literature, however, remains atomized, and attention to shared concerns about causation among the major thinkers of the seventeenth and eighteenth centuries is often overlooked in favor of articulating a particular philosopher's understanding of causation.[1]

There are a couple of obvious reasons for scholars' delay in turning to the causation debate in modern philosophy. First, Descartes, who plays such an important role as a founder of this debate, is notoriously obscure in his remarks about the nature of causation, and this obscurity tends to infect the entire debate. Second, there are so many distinct threads in this debate that any effort to gather them into a continuous account of the debate is difficult and frustrating. But just as we gain a certain perspective on the philosophies of this period by looking at their struggle with skepticism or their transformation of the concept of substance, so we gain a unique perspective if we focus on their general concern with causation.

This book is an introductory overview of the modern debate about causation. The dates selected for this debate span the years 1637, when Descartes published his *Discourse on the Method, with Optics, Meteorology and Geometry*, to 1739, when Hume published *A Treatise on Human Nature*. Descartes represents the beginnings of the modern concern about causation, and he makes a conscious effort to transform philosophical thinking about causation. Hume, on the other hand, represents the culmination of several tendencies in the debate, especially the simplification, secularization, and epistemological treat-ment of causation. Although this book offers an introduction to the debate, it includes several of my own observations about crucial issues within the debate; these observations may be of interest to more advanced scholars of this period.

Throughout this book my treatment of the debate is built around two grand problems.

The first is *the metaphysical problem of causation*. Sleigh describes this prob-lem as an attempt "to state what conditions obtain at the level of ultimate metaphysical reality when causal statements are employed" (1990b, 163). Suppose, for example, that a modern philosopher thought that when an oven (a substance) bakes bread (a substance), it warms the bread through the trans-fer or communication of heat (an accident) to the bread—that would be one example of how causation works at the metaphysical level. Such an account of causation obviously makes numerous assumptions about the kinds of enti-ties that exist and how they relate to one another.

The second grand problem is *the epistemology of causation*. This grand prob-lem has two subproblems. The first is obviously how we can know what goes on at the metaphysical level. And a failure to show that the metaphysics of causa-tion can be known may translate into an abandonment of that metaphysical view. Thus, the early moderns, for example, reject Scholastic accounts of causa-tion in part because the explanatory principles—substantial forms—are not knowable. But a second epistemological problem of causation is how we know that an *apparent* causal interaction is a genuine causal interaction. Obviously, unless we can correctly identify causal connections, we do not know where to apply the metaphysical analysis. Furthermore, since modern philosophers gen-erally hold that causes explain effects, until there are ways to recognize genuine causal interactions, there is no way to distinguish genuine explanations from pseudoexplanations. For modern philosophers, who seek to understand the material and mental worlds, identifying true or proper causes is necessary in order to make the universe intelligible.

Not all modern philosophers discussed in this essay are concerned with giv-ing what Sleigh calls the "metaphysically correct" account of what happens when two things are related as cause and effect (Sleigh 1990b, 163). But if they do not offer a positive account of their own, they, at least, are clear about which accounts they consider to be incorrect. And they often try to formulate episte-mological criteria by which true or proper causal processes can be demarcated from pseudocausal processes. Their examples of purported causal processes are often mundane ones, such as the baking of bread, the sun melting wax, a per-son voluntarily raising her arm, or one body pushing or pulling another.

However, as modern science becomes more successful, the examples become more complex and the importance of making one's account of causation agree with scientific examples increases.

Throughout the approximately one hundred years of the debate three great transformations occur in the thinking about the nature of causation. First, the concept is greatly simplified; second, it is secularized; and third the problem of identifying true or proper causal connections replaces philosophical concern about the metaphysical problem of causation. In the simplification process, many complexities and ambiguities are abandoned. The moderns discard talk about the four causes in favor of explanations in terms of efficient causation only. Hume takes it as a corollary of his definition of cause that "all causes are of the same kind" (EHU, 156). Furthermore, causes are no longer seen as logically or metaphysically necessary to their effects, and, accordingly, effects do not have to preexist in their causes. The ambiguity between cause-as-thing and cause-as-premise in a scientific explanation lessens as modern philosophers sharpen the distinction between language and the world. The secularization of the concept of cause is complete by 1739; in Hume's philosophy, God ceases to be the paradigm of a true cause and becomes irrelevant to proper causal explanations. Third, and finally, interest in the metaphysical problem of causation wanes because it is increasingly seen as an insoluble problem of little importance. At the same time, science prevails over metaphysics; *the* paramount philosophical conception of cause becomes that which is so identified in an accepted scientific explanation.

In part, these changes in thinking about causation are motivated by a growing success in understanding and controlling nature. Francis Bacon realized in 1620 that "human knowledge and human power meet in one; for where the cause is not known the effect cannot be reproduced. Nature to be commanded must be obeyed; and that which in contemplation is as the cause, is in operation as the rule" (Bacon 1620, 3). If God is the real cause of natural changes, then understanding nature becomes more difficult and controlling nature becomes impossible; even the early modern Hobbes cites such concerns for removing the "doctrine of God" from knowledge of cause and effect (MO I, 10). Further, if cause and effect are metaphysically or logically linked, then given that the initial state of the universe is already set, control of natural processes again becomes impossible. Both understanding and control of nature, however, depend directly upon the correct identification of causal processes as does the all-important experimental philosophy that emerges with Boyle and Newton. Thus, the focus on identification of genuine causal processes fits tightly with the search for understanding and control over diseases, bodies in motion, and other critical problems that are the ultimate goals of natural philosophy.

Metaphors that contribute to the belief that causal processes can be identified and controlled become increasingly common; nature is a machine, often like a clock (Freudenthal 1986, 53–55; Laudan 1966). Clocks are understood, their causal workings, whether by springs or pendulums, are known, and they can be repaired and adjusted. (Some theistic philosophers even hope to gain insight into the nature of the creator by understanding his clock.) "Mechanism" or "the mechanical philosophy" is often used to describe the seventeenth-century view of nature as a machine. But "mechanism" is only a direction in thinking about causation that appears at this time; as we shall see, there are many seventeenth-century "mechanical philosophies." They all share an anti-Scholastic metaphysics, but in other respects they differ metaphysically and epistemologically. Metaphysically, some (classical mechanists) hold strictly to a push-pull model of causation at least in the physical world. Some mechanist metaphysics are wholly materialistic, others are only partially materialistic. Some admit forces of repulsion and attraction as basic forces of nature. Some believe that causation in the microworld, the world below sense perception, is precisely the same as that in the macro world of ordinary perceptual objects, while others posit special processes below the threshold of the senses. Ultimately, in order to determine the extent to which the one hundred years of this period may be identified as mechanistic, there must be a philosophically satisfactory explication of the various mechanical philosophies. And as McGuire notes, "no adequate analysis of the various meanings of 'the mechanical philosophy' has yet been given" (McGuire 1972, 523). That task lies beyond the scope of this book, although it is hoped that a better understanding of the causation debate will contribute toward that end.

Three arenas of discussion dominate the modern debate about causation, although they are not all equally important to every participant in the debate:

The first is how to explain metaphysically the apparent interaction between bodies. Physics is the science of the day, and the laws of motion dominate much of that science. Early modern philosophers quickly came to agree on a generalized understanding of inertia, that is, they agree that a body at rest will remain at rest unless acted upon and a body in motion will continue in motion in a straight line (or, in some cases, in a circle) unless acted upon (Dijksterhuis 1961, 366; Gabbey 1980; Woolhouse 1993, 102-103). But while this concept of inertia ended certain of the most pressing issues as to why bodies continue in motion or at rest, it immediately suggests that there are causes (external forces) that explain why bodies change direction and accelerate or decelerate. In Gabbey's words several modern philosophers and scientists came to view the dynamic world as one in which "interactions between bodies were seen as contests between opposing forces, the larger forces being the winners, the smaller forces being the losers. . ... Furthermore, it was held that the resultant forces continue indefinitely in the absence of further collisions . . ." (1980, 243).

Once the arena of physical dynamics is identified as one of forces that change or alter rest or direction, philosophers and scientists debate on two levels. At one level they disagree about the laws of motion, how to formulate them, and what is conserved in motion (Dijksterhuis 1961; Woolhouse 1993, 102-33). At another level, the metaphysical level, they disagree about what the motive force (*vis movens*) is and through what processes that force is distributed throughout the world of dynamic bodies (Gueroult 1980, Hatfield 1990). The first level of disagreement, the scientific debate, is relevant to our project only to the extent that it throws light upon the second, which is where the two great problems of causation are most apparent.

The second arena is the debate about how to explain the correlations between mind and body. None of the modern philosophers deny that there is a "connection" between mind and body. They do question the nature of that connection, that is, whether it is a causal interaction or some other kind of relation. The mind-body connection, itself, divides into two subissues: (1) the relationship of minds to bodies and (2) the relationship of bodies to minds. Some moderns treat the former, but not the latter, as a causal connection; some deny that either is a genuine causal interaction; and some hold that both are causal interactions. Mind-body interaction is a particular problem if mind and body are very different kinds of things; thus, some philosophers embrace a monism that posits only one kind of substance, and in that way try to dissolve the problem. Later modern scientist-philosophers such as Boyle and Newton tend to move the whole issue of mind-body interaction outside of scientific discourse. Their focus then is on the causal connections and scientific explanations of the physical or material world.

The third arena is a set of questions as to how to divide up the causal network between God and God's creations. For the most part modern philosophers do not doubt that it makes sense to speak of God as the creator and at least a partial cause of everything, although they do not claim to understand fully the nature of God's causal powers, and they describe God's role in different ways. But since God is a cause of everything and since they, for the most part, also believe that created things are causes, some determination of the relationship between God and these finite causes is needed. Does God enjoy a prolonged retirement after creation while his creatures do the work? Do God and created things collaborate in producing change in the world? Does God do it all, while created things only serve as epistemic guides to what happens next? Each of these questions was answered in the affirmative by some modern philosopher. Furthermore, if God is a causal factor in producing various changes, how much about God must be understood or included in a proper explanation of these changes? Since there are sharp disagreements about the epistemological accessibility of God, the inclusion of God in any explanations brings with it controversy about just how intelligible the universe really is. At the same time, there is a major shift in the debate in this arena. The early moderns, with the exception of Hobbes, hold that some knowledge of God is critical to understanding nature and natural laws. The later moderns generally dismiss God as a part of scientific understanding but hold, at the same time, that understanding nature is a good way to gain an understanding of God.

Lying behind their efforts to solve the issues in these arenas is a multiple legacy derived from Aristotle and the Scholastics. From Aristotle comes the idea that proper explanations are in terms of the actual causes of things and that there are four kinds of causation. In Aristotle these causes appear in the scientific syllogisms that are used to explain phenomena. The Scholastics reinforced these Aristotelian ideas and add the theological thesis that God is the true author (creator) of everything (see Wallace 1972 I).

While many of the early modern philosophers accept the division of causation into four types, they abandon the metaphysics of substance, essence, and accident that underlies that division. At the same time they must abandon the Aristotelian/Scholastic model of a proper causal explanation. Having the Aristotelian/Scholastic legacy without its ontology makes the labor of reconstructing a theory of causation even more herculean. From Aristotelian/Scholastic philosophy moderns inherited the idea that God is an active cause in His creation; modern philosophers, who would keep God as a cause, must explain how they can retain their new-found, scientific explanations of phenomena, explanations that often do not refer to God. Their dilemma is obvious. On the one hand, if God is a true cause of everything; then the new scientific explanations are not proper explanations. On the other hand, if the new scientific explanations are proper, then God is not a true cause of everything. Most of the debate from Descartes through Hume centers around how modern philosophers can free themselves of this legacy and whether one philosopher is more successful than another in that task. Ultimately, the legacy of Aristotelian/Scholasticism is jettisoned in favor of explanations without God, substantial forms, or even substances.

A great many philosophers participate in this debate. This essay does not pretend to exhaust every contribution of every philosopher; instead, I seek to reveal "the big picture" by highlighting certain figures. Among the early debaters I include Descartes, Hobbes, Gassendi, Le Grand, Malebranche, Spinoza, and Leibniz. The lesser-known Anthony Le Grand is included because his philosophy provides a bridge from Descartes to Malebranche and Locke. Among the later debaters, Hume is treated as most significant, but Berkeley and Locke certainly deserve mention. The activity of science and the activity of philosophy were less distinct in the seventeenth and eighteenth centuries than they are today; many of those named were philosophers as well as scientists; even the "pure" philosophers read the science of their day. But there is another category among the moderns better described as scientist-philosophers, those whose major contribution is to science but who through their scientific work substantially contribute to the philosophical debate about causation. Indeed, much of the causation debate is a matter of adjustment between an emerging philosophy and an emerging science. Scientists must adjust their thinking to the philosophical conditions placed on causation, and philosophers must adjust their views on the nature of causation to the newest scientific explanations. Accordingly, I include a chapter on the contributions of Boyle, Rohault, and Newton, three scientist-philosophers who help to direct the debate in new and scientifically useful directions.

Of course, within each group there are other figures who may only be mentioned, but whom other scholars view as deserving of more attention than they receive in this book. There is always more than one way to tell a story, and I would encourage anyone who would identify different protagonists in this debate to tell their story as well. For an issue as complex as the modern debate about causation there is a need for multiple versions of this history.

Roughly speaking, the debate has three stages, namely, the early debate (roughly the second third of the seventeenth century), the scientific impact (the last third of the seventeenth century), and the later debate (the first third of the eighteenth century). In the early debate, philosophers are preoccupied with the metaphysical problem of causation and how to resolve it against the deep legacy of the Aristotelian/ Scholastic tradition. The scientific impact through the efforts of Rohault, Boyle, and Newton diminishes metaphysical speculations about causation and makes successful scientific explanation the principle criterion of accepting something as a cause. The late debate accepts many of the conclusions that come from the previous stages. At this stage the Aristotelian/Scholastic legacy is abandoned, but so is the metaphysical problem of causation. The late moderns, particularly Hume, take the problem of causation back from science but shift the emphasis to the question of how to identify genuine causal connections. But this abandonment of the metaphysical problem carries with it its own risks; once one gives up trying to say what causation is, any effort to simply identify true causal connections becomes problematic. How can one identify that for which there is no clear metaphysical conception?

I use the word "debate" to refer to the modern discussions because the thinkers in this period possess a clear sense of the ideas of their near contemporaries. When possible, they correspond with one another. And many participants write essays in direct response to the writings of others. It is this level of engagement that makes "debate" seem the appropriate term.

In the end this story contains some ironies. For example, the seventeenth century begins with a notion of cause that is so metaphysically restricted that it is useless, or nearly so, in scientific explanation. The occasionalist philosophers of this period reach the conclusion that given these conditions on causation, only God can be a real cause. In the late seventeenth century, most of these restrictions are removed; in fact, so many have been removed that the extension of the concept becomes too generous, thereby also limiting its usefulness to scientific explanation. It has been an ongoing problem of twentieth-century philosophy of science to find ways of restricting the too generous notion that emerges from this debate.

A second irony is that mechanism, which arose in part in an effort to offer a particular kind of view of causation free of occult forces, proves so inadequate to the task that either it is abandoned in favor of "occult forces" or, as happened in the late debate, philosophers completely abandon the metaphysical task of providing any account of how causation works.

A final irony is that Descartes, who is often identified as the father of modern philosophy and founder of the mechanistic philosophy, initially won out in the struggle for prominence and influence against other mechanists such as Gassendi and Hobbes (Lennon [1993a] calls this the battle between Gods and giants). But in the crucial debate about causation Descartes's views take a beating; they are abandoned in a wholesale fashion both by those who continue to call themselves Cartesians and by those who reject Cartesianism. The view of causation at the end of the debate is much closer to that of Descartes's antagonists, Gassendi and Hobbes, than it is to that of Descartes himself.

A DUAL LEGACY: ARISTOTLE AND THE SCHOLASTICS

Aristotle

In the *Physics* Aristotle notes that the number of causes is the same as "the number of things comprehended under the question 'why'" (B, 338). In summary form he identifies the four causes as "the matter, the form, the mover, that for the sake of which," or, more simply, the material cause, the formal cause, the efficient cause, and the final cause (B, 338). Aristotle offers almost identical accounts of the four causes in the *Physics*, the *Generation of Animals*, and the *Metaphysics*.

The doctrine of the four causes is used by Aristotle to explain change—either the coming into being of a substance or the alteration of a substance (compare Wallace 1971, 1972, I, 13–15). It matters not whether the substance is a natural thing such as a human or an artificial thing such as a statue. In every change there are four causes: the *material* cause is that out of which a thing is made. Natural things are made out of the four elements of earth, air, fire, and water; the statue may be made of bronze or marble (B, 334). The *formal* cause is the essence of a thing, those properties without which it could not continue to exist. The formal cause preexists in the *efficient* cause, or the maker of the thing that comes to be. Efficient causes are always particular substances; thus, the father is the efficient cause of a human, whereas the sculptor is the efficient cause of the statue (B, 334) The *final* cause is the telos (end or purpose) of the thing. In the case of natural things the end is often nothing more than the realization of its form or essence (B, 339–40). Thus, formal and final causes are especially likely to be one and the same. And in some cases all the causes coincide in a single entity: the *essence* (B, 1111).

As in other cases of change, the movement of a body must also have four causes. Yet much of Aristotle's discussion of motion focuses on a search for the efficient cause of motion, the *motor.* The motions of bodies may be either natural or enforced. The natural motion of heavy bodies (associated with the elements earth and water) is to move toward Earth (the natural center of the universe); the natural motion of lighter bodies (associated with the elements air and fire) is to move up or away from Earth (Aristotle, *On the Heavens*; Dijksterhuis 1961, 27). In natural motions the efficient cause is in the body itself. And in living things, Aristotle tells us in *Physics* VII, the animate soul produces local motion. Inanimate bodies that are not undergoing natural motion must have an external mover, an efficient cause, that is acting on them in order to keep them in motion. This mover is distinct from the change of place (*motus localis*) which the body undergoes (Dijksterhuis 1961, 21). Thus, for Aristotle there is no inertia (*vis inertiae*), that is, bodies do not continue in motion (or rest) unless acted upon by an external cause; bodies that continue in motion (or rest) are being acted upon by an efficient cause. Ultimately, for Aristotle, the chain of efficient causes terminates in primary movers; movers that can produce motion in other things without having motion in themselves (B, 343; B, 1695).

But Aristotle's account of motion left serious questions for Scholastic and modern students of physics. Why do bodies accelerate when falling? How does the spear-thrower transmit motion to the spear once it leaves the hand? In short, identifying the efficient cause in many cases of motion is difficult or impossible within Aristotelian physics (Dijksterhuis 1961, 27–28).

Theoretical knowledge—knowledge pursued for its own sake—is divided by the subjects of knowledge. Physics looks at things that can change, and explanations in physics take the form of explanatory syllogisms whose premises state the causes. Something is not known until the "why" of it is grasped (B, 332). In some cases an explanation of a change is given in terms of something else which produces that change, for example, the efficient cause. In other cases the explanation is not in terms of something else; for example, the formal cause of growth in a plant is the realization of its own form (B, 154). And only some syllogisms are explanatory of *why* phenomena occur—these are properly causal and, hence, explanatory. Others simply establish *that* phenomenon occurred.

> But if it is not possible for things to be explanatory of one another (for the explanation is prior to what it is explanatory of), and the earth's being in the middle is explanatory of the eclipse, but the eclipse is not explanatory of the earth's being in the middle—so if the demonstration through the explanation gives the fact, you know that it is in the middle but not why. And that the eclipse is not explanatory of its being in the middle but the latter of the eclipse is evident: for its being in the middle belongs in the account of the eclipse; so that it is clear that the latter becomes familiar through the former and not the former through the latter. (B, 163)

In explanatory syllogisms it is the middle term which links the subject and predicate of the conclusion (B, 156–57)

> And why did the Persian war come upon the Athenians? What is the explanation of the Athenians' being warred upon? Because they attacked Sardis with the Eretrians; for that initiated the change. War, A; being the first to attack, B; Athenians, C. Thus B belongs to C (being the first to attack to the Athenians), and A to B (for men make war on those who have first done them wrong). . . . Therefore here too the explanation, what initiated the change, is a middle term. (B, 156).

Aristotle's views on causation had a far-reaching effect in the causation debate of the seventeenth and eighteenth centuries. His view that there were four types of causation becomes a focal point of the early debate concerning the number of kinds of causes. Aristotle's idea that the efficient cause is a particular substance creates considerable mischief throughout much of the debate, since it runs counter to modern scientific explanations that typically identify states of substances as the (efficient) cause. Aristotle views explanations as deductively inferential, and those inferences are syllogistic. Some early modern philosophers, specifically Hobbes and Descartes, retain the idea that explanations are deductively inferential, but both reject syllogistic argument patterns; consequently, they have to formulate their own theories of inference. In Aristotle the form of a thing that comes to be must *preexist* in the efficient cause; thus the form of the statue exists in the mind of the sculptor. A version of this causal principle is retained by the early moderns in spite of the fact that they have given the principle an entirely new metaphysical meaning, since they unanimously reject substantial forms in the Aristotelian or Scholastic sense.

For Aristotle some causes are *prior* to that which they explain and some are *simultaneous* with it; thus the letters of the alphabet are simultaneous with the syllables they cause, whereas the builder is prior to the house (B, 333). The early moderns, too, thought that efficient causes could be either simultaneous with or prior to their effects. As the interest in prediction and control becomes even more dominant, however, causes are treated by the late moderns as prior to their effects.

Finally, Aristotle allows an equivocation on "cause" (*aitia* or *causa*) which is retained by the Scholastic philosophers, the early moderns, and even, occasionally, by scientist-philosophers. Throughout Aristotle's writing the middle term and the thing which it represents are both said to *explain* the effect or the conclusion. Thus, cause is used to stand both for things in the world—things that have properties and act or are acted upon—and for premises in a causal explanation that have consequences and entailments (compare Grene 1963). In Aristotle, all "sciences come about through definition," the discovery of middle terms (B, 164). And middle terms are also taken as the causes which explain why. For example, the shedding of leaves is explained by the middle term (formal cause), namely, the solidifying of sap at the connection of the seed (B, 164). Perhaps no other Aristotelian doctrine has a greater impact on the causation debate in modern philosophy than Aristotle's willingness to count both middle terms *and* physical things as explanatory causes without drawing a sharp distinction between them (see Gaukroger 1989, 16-17). This doctrine has a consequence which also plays a major role in the debate, since premises are necessary to their conclusions, and causes are premises and conclusions are effects, it makes it easier to defend the view that causes are necessarily linked to their effects—a position against which Hume is in full rebellion.

The Scholastics

Scholastic philosophers such as St. Thomas Aquinas generally endorsed Aristotle's doctrine of the four causes. But, for these Scholastics, God replaces the unmoved mover(s) (ACP II, 113). In the *Summa Theologica* Aquinas notes that God is the efficient cause of all things, a point on which Suarez says that all Catholics agree (ACP I, 426-28; Suarez 1597a, 113). God acts by knowledge and will, which are identical and contain "the effective power of God" (ACP I, 260). The introduction of an all-powerful being, who is the efficient cause of all things and who is efficacious merely by an act of will introduces a difficulty, which Aquinas summarizes in the *Summa Contra Gentiles* as follows:

> If God produces the whole natural effect, nothing of the effect is left for the natural agent to produce. Therefore, it seems impossible that God produce the same effects as natural things. (ACP II, 129)

Medieval philosophers respond to this difficulty in one of three ways (compare Suarez 1597a, 124–27). For some, God is only the first cause, the being who brings the universe at the time of the initial creation and sustains it, but all changes and motions (except miracles) in the world after the initial creation are the immediate effects of created things. This view I shall refer to as *deism*; it makes God's involvement in the world minimal. A second broad category is Scholastic *occasionalism*. In this view the distinction between God and secondary causes is metaphysically unimportant, since God's will is the immediate cause of the creation and everything which happens thereafter. A third view, which tries to chart a course between deism and occasionalism is *concurrentism* (Shannahan 1990). This is the view of Thomas Aquinas and probably of Suarez. According to concurrentism, "the same effect is ascribed to a natural cause and to God, not as though part were effected by God and part by the natural agent; but the whole effect proceeds from each" (ACP II, 130). The metaphor typically used by concurrentists is that God is the craftsman whose instruments are created things and their properties; thus, both God and created things are among the immediate causes of any noninitial change (ACP II, 129; Suarez 1597a, 135). Many of the moderns are also concurrentists, but for these thinkers God's concurrence comes to mean that God *preserves* the secondary substances that cause changes in other secondary substances.

With the introduction of God as cause—not to mention other higher spiritual beings such as angels—scholastic philosophers introduce the further problem of how to talk about the metaphysics of the actions of these higher or more perfect beings on the lower or less perfect beings. To this end, Aquinas and others introduce an influx model according to which what moves from cause to effect is a likeness or replica, causes are ontologically superior to their effects, and the effect coexists with its cause (O'Neill 1993, 36). To these conditions, O'Neill notes, the Scholastic influx model adds that the influx "does not take place through a contact of surfaces," "there is no time at which the influx takes place," and "there is no locus of influx" (1993, 37) These latter features make the influx model particularly inappropriate as a model for the interactions of temporally and spatially bound individuals.

Thus, while the Scholastic philosophers generally restricted influx theory to an account of how God and higher beings such as angels interact with the mundane world, late Scholastics and early moderns modified the model so that it would be more appropriate to created things (O'Neill 1993). Generally, modern philosophers do not attempt to answer the metaphysical problem of causation for God and higher beings, but they accept as given that God is a first and sustaining cause.

Some Scholastics, Walter Burley, for example, hold that in motion there were two things, namely, the change of place and the "forces" (*fluxus formae*) that produce changes of place and are distinct from either the body moved or its locations (Wallace 1971, 1972 I, 57). William Ockham, who tries to avoid talking about influxes, denies that motion was anything except change of place (Wallace 1971, I, 55). Roger Bacon holds that in perception the object of perception gives off a species which is a corporeal likeness of the object, a *defluxus* (O'Neill 1993, 45-49). And the early mechanists such as Hobbes, Gassendi, and Charleton develop their own influx models of causation within the physical realm (O'Neill 1993: 42-43). Later scientist-philosophers hold considerable debate on whether there are influences and of what kind—some allow only a physical sharing while other posit attractive and repulsive forces.

Aristotle, as we have noted, often treats causation as involving something passing from cause to effect; this intuitive notion of causation was defended in various influx models by the Scholastics and taken up as a way to conceptualize causal connections by the early moderns. The claim that in causation something is communicated was especially attractive in the case of transitive change wherein one thing acts upon another (Des Chene 1996, 41). Such a view of change is particularly supported by theories of impetus such as those of Jean Buridan in which impetus is conceived as a property that can be transmitted from a cause to an effect—movement of a ship gives impetus to all objects on the ship. Once transmitted, an impetus can become a permanent property (inertia), which survives other actions upon it (Wallace 1972, I, 104-11).

Scholastic philosophy, although hardly monolithic, transmitted other Aristotelian doctrines more or less intact, including the conflation of the cause-as-thing and the cause-as-premise of an explanatory argument (Des Chene 1996). For example, in his commentary on the *Posterior Analytics*, Thomas Aquinas speaks of "a demonstration whose middle is a cause" (Thomas Aquinas 1970, 192). Aquinas also notes that arguments proceed from the cause (*causa*) to the effect (*effet*); others from the effect to the cause (Thomas Aquinas 1970, 228-29). Thus the notion of cause, inherited by the early moderns, could be either a substance capable of acting (by emitting an influx) or a premise describing that substance in an explanatory inference, and an effect could be either a substance being acted upon (by an influx from another substance) or the conclusion or entailment from a scientific premise.

KEY THEMES OF THE CAUSATION DEBATE, 1637–1739

The causation debate is a maze of metaphysical and epistemological paths and dead ends. It is useful, therefore, to have in mind some key propositions that serve as compass points in the debate. We will return to these themes in each chapter:

(1) There are four kinds of causation—material, efficient, formal, and final.
(2) Forms preexist in efficient causes.
(3) Causation requires that something is "communicated" from the cause to the effect.
(4) Proper explanations are deductively inferential.
(5) Cause and effect are necessarily linked.
(6) Causes and effects are substances.
(7) Some substances are active (self-moving causes).
(8) Causation may be instantaneous.
(9) Proper explanations are in terms of the true or proper causes of change.
(10) God is the total efficient cause of everything.

Each of these key propositions is abandoned in the course of the debate; only proposition (9) survives by the end of the debate, but what counts as true or proper cause is significantly changed by 1739.

2.
Descartes: The Metaphysics of Causation

PLACE IN THE DEBATE

René Descartes (1596–1650) is the acknowledged founder and inspiration for the causation debate. Throughout the debate the participants refer to him as the "famous," "the epitome of all," and a person of "such a singular genius, that he alone discovered more philosophical truths, than ever were discovered in all foregoing ages" (LG Preface; RS Preface; Charleton 1654, 3). Descartes corresponded with Hobbes and Gassendi. Le Grand and Rohault were openly his disciples. Malebranche and Spinoza count themselves as Cartesians. Even Newton was a Cartesian for many years. Boyle counts Descartes as the founder of the mechanical philosophy and regularly refers to him as the "ingenious" or "excellent" (S, 10, 14). And Leibniz's own thinking about causation was dramatically spurred by his visit to Paris in the 1640s where he learned of the writings of Descartes and the occasionalists. Only in the late stages of the debate does Descartes lose some of his luster, but by that time his ideas and positions are so imbedded that the late moderns (Berkeley, Locke, and Hume) constantly concern themselves with ideas that are essentially Cartesian in origin.

In many ways Descartes's works set the paradigm for the entire debate. Descartes directly addresses the metaphysical problem of causation and offers an alternative model of a causal explanation. Descartes, above all, struggles to free discussions of causation and the knowledge of causation from the legacy of Aristotle and Scholasticism (compare Garber 1988). He focuses the debate on efficient causation. And having discussed the nature of causation, Descartes does not hesitate to use that discussion to address a variety of philosophical topics in metaphysics, epistemology, and theology (Voss 1993). For example, in the "Third Meditation" Descartes concludes that he is not alone by arguing that only a being such as God could *cause* in us the idea of a perfect being. In both the "Fourth Meditation" and the "Sixth Meditation," Descartes argues that we can trust clear and distinct ideas as well as many ideas about the material world because we have a strong inclination to believe that our ideas are like their purported causes. (If ideas were caused in us by anything that did not resemble them, God would be a deceiver for giving us such an inclination.) Finally, Descartes's discussion of the three central problems—body-body interaction, mind-body interaction, and the role of God—becomes the standard in the seventeenth and eighteenth centuries, and no participant in the debate can be ignorant of Descartes's answers to these problems.

Throughout his writings, Descartes displays an insatiable scientific curiosity about causes and their effects; he offers hundreds of examples. Sometimes his speculations about the cause are based on the study of its effect, in other places his explanations of the effect are grounded in his study of their causes. Descartes is concerned with such diverse causal sequences as the way the body produces pain or "titillations" of the mind, the effects of magnets on iron, the communication of motion from body to body, the motions of the heavenly bodies, and the cause of our idea of God (CSM I, 52, 103, 105, 240–43, 254; CSM II, 28–30). In this way, Descartes goes further than any mere philosophical concern about causation; he actually tries to build a science upon his metaphysics and epistemology of causation. Thus, his name and his ideas occur more often on the pages of the debate—scientific or philosophical, in agreement or disagreement—than anyone else.

Causation was so central to Descartes's thinking that causal reasoning became the core of rational thought in the study of logic. In the wake of Descartes's writings, Antoine Arnauld and Pierre Nicole's *Logic or the Art of Thinking* (1664), which draws heavily on Descartes's *Rules for the Direction of the Mind* (1628), recognizes only four modes of inference, namely, reasoning from cause to effect, from effect to cause, from whole to part, and, lastly, from part to whole. Rohault supposes that all of natural philosophy is reasoning from cause to effect or effect to cause (RS Preface). And Hobbes identifies knowledge as knowledge of cause and effect (MO I, 65-66).

THE METAPHYSICS OF CAUSATION

There is nothing particularly problematic in Descartes's generic idea of cause, namely, that something is caused when it "derives its existence from another"

(CSM II, 166). That there are material, formal, efficient, and final causes remains a working assumption for Descartes as well as for his regular correspondents, philosophers such as Caterus, Mersenne, and Gassendi. But Descartes takes a significant first step toward the simplification of the Aristotelian/Scholastic division of causes. Final causes need not be considered for the simple reason that they are unknowable. Descartes equates final causes with God's purposes, and he believes that God's purposes are all ". . . equally hidden in the inscrutable abyss of his wisdom" (CSM II, 258; CSM III, 341).

As a further (textual) simplification, Descartes says almost nothing about the nature of material causes. He seems to agree that there are material causes and that the material cause of something is the matter out of which it is composed (CSM II, 252). But beyond this acknowledgment, Descartes directs our attention specifically toward efficient causes in the following way. Formal causes require essences or substantial forms in the Aristotelian/Scholastic ontology. And Descartes believes he has good reason to reject forms or essences in this sense. He notes that these forms ". . . were introduced by Philosophers to explain the proper action of natural things, of which action this form is the principle and the source" (CSM III, 205). And he argues that such forms are unnecessary, for scientific explanation, that "no natural action at all can be explained by these substantial forms, since . . . they are occult . . ." (CSM III, 205, 208). The abandonment of substantial forms and formal causes, the neglect of material causes, and the unknowability of final causes naturally places the focus on efficient causation. But having placed that focus, Descartes must find a substitute metaphysical account of efficient causation, since in the Aristotelian/Scholastic ontology the efficient cause is the agent that places the form in the effect for some purpose and he has ruled out forms and purposes. Descartes's alternative account depends upon his well-known but difficult causal principle: "There must at least be as much (reality) in the efficient and total cause as in the effect of that cause" (CSM II, 28). In the ensuing discussions we shall uncover some of the ways in which this causal principle can be understood. This understanding is important because much of the debate, especially in the early modern debate, makes use of one or more versions of this principle.

Aristotle and most Scholastics talk about the form preexisting in the efficient cause. The father, who is the efficient cause of a child, contributes the form of the child in his sperm. The builder of the house contains the form (plans) in his mind before construction. And although Descartes does believe that the essence of matter is extension and the essence of mind is thought, he is explicit in his rejection of these Aristotelian/Scholastic forms and essences that might constitute the defining properties of natural kinds (CSM III, 205-

09; compare Garber 1992, 103-11). What, then, can it possibly mean within Descartes's causal principle when he says that there is as much reality in the cause as in its effect?

Let us begin our examination with some of Descartes's other statements of his causal principle. These formulations make it clear that there is no sharp distinction to be drawn among form, reality, and perfection, though Descartes has a strong preference for the terms "reality" and "perfection" over "form" and "formal cause," perhaps because the latter suggests the Aristotelian/Scholastic ontology.

> In this passage, however, we are talking about the total cause, the cause of being itself. Anything produced by this cause must necessarily be like it. (CSM III, 340)

> Whatever reality or perfection there is in a thing, is present either formally or eminently in its first and adequate cause. (CSM II, 116)

> There is nothing in the effect that was not previously present in the cause, either in a similar or in a higher form. (CSM II, 97)

> There is nothing [perfection of form] in the effect which did not previously exist in the cause. (CSM II, 252)

We can gain further insight into the meaning of this principle by looking at Descartes's own examples of such "preexistent" entities. These examples make it clear that by the terms "perfection," "form," and "reality" Descartes means the accidents or properties which substances possess. Thus, in the *Meditations*, by way of explaining his principles, Descartes offers the following illustration:

> A stone, for example, which previously did not exist, cannot begin to exist unless it is produced by something which contains, either formally or emi- nently, everything to be found in the stone [i.e. it will contain in itself the same things as are in the stone or other more excellent things (added in the French version)]; similarly, heat cannot begin to exist unless it is produced in an object which was not previously hot, except by something of at least the same order (degree or kind) of perfection as heat, and so on. (CSM II, 28)

There is also more than an echo of his causal principle in Descartes's laws of motion, especially his conservation principle that requires not only that the general quantity of motion (size times speed) in the universe remain constant, but also that in particular causal interactions a body cannot impart a quantity of motion to another body unless it has at least that quantity of motion in it (CSM I, 242).

In each of these examples it is a qualitative state of one particular that constitutes its reality or perfection. The suggestion that properties in the widest sense are what Descartes is referring to by "reality" and "perfection" is the correct one. Furthermore, it is the only possible one, since Descartes's ontology is exhausted by substances and their properties. As I have argued in an earlier paper:

> In general, realities are the properties, qualities, modes, accidents, or attributes of substances. For it is "properties [*proprietas*], qualities [*qualitas*], or attributes [*attributa*]" which exist formally or eminently in substances, and these are the only things which exist formally or eminently in substances (CSM I, 208–09; CSM 11, 114). And it is such things as motion, extension, figure, and volition which serve as examples of realities and also as examples of properties, qualities, and attributes (CSM II, 28–31; 114; III, 205–209).[1]

Most readers of Descartes have been taught to distinguish attributes—essential properties of things such as extension or thought—from modal or accidental properties of things such as being square or thinking of chiligons. Unfortunately, Descartes is simply not consistent in his use of these terms; In places, attributes are also called "accidents" or "modes" or "non-essential"; in others places essential realities are called "qualities" or "accidents" (CSM II 31, 155). Descartes himself seems to give incompatible definitions of "attribute"—he defines it as what is essential to substances (CSM III, 279–80) and as *whatever* "can be affirmed" of a substance (CSM I, 297).

Descartes occasionally shows an awareness of the ambiguity of his terms, especially in his use of "attribute":

> We must take care here not to understand the word "attribute" to mean simply 'mode', for we term an 'attribute' whatever we recognize as being naturally ascribable to something, whether it be a mode which is naturally ascribable to something, whether it be a mode which is susceptible of change, or the absolutely immutable essence of the thing in question. Thus God has many attributes, but no modes. (CSM I, 297; compare CSM III, 279-80)

To standardize our usage when talking about Descartes in a way that is familiar to most readers, I shall adopt the following distinction.[2] Realities can be divided into three categories: (i) attributes or essential properties, such as extension, thought, or divine wisdom; (ii) modes or accidents, or particular figures, motions, or thoughts; and (iii) qualities—what Locke would call secondary qualities—such as being soft, white, or having a smell (compare CSM I, 211; CSM II, 31; CSM III, 279–80). "Properties" is a generic term I shall use when such distinctions among realities are unimportant.

The causal principle, then, states a necessary condition for efficient causation. In the simple examples cited above, Descartes suggests that for a stone to become warm, its cause must have at least that degree of heat. And for a stone to come into existence, it must come from a cause, for example, another stone from which it is a chip that also has the properties of that stone, say, hardness, temperature, density, etc. Although Descartes's principle applies both to the alteration of an existing substance and to the coming to be of a substance, the principle only requires that the properties of the effect in some way preexist in the cause. Hence, in my formulations of the causal principle I shall overlook whether the effect is a substance being brought into existence or a substance being altered. In either case the cause must have the properties that come to be in the effect. Stated in this way, the causal principle seems to require a resemblance or similarity between cause and effect, which Descartes sometimes acknowledges (CSM III, 340).

Simply stated, **Version I**: An efficient cause must have the properties that are found in its effect.

Such a version works for realities such as heat or quantity of motion. In Version I even a *potential* cause of heat in the bread must have either that degree of heat or some greater degree of heat. To use Descartes's language, in Version I the realities or properties in the cause exist in the cause *formally* or *actually*. However, Descartes makes it clear in most versions of the causal principle that the cause need not actually have the properties of the effect but may have them only *eminently*. Thus, if we are going to make headway in understanding this principle, we must explicate the difference between having a property formally and having that property eminently.

Descartes's definition of formal inherence is complex:

> Whatever exists in the objects of our ideas in a way which exactly corresponds to our perception of it is said to exist *formally* in those objects. (CSM II, 114)

Descartes's epistemological language somewhat obscures his intention—obvious elsewhere—to equate formal inherence with actual inherence (CSM II, 28, 32, 116). But his epistemological definition is useful when talking about qualities. Since we have ideas of qualities, such as whiteness, that exist in our minds but the cause of these ideas is not a property of things that actually (formally) exists in the things, qualities do not formally exist in substances (compare Wilson 1991). Descartes's language also rules out the possibility that an effect can be produced by a reality that is only potentially in an object, since potential properties also fail to correspond exactly to our ideas of them. Thus, Descartes argues: ". . . the objective being of an idea cannot be produced merely by potential being, which strictly speaking is nothing, but only by actual or formal being" (CSM II, 32). We conclude that to formally exist in an object, the object must have an actual property (that is like our idea of it)—both qualities and potential properties fail this test.

The definition of "eminent existence" makes reference to how the property corresponds to our idea of it; but in this case, the idea does not correspond to that of which it is an idea.

> Something is said to exist *eminently* in an object when, although it does not exactly correspond to our perception of it, its greatness is such that it can fill the role of that which does so correspond. (CSM II, 114)

Elsewhere Descartes substitutes "some higher form" for "eminent" (CSM II, 97; compare CSM II, 28, notes 1 and 2). God, for Descartes, contains all properties either formally or eminently; he contains his own perfections formally and other realities eminently (CSM II, 31–32). Hence, God satisfies the necessary condition for causing any change or creation, and Descartes readily identifies God as the total efficient cause of everything (CSM III, 25). For example, God contains divine wisdom and intellect which is far grander than human intellect, and, at the same time, God's intellect fills the same role for God that human intellect does for humans, hence God satisfies the necessary condition to be the cause of wisdom in the human intellect. The more literal Haledane and Ross translation highlights this stipulation that the eminently inhering property must play *the same role* in the cause as the property that is produced does in the effect:

> It exists eminently when though not indeed of identical quality, it is yet such amount as to be able to fulfill the function of an *exact counterpart* [italics mine]. (HR II, 53)

In light of the above explication, we may now make the allowable substitution of "actual" for "formal" and "grander counterpart" for "eminent."

Thus, **Version II** of the causal principle reads: An efficient cause must have either actually or in the form of some grander counterpart the properties that are found in its effect. (Note that Version II entails Version I.)

Most of Descartes's examples of causal interaction can be brought under Version II of his causal principle. Even ideas that contain properties objectively are treated as effects that need ". . . a cause which contains this reality formally or eminently in its first and adequate cause" (CSM II, 116). When I have an idea of a stone and an idea of the hardness of the stone, the stone and the hardness exist in my mind only as representations (objectively), but even so these representations need a cause with at least as much reality as that which is represented (CSM II, 28; compare CSM II, 75). This corollary of Version II is clearly the corollary that gets Descartes to God's existence from the idea of God, since my idea of God is a representation of an object with so much reality that only God could be the cause of such an idea (CSM II, 118).

However, Descartes does introduce cases of causal interaction that do not fit well under Version II. For example, he allows that the mind can causally affect the body in a variety of ways causing movement and sensations (CSM III, 190; CSM I, 340 ff.). The mind does not contain formally or in a grander form the properties of the body. Indeed, except for being a substance (and perhaps having duration), the mind has nothing in common with the body. Yet Descartes believes that the mind can act upon the body. In the "Third Meditation" Descartes argues that a mental substance has sufficient reality to cause in itself the idea of material substance even though it does not actually contain formally or eminently any of the properties of a material substance (CSM II, 30–31; compare Wilson 1991). In a letter to Chanut, Descartes argues that certain bodily states and mental states are "naturally connected" though the substances are not at all alike (CSM III, 307). Elsewhere, Descartes denies that "two substances whose nature is different" are prevented "from being able to act on each other" (CSM II, 275) How, then, is the causal principle satisfied in these cases?

In fact Descartes does believe that the causal principle is satisfied in such cases as mind-body interactions, but in order to do so he must introduce yet a third version of his causal principle. Toward that end, he invokes an ontological hierarchy in which each entity is assigned a "degree of reality," which he understands as the capacity to exist independently. God has the greatest degree of reality. Created substances depend only upon God for their existence, so created substances have the next-greatest degree of reality. Finally, modes and attributes depend for their existence not only on God but also on created substances, so they have the least degree of reality (AG, 192). In Descartes's words:

> There are various degrees of reality or being: a substance has more reality than a finite substance. Hence there is more objective reality in the idea of a substance than in the idea of an accident; and there is more objective reality in the idea of an infinite substance than in the idea of a finite substance. (CSM II, 117).

When Thomas Hobbes questions Descartes's hierarchy by asking if reality admits of more or less, Descartes responds as follows:

> I have also made it quite clear how reality admits of more and less. A substance is more of a thing than a mode; if there are real qualities or incomplete substances, they are things to a greater extent than modes, but to a lesser extent than complete substances; and finally, if there is an infinite and inde-

pendent-substance, it is more of a thing than a finite and dependent sub-stance. All this is completely self-evident. (CSM II, 130)[3]

Descartes's degrees of reality hierarchy allows us to formulate **Version III** of his causal principle: An efficient cause must have at least the same degree of reality (capacity for independent existence) as its effect. Version III makes Descartes's causal principle into a weaker principle than Version I or Version II; it only requires that metaphysically, where there is a causal interaction, the cause and effect are at the proper ontological levels.

Because of its generality, Version III is less useful than earlier versions of the causal principle. Version I, for example, allows one to pick out the cause of the warm bread, namely, the only warm stove in a room where the others stoves are cold. Similarly, it allows one to identify the candidates for causing a certain body to move with a certain quantity of motion (if we know their histories). Version III is satisfied by every stove in the room or every body, whether it is in motion or not. Thus, Version III lacks a certain utility; it is overly generous. It seems designed largely to cover the apparent exceptions—causal interactions among very different ontological kinds.[4]

Descartes consistently holds that the causal principle, in one version or another, is a metaphysical precondition for efficient causation. Even in the case of God, Descartes argues that God can be his own efficient cause precisely because his essence contains enough reality to produce his existence (CSM II, 34, 167). To avoid the argument that God cannot be his own efficient cause, because God would have to exist prior to himself, Descartes denies the condition that an efficient cause must exist prior to its effect.

> I said that in this context the meaning of "efficient cause" must not be restricted to causes which are prior in time to, or distinct from, itself; and secondly, the restriction "prior in time" can be deleted from the concept while leaving the notion of an efficient cause intact. (CSM II, 167)

Descartes offers very little by way of a defense of his causal principle. He seems to think it is so obviously true that no real defense is needed (CSM III, 340). At first glance, Descartes's meager defense seems to take two forms. First, in the "Third Meditation" Descartes defends the principle as "manifest by the natural light" (CSM II, 28). Second, in response to Mersenne, Descartes suggests that the principle derives from a further common notion.

> The fact "there is nothing in the effect which was not previously present in the cause, either in a similar or in a higher form" is a primary notion which is as clear as any that we have; it is just the same as the common notion "Nothing comes from nothing." For if we admit that there is something in the

effect that was not previously present in the cause, we shall also have to admit that this something was produced by nothing (CSM 11, 97).

However, in the "Second Set of Replies," where Descartes formulates his arguments in geometrical fashion, it becomes clear that axioms or common notions are the same and that both are clearly and distinctly known, that is, manifest by the natural light (CSM II, 116; compare CSM II, 105). Thus, the claim that the principle is known by the natural light is equivalent to the claim that it derives from the common notion that nothing comes from nothing. In the next chapter we shall have more to say about why Descartes regards this principle as so obvious.[5]

Descartes's metaphysical speculations about causation, especially surrounding his multiple-versioned causal principle, have generated three distinct lines of interpretation, each of which has been in existence since shortly after the publication of the *Meditations*.

The first line of interpretation is that Descartes offers an unworkable theory of causation—he is a failed interactionist. His theory of causation is so unworkable—owing to the causal principle—that it leads to the collapse of orthodox Cartesianism and the emergence of occasionalism (Watson 1966; Radner 1978). The second line of interpretation is that Descartes is, in fact, an occasionalist (or, at least, a proto-occasionalist or partial occasionalist) and his occasionalist followers are simply being faithful to this aspect of Descartes's metaphysics (Le Grand 1694; Hatfield 1979; McCracken 1983; Broughton 1986; Garber 1993). A third interpretation, probably the most prevalent over the years, is simply that Descartes's views on causation, especially his causal principle, are so muddled that no coherent view can be attributed to him. This view, unlike the second, does not doubt that Descartes was a causal interactionist, that is, he believed that causal connections between and among created substances did occur, but he had no idea how they occurred. That is to say, he had no coherent response to the metaphysical problem of causation (Bedau 1986; Williams 1978; Curley 1978; Anscombe and Geach 1971). As a result, his followers were free to embrace occasionalism or interactionism without contradicting his (nonexistent) views on causation.

The first line of interpretation, simply stated, is that Descartes's metaphysics of causation fail to allow the very interactions that he wants to allow. This part of the debate usually begins by attributing a particular theory of causation to Descartes and then showing that he allows causal interactions that do not conform to this theory. Margaret Wilson summarizes this objection as follows:

> From Descartes' time to the present his critics have interpreted his system as a form of dualistic interactionism that fails to provide answers to crucial questions concerning the "how" of interaction between substances of distinct types. Princess Lizabeth wondered how an immaterial thing, which could not be conceived either as extended or as in physical contact with any body, could be supposed to cause physical movement. (Wilson 1978, 205)

Thus in the late 1600s the skeptic Simon Foucher argued that Descartes's causal principle requires an essential likeness between cause and effect, obviously a requirement that fails in the case of mind-body interaction, and if it fails in mind-body interaction, then minds cannot interact with the material world which makes knowledge impossible. Thus, Descartes's causal principle should lead him to skepticism (Watson 1966, 36–37).

Daisie Radner offers another version of this argument in her book *Malebranche*:

> According to Descartes, anything which acts as a cause must contain in itself what it produces in another thing. Why? Because otherwise there would be a violation of the common truth that something cannot come from nothing. Causation, for Descartes, is a matter of communication or impartment, and a thing cannot communicate or impart to another what it does not possess in itself.

> Given Descartes' view of causality, it seems to follow that the substance which acts and the substance acted upon must resemble one another, at least to the extent of being able to possess the same sorts of modifications. Nevertheless, Descartes wishes to maintain that minds and bodies act upon one another. . . . Faced with the changes in one another if they are totally different in nature, Descartes answers that [they] interact by virtue of their union . . . [which] he says he cannot explain. (Radner 1978, II, compare Watson 1966, 36)

Rader interprets Descartes's theory of causation as a theory of communication or impartment—an influx theory in which a cause literally passes on a property (usually a mode) to its effect. In the case of mind and body this communication is clearly impossible since mind and body, being essentially different, do not share any modes or accidents.

Leibniz, possibly influenced by Foucher, raises a variation on this objection in *A New System of Nature* and his letter to Beauval, although as O'Neill has warned us, Leibniz is not rejecting only Cartesianism when he argues for the impossibility of the way of influence (1993, 53–54). But Leibniz does hint that Descartes's views on causation require the transfer of a property from one substance to another, and he suggests that Descartes's account of the interaction of the soul with the body was defeated by the assumption that such a transfer is metaphysically possible.

> But when I began to think about the union of the soul and body, I felt as if I were thrown again into the open sea. For I could not find any way of explaining how the body makes anything happen in the soul, or vice versa, or how one substance can communicate with another created substance. Descartes had given up the game at this point, as far as we can determine from his writings. (AG, 142)

> The way of influence is that of the common philosophy; but since we can conceive neither material particles nor immaterial qualities or species that can pass from one of these substances to the other, we must reject this opinion. (AG, 148)

Certainly, if Descartes held a theory of causal interaction which required that properties in the effect must preexist in the cause and that causation is literally the communication of a property from one substance to another, then Descartes would be required to hold: (1) that there must be a strong resemblance between cause and effect—the cause must literally share with the effect the property which it produces in it as in Version I of the causal principle *and* (2) that the transfer of a property from one substance to another is metaphysically possible. It is worth noting at this point that if the properties shared by two substances are accidents, then in Descartes's metaphysics that requires that the substances share an essence, the converse is not the case, that is, two substances could have the same essence and distinct accidents. Let us call these interpretations of the causal principle the transference model.

On behalf of the transference model we can say first that it provides a clear answer to the metaphysical problem of causation. Second, Descartes certainly gives examples where a like property, say, the quantity of motion that comes to exist in the effect, was possessed by the cause. But such interactions, as we have seen, are only a portion of the various kinds of possible causal interactions. To see why Descartes cannot hold to such a simpleminded version of the causal principle, consider its implausible consequences, namely, only red things could give rise to red things, only tall people could have tall children, etc. Obviously Descartes does not hold such a naive view.

But there is a more sophisticated version of the transference model; Radner herself pursues this line (Radner 1978, 8). Descartes clearly seems to hold that in the material world there is a fixed quantity of motion which is parceled out among the different individual bodies (CSM I, 240). Causation, then, among bodies is of the transfer or impartment variety, that is, a body can gain only as much quantity of motion as its "cause" gives up (CSM I, 242; compare Garber 1990, 289ff.). Descartes's laws of motion presuppose that the cause must have at least the quantity of motion found in its effect. Add to this view of motion a strong reduction principle to the effect that all change in the material world reduces to this transfer of motion and one can begin to make a case for the transference model at least in the material realm. Descartes certainly seems to entertain such a reductionist principle: "The matter existing in the entire universe is thus one and the same, and it is . . . matter simply in virtue of its being extended. All the properties which we clearly perceive in it are reducible to its divisibility and consequent mobility in respect of its parts" (CSM II, 232). Also, in his conversation with Burman, Descartes adopts just such a reductionist strategy. In response to the objection that a builder is not like a house Descartes argues that the builder "applies active forces to what is passive and so there is no need for the product to be like the man" (CSM III, 340).

Further support for Descartes's reductionism is easy to find. The transfer of heat reduces to the transfer of quantity of motion among corpuscles. Indeed, Descartes's thesis expressed in *The World* is simply that *fire, heat,* and *burning* are but "finer parts" in "violent motion" which separates them from "coarser parts" (CSM I, 83–84). Color, too, is simply "nothing other than the various ways in which the bodies receive light and reflect it into our eyes" (CSMI, 153). This reductionism reflects Descartes's basic commitment to mechanism. Regardless of how one interprets the metaphysics of causation, Descartes is clearly a classical mechanist. He describes the physical world as a machine in which cause is by contact of the push-pull variety and changes in bodies are due to matter (corpuscles) of different shapes and sizes in motions that lead them to contact one another (CSM I, 279 ff.).

However, even granting this mechanistic-reductionist reading, the transference model faces serious obstacles.

First, textually, Descartes seems to reject the view that only essentially like substances can interact. In response to such an objection, Descartes writes to Clerselier:

> As for the two questions added at the end, namely: *how the soul moves the body, if it is not at all material? & how it can receive the species of corporeal object?* . . . I will tell you privately, that all the difficulty they contain only proceeds from a supposition which is false, and which cannot at all be proved, namely, that if the soul and the body are two substances of different nature, that prevents them from being able to act the one upon (contre) the other. (CSM II, 275)

A second point is that while Descartes does give many examples of the causal principle that do conform to the transference model, he also gives examples, particularly concerning sensation, where it is clear that the ideas caused in us by things represent things not through sharing properties but as signs of those things (CSM I, 167). And if the defender of the transference model of causation tries to fall back on eminent inherence, as Wilson notes, "It seems highly implausible to ascribe to him the view that body contains 'perfection more excellent than' mental modes, since he explicitly says that the human mind is "much nobler than the body" (1991, 300).

Third, Version III of the causal principle clearly allows that unlike substances can causally interact if only because they exist at the same degree of reality. At this point Radner and other defenders of the transference model might argue that this version of the causal principle is ad hoc, that is, Descartes offers it solely to make it appear as if causal interactions conform to his theory of causation. But to argue this way, those who think Descartes holds such a theory need to produce evidence that Version III is ad hoc or that he brings it up only in contexts where he is concerned about the interactions of unlike substances. In fact, Descartes never seems to clearly separate the different versions of his causal principle.

A final concern is that the transfer model needs to demonstrate that when Descartes talks about the communication of motion and other accidents, he *literally* means it. Only if Descartes thinks of the causal interaction among bodies—forget for the moment all other kinds of purported interaction—as the literal giving of the accident of motion from one body to another, does the transference model have any plausibility. This consideration brings us to Leibniz's objection.

Leibniz himself rejects the transfer model, because he believes that the transfer of accidents from one substance to another is ontologically impossible. And as we have seen, he thinks that if Descartes holds such a model, his theory of causation fails metaphysically to explain causal interaction. As Leibniz says, "An accident, however, needs not only some substance in general but that very one in which it inheres, so that it cannot change it" (LL, 390).[6] Contrary to Leibniz's reading of Descartes, there is a case to be made that Descartes agrees with Leibniz about the impossibility of modes or accidents being communicated from one substance to another. Descartes's reasons are the same as Leibniz's, namely, modes or accidents are individual (or, at least, cannot exist apart from the very substance which has the accident), hence they cannot transfer literally from one substance to another even though Descartes sometimes talks this way. For example, consider the following passage:

> And supposing together with this [i.e., that God placed a certain quantity of motion(s) in matter at creation] that from the first instant, the different parts of matter, in which these motion are found unequally dispersed, began to retain them or transfer them from one to another, according as they had the force to do so. (As in Garber 1992, 289: compare AT XV, 43)

Yet, there are other texts that suggest that such language is not to be taken literally. The first comes out in Descartes's warning that there are no real accidents, that is, accidents that survive the loss of their substance and get attached to another substance, as is sometimes used to explain transubstantiation (CSM II, 176). To suppose such a transfer is if not a verbal contradiction, a conceptual one (CSM II, 176).

The second argument derives from Descartes's famous remarks to Henry More. In his letter to Descartes, More wonders whether "numerically the same motion can occupy now a larger body, now a smaller one" (CSM III, 382). More does not understand "how something that cannot be outside the subject as all modes are, passes nevertheless into another subject" (CSM 111, 382). Descartes responds:

> You observe correctly that a motion being a mode of a body, cannot pass from one body to another. But that is not what I wrote; indeed I think that motion, considered as such a mode, continually changes. For there is one mode in the first point of a body A in that it is separated from the first point of a body B; and another mode in that it is separated from the second point; and another mode in that it is separated from the third point; and so on. But when I said that the same amount of motion always remained in matter I meant this from the force which impels its parts, which is applied at different times to different parts of matter. CSM III, 382)

Descartes's response to More is complicated by the fact that throughout his writings, Descartes uses the concept of motion ambiguously (compare Hatfield 1979; Clatterbaugh 1980; Garber 1992). On the one hand, motion is "the force or action of transference" whose measure is the quantity of motion transferred from body to body (CSM I, 233). On the other hand, motion is "the translation of a piece of matter, or body from the vicinity of the bodies immediately touching it, these being regarded as at rest, to the vicinity of other bodies" (CSM I, 233). Motion as force or power to move (*vis movens*) is the cause of motion as translation (Garber 1992, 160). Descartes is certainly aware of these two notions, though he is not always careful to distinguish them. Hereafter I shall speak of the first notion of motion as *force* and the second as *translocation*.

> And I say "the transfer" as opposed to the force or action which brings about the transfer, to show that motion is always in the moving body as opposed to the body which brings about the movement. The two are not normally distinguished with sufficient care; and I want to make it clear that the motion of something that moves is, like the lack of motion in a thing which is at rest, a mere mode of that thing and not itself a subsistent thing, just as shape is a mere mode of the thing which has shape. (CSM I, 233)

The translocation of a thing or its rest (relative to other bodies) is a mode.

Descartes in his response to More seems to take motion to be translocation, and, certainly, it makes no sense to think of motion as translocation as the kind of thing that is transferred from one substance to another. And Descartes is unwilling to say much about motion as force, which is the logical candidate for that which is communicated from one substance to another. In the *Principles*, Descartes denies that he is concerned about the ordinary sense of motion, meaning "the action by which a body travels from one place to another"; instead he claims to be concerned only with motion as translocation, that is, "the transfer of one piece of matter, or one body, from the vicinity of the other bodies which are in immediate contact with it, and which are regarded as being at rest, to the vicinity of other bodies" (CSM I, 233).

Clearly, if Descartes would have responded to More by saying that force is a mode or accident and that it is numerically the same *force* that gets communicated, or if he were to deny that it is numerically the same *force* that gets communicated, then we would have a definitive answer to the question: does Descartes think of causation in terms of the literal communication of modes or accidents from one substance to another? However, Descartes's understanding of motion as translocation and his refusal to call moving forces modes or accidents places the Rader/Leibniz reading in serious doubt. For if we speak of motion as translocation, then it is not transferred because such a reading of motion into the laws of physics is nonsense. If we speak of motion as force, then it is not the transfer of an *accident* or *mode* that happens when bodies interact because force, as Garber has clearly demonstrated, has no ontological status as a mode or accident of bodies in Descartes metaphysics (1992).

In the end, Descartes's seeming refusal to grant ontological status to force makes it easier to read him as an occasionalist. The force must come from somewhere, and the most likely agent for the material world outside the reach of our bodies is God. But his same refusal to grant ontological status to force makes the transference model problematic, since there is literally nothing to be transferred.

DESCARTES AS OCCASIONALIST

Occasionalism is a metaphysics that presupposes the distinction between uncreated (infinite) substance (God) and created (finite) substances (minds and/or bodies). As I shall use the term, "occasionalism" is the view that (1) there can be no causal relations among finite substances and (2) God is the immediate cause (proximate cause) of all alterations of substances. An *interactionist* view, on the contrary, affirms that finite substances are the immediate or proximate or partial causes of changes in other finite substances.

On the face of it, it seems hard to read Descartes as anything but an inter-actionist. As we have noted, examples of causal interactions permeate his writing. His stated goal in *The World* is to formulate a set of rules that will enable readers to "recognize effects by their causes" (CSM I, 97). His mechanistic reductionism requires a causal order among the bits of matter that in turn cause the mind to have the ideas and sensations that it does (CSM I, 232–33). His doctrine of the will clearly requires that the mind is a cause of movements in the body (CSM III, 246).

When interpreters make the claim that Descartes is an occasionalist, they often mean very different things. One view is that Descartes is a full-blown, conscious occasionalist. A second view is that Descartes is at least a partial occasionalist, that is, he ultimately denies causal interactions among at least some types of created substances, for example, among bodies or between minds and bodies. A third claim, perhaps the most plausible, is that Descartes is a proto-occasionalist, that is, his metaphysics contains certain requisite occasionalist principles that he either fails to recognize or that he ignores.

The first view is the hardest to defend. It requires that all of Descartes's causal language and causal reasoning is a sham. It is unsupported by any explicit denial that there is real causation among created substances. Yet such a reading of Descartes has been offered. The anonymous author of "Lettre d'un philosophe à un Cartesian" claims "all Cartesians agree that God alone is able to cause motion" (Gilson 1937, 20). And among Descartes's near contemporaries, the occasionalists Le Grand and Malebranche pretend that they are simply carrying through Descartes's views on causation. The title of Le Grand's occasionalist work is *An Entire Body of Philosophy, According to Principles of the Famous Renate de Cartes* (Le Grande 1694). Malebranche suggests that Descartes recognizes "as do all those who follow the light of reason, that no body can move itself by its own forces, and that all the natural laws of communication of motion are but the consequences of the immutable volitions of God" (LO, 466).

One reason for reading Descartes as a straightforward occasionalist is that he so readily acknowledges that God is "the efficient cause of all things"; indeed, he says that God is the "efficient and total" cause of all things (CSM I, 202; CSM III, 25). If God is the total and efficient cause of all things, what is left for created substances to do? But in other places, Descartes acknowledges that there is a need for created substances and their states to serve as causes; because God's actions are immutable, "there must be many changes in its [matter's] parts which cannot, it seems to me, properly be attributed to the action of God (because that action never changes) . . ." (CSM I, 93). And Descartes claims in the *Principles*: ". . . we understand very well how the different size, shape, and motion of the particles of one body can produce various local motions in another body" (CSM I, 285).

Whatever weight we put on Descartes's claim that God is the total efficient cause of everything, it cannot bear the entire burden of making Descartes into a full-blown occasionalist. Descartes gives too much causal responsibility to created substances, and nowhere does he claim that these causal claims are fictions. It remains—in the next chapter—to show how Descartes can make such a claim about God and give real efficacy to things other than God; but it is indisputable that Descartes strives to maintain causal efficacy for both God and created things and cannot therefore be classified as a full-blown occasionalist.

The second interpretation that Descartes is a partial occasionalist is less at odds with Descartes's writings. This view does not deny that Descartes is an interactionist with respect to some created substances, but the view insists that sometimes Descartes is forced to admit that apparent causal interactions are in fact God acting on created substances. Hatfield argues that having excluded force from matter, there is little else that Descartes can do:

> In the end, then, the view that signs to Descartes a wholly geometrical treatment of matter and motion—a treatment of matter as inert extended substance and a kinematical treatment of motion—stands; Descartes removed causal agency from the material world and placed it in the hands of God and created minds . . . (Hatfield 1979, 134–35)

Garber makes a similar claim but reaches this conclusion from the Cartesian doctrine of continual re-creation.

> I think that it is reasonably clear, then, that in the material world, at least, God is the only genuine causal agent. (1993b, 14)

Hatfield sees Descartes as having reached a dead end. Having denied that matter has no properties except the properties of extension, Descartes has no dynamic force by which he can account for its kinematical properties (Hatfield 1979; CSM I, 224). As a result he must give God the role of cause in explaining the particular motions and rests of particular bits of matter. Garber, in *Descartes' Metaphysical Physics*, agrees with Hatfield's conclusion that God is responsible for the motion and rest of matter (Garber 1992, 364). But Garber's reading differs from Hatfield's in where to locate the force which causes movement. Hatfield directly makes God the only real cause of the kinematical properties of bodies. In Hatfield's view, which Garber terms "the cinematic view," God recreates the universe at each moment and locates bodies at different places or at the same place in the case of rest. Thus, the movement of bodies is nothing more than a series of acts by the divine will (Garber 1992, 282). Garber finds this account puzzling; why would an unchanging God, who always wills in the same way, create motion at all? Garber further notes that Descartes, in the few passages when he does talk about force, is willing to attribute force to bodies themselves, while the cinematic view attributes force only to God (Garber 1992, 282).

In Garber's preferred reading, force is the "divine impulse"; "God causes motion by sustaining a divine shove, an action quite distinct from the action by which he sustains bodies in their existence" (Garber 1992, 297). In this view "God directly conserves . . . not the quantity of motion itself, the effect, but its cause, the impulsion he introduced into the world at its creation, the cause that results in motion" (Garber 1992, 283). Elsewhere, Garber calls this impulse a "divine shove" or an "imaginary force" which "has no place in Descartes' world" (Garber 1992, 297).

> By law 1, God will act on the world in such a way as to keep moving bodies moving, and resting bodies at rest. This can be *described* by saying that bodies, *as it were*, have a force to continue their motion, or exert a force to maintain their rest. But this is not to attribute anything real to bodies over and above the fact that God maintains their motion and as a consequence they obey a law of the persistence of motion. (Garber 1992, 298)

This force is neither in bodies as a mode nor in God, it is "nowhere at all" (Garber 1992, 297). This view, as Garber is aware, hardly counts as a solution to the metaphysical problem of causation. If anything, it is an acknowledgment that Descartes offers no solution; after all, change in the physical world reduces to matter in motion, and matter in motion is left a mystery. And Garber's view fares no better than Hatfield's with respect to locating force in bodies—Hatfield locates the force in God and Garber locates the force nowhere. In either view the language of communication and the attributions of force are as much a sham as in any occasionalist interpretation.

Wagner, following Gueroult, suggests a different strategy. Hoping to make Descartes's view appear to be less occasionalist and more interactionist, Wagner thinks that in addition to modes and attributes in matter Descartes also postulates forces or powers in matter (Wagner 1993; Gueroult 1980). There is no doubt that Descartes sometimes talks about the force which is in bodies, though he tends to identify that force with the power of God to act on matter.

> The transfer which I call "motion" is no less something existent than shape is: it is a mode in a body. The power causing motion may be the power of God himself preserving the same amount of transfer in matter as he put in it in the first moment of creation; or it may be the power of a created substance, like our mind, or of any other such thing to which he gave the power to move a body. In a created substance this power is a mode, but it is not a mode in God (CSM III, 381).

Just what such passages amount to is unclear. Gueroult wants to distinguish modes from powers, but the above passage suggests that Descartes is less precise than this distinction would require (Gueroult 1980, 196–97). Gueroult also wants to identify force with the existence and duration of each material substance—the force is its creative force (Gueroult 1980, 197). But as Garber argues against this view:

> The forces of motion and rest that enter into the impact law as force for proceeding and force of resisting . . . cannot simply be identified with existence and duration, as Gueroult seems to want to do; unlike existence and duration, the forces of motion and rest are variable, existing sometimes with one value, and sometimes with another in a given body. (Garber 1992, 296)

Thus the effort to give some clear ontological status to force in Descartes collapses, although the temptation to introduce them is, for some scholars, irresistible.

If force is something extrinsic to matter and that force is the cause of motion, then Descartes's talk about one body acting on another is not literally true. It is a metaphor or shorthand for an account that at some level seems to involve divine action. Descartes has no way to ground his so-called mechanical philosophy except in divine action. As long as Descartes's cause of motion is either God's intervention or a divine shove or a force brought into existence at each moment by God's continual creation, Cartesianism mechanism is animated by mind.

Broughton finds Descartes to be a partial occasionalist in another sense. She pursues an argument very close to Radner's, except that she thinks Descartes, because of the causal principle, is so hard pressed to explain causal interaction between bodies and minds that he ultimately abandons the role of bodies in causing sensations and ideas (Broughton 1986, 116). Broughton cites a passage from *Comments on a Certain Broad Sheet*:

> . . . there is nothing in our ideas which is not innate to the mind or the faculty of thinking, with the sole exception of those circumstances which relate to experience, such as the fact that we judge that this or that idea which we now have immediately before our mind refers to a certain thing situated outside us. We make such a judgment not because these things transmit the ideas to our mind through the sense organs, but because they transmit something which, at exactly that moment, gives the mind *occasion* [italics mine] to form these ideas by means of the faculty innate to it. (CSM I, 304)

Broughton, like Radner, wants to commit Descartes to a particular theory of causation, namely, causation that involves the transference of a property from the cause to the effect. She argues that having endorsed such a theory, Descartes comes to realize that in the case of matter acting on mind, such a migration cannot occur. Furthermore, Broughton argues, Descartes cannot appeal to the possibility that bodies eminently contain the properties that are transferred to the mind because he believes that "mind-body interaction involves only formal containment" (Broughton 1986, 111). Broughton relies heavily on Descartes's argument in "Meditation VI" where he asks about the source of the many ideas which come to his mind, often without any act of will on his part. He concludes:

> The only alternative is that it is in another substance distinct from me—a substance which contains either formally or eminently all the reality which exists objectively in the ideas produced by this faculty. . . . This substance is either a body, that is, corporeal nature, in which case it will contain formally—and in fact—everything which is to be found objectively—or representatively—in the ideas; or else it is God, or some creature more noble than a body, in which case it will contain eminently whatever is to be found in the ideas. (CSM II, 55)

At the end of that same paragraph Descartes makes it clear that bodies formally (actually) possess the mathematical properties that are contained in our ideas of them. Other ideas are "obscure and confused"; hence the world does not actually contain what these ideas objectively represent.

Garber gives some support to Broughton's conclusion when he argues that while the Descartes of the *Meditations* did indeed believe that bodies can cause sensations in the mind, by the time of the French version of the *Principles*, Descartes had changed his mind. Compare these two passages from the *Principles*, first the Latin version and second the French:

> We seem to ourselves clearly to see that its idea comes from things placed outside of us . . . (as in Garber 1993b, 21)

> . . . it seems to us that the idea we have of it forms itself in us on the occasion of bodies from without. (as in Garber 1993b, 22)

Yet there are other passages in Descartes's writings that clearly contradict the occasionalist spirit of the *Comments*. And given the mixed messages of "Meditation VI," which also clearly states that material things are the cause of ideas and sensations in the mind, Broughton might have chosen some of these other passages to support her view (CSM II, 58). For example, in the *Treatise on Man* Descartes writes that "the [nerve] fibres cause a movement in the brain which gives occasion for the soul to have the sensation of pain" (CSM I, 103). Even here the *language* of occasionalism does not suggest the *doctrine* of occasionalism. Throughout his writings, as we have seen, Descartes clearly holds that the mind and body do interact.

There are two issues in this debate that should be kept separate. One is whether Descartes is in the area of body-mind interaction an occasionalist or perhaps whether he drifts into occasionalism. The other is *why* he holds or drifts into such position, if he does. Broughton argues that Descartes holds a transference model of causation and therefore comes to see that he cannot not hold that bodies act on minds. However, we have already seen that there are good reasons to suppose that the transference model is not Descartes's theory of causation. Thus, Broughton's arguments that Descartes is driven to some form of partial occasionalism are hardly conclusive (compare Bedau 1986; Wilson 1991, 320). And to the extent that these reasons are not compelling, they may not have driven Descartes to such a position.

Wilson has argued that once one abandons a strong causal principle or a transference model in interpreting Descartes, one can see that Descartes clearly allows causal interaction between bodies and minds. In Wilson's "presentational model" Descartes sees the mind activated (caused) by signals in the brain to present an (innate) picture which is intermediary between the signals of the nerves and the purely mental idea (1991, 303–04). Thus, there are alternatives to the Broughton interpretation that fit better with the texts; indeed, Descartes rarely talks in the language Broughton requires while the presentation model is "extremely pervasive" (1991, 309). There are many oddities with the presentation model—the mind perceives external objects by perceiving something innate to itself—but Wilson's presentation model is textually sound, and it is clearly an interactionist not an occasionalist interpretation (1991, 308–09).

I now turn to the third alternative, namely, that Descartes is a proto-occasionalist. That is to say, Descartes embraces a metaphysical position which makes causal interaction among created substances unnecessary and which, if taken seriously, entails that such interactions are impossible. This view need not hold that Descartes sees the implications of this argument—others certainly thought they did—or that Descartes does not continue to hold that interaction is possible. It is evidence, as McCracken notes, that Descartes's system contains the "seeds of occasionalism" (1983, 91–96). The proto-occasionalism that many find in Descartes derives especially from his argument (the divine *concursus* argument) in the "Third Meditation" that God must continuously create and recreate the universe:

> For a lifespan can be divided into countless parts, each completely independent of the others, so that it does not follow from the fact that I existed a little while ago that I must exist now, unless there is some cause which as it were creates me afresh at this moment—that is, which preserves me. For it is quite clear to anyone who attentively considers the nature of time that the same power and action are needed to preserve anything at each individual moment or its duration as would be required to create that thing anew if it were not yet in existence. (CSM II, 33)

It is possible to read a Malebranchean argument for occasionalism into such texts (compare Garber 1993b, 14). Compare the above passage, for example, with passages from the occasionalists La Forge and Malebranche.

La Forge argues:

> I hold that there is no creature, spiritual or corporeal, that can change (the position of a body) or that of any of its parts in the second instant of its creation if the creator does not do it himself, since it is he who had produced this part of matter in place A. For example, not only is it necessary that he continue to produce it if he want it to continue to exist, but also, since he cannot create it everywhere, nor can he create it outside of every place, he must himself put it in place B, if he want it there, for if he were to have put it somewhere else, there is no force capable of removing it from there. (as in Garber 1993b, 16)

Malebranche's version is:

> Creation does not pass: the conservation of creatures is on the part of God simply a continued creation, simply the same volition which subsists and operates unceasingly. Now, God cannot conceive, nor consequently will, that a body be nowhere or that it not have certain relations of distance with other bodies. Hence, God cannot will that this chair exist and, by this volition, create or conserve it without His placing it here or there or elsewhere. Hence, it is a contradiction that one body be able to move another. I say further: it is a contradiction that you should be able to move your chair. . . . Hence, no power can transport it where God does not transport it, nor fix or stop it where God does not stop it, unless it is because God accommodates the efficacy of His action to the inefficacious action of his creatures. (D 157)

As we shall see in Chapter 4, there is little doubt that Malebranche and Le Grand use the doctrine of continuous creation or divine *concursus* to support their claim that no created substance can be a real cause or effective cause of a state in another created substance. But Descartes's statement of continuous creation is significantly more cautious than Malebranche, La Forge, or Le Grand; Descartes only states that the continued existence of substances requires God's continuous creation; he says nothing about the need to re-create all its states (CSM I, 200). In fact, in the "Second Set of Replies" Descartes hints that only the act of preserving a substance is worthy of God.

> IX. It is a greater thing to create or preserve a substance than to create or preserve the attributes or properties of that substance. However, it is not a greater thing to create something than to preserve it, as already been said. (CSM II, 117)

What this passage together with the very wording of Descartes's theory of continuous creation suggests is that Descartes may hold a weaker version of the doctrine of continuous creation than that of Malebranche, and others, a version that does not entail even proto-occasionalism. As Garber notes, God's activity in sustaining substances is distinct from the activity of causing motion, so ". . . there is no reason there cannot be causes of motion distinct from God" (1993b, 17).

In fact there seem to be two readings of Descartes, each of which falls short of proto-occasionalism[7]. These are:

> (P) For any finite individual substance x and a time t, if x exists at t, then God is the immediate cause of x existing at t.

> (Q) For any finite individual substance x and a time t, there exists a property f at t, such that God is the immediate cause of x existing at t and x being f at t.

For the sake of completeness I shall mention the Malebranche/La Forage/Le Grand thesis:

> (O) For any finite individual substance x and a time t, and for any property f of x at t, God is the immediate cause of x existing at t and x being f at t.

If Descartes holds (O), then it is hard to see how he could fail to be a proto-occasionalist. However, Descartes could hold (P) or (Q) and avoid that label since each allows that some states of any substance may be caused by other created substances.

Throughout much of his writing, especially in the *Principles of Philosophy* and the *Mediations*, Descartes writes as if God acts only to preserve the existence of substances (P). Thus in the *Principles* he notes:

> From the fact that we now exist, it does not follow that we shall exist a moment from now, unless there is some cause—the same cause which originally produced us—which continually reproduces us, as it were, that is to say, *which keeps us in existence* [emphasis mine]. For we easily understand that there is no power in us enabling us to keep ourselves in existence. (CSM I. 200)

Since Descartes also makes it clear that minds may produce ideas, volitions, or passions in themselves or other minds, that bodies may produce ideas and sensations in us, and that bodies may produce motion in other bodies, there is good reason to think that Descartes embraces at most something like (P) or (Q). For example, in talking about motion Descartes clearly embraces the thesis that God preserves the quantity of motion (its existence) in the world, but it is individual bodies that cause the redistribution of the quantity of motion among particular things:

> After this consideration of the nature of motion, we must look at its cause. This is in fact twofold: first there is the universal and primary cause (God)— the general cause of all the motions in the world; and second there is the particular cause which produces in an individual piece of matter some motion which it previously lacked. (CSM I, 240)

In other places, however, Descartes seems more tempted by (Q). He states in *The World* that "God alone is the author of all the motions in the world in so far as they exist and in so far as they are rectilinear" but it is the "various dispositions of matter" which "render them irregular and curved" (CSM I, 97). Is God, then, the author of those motions (rectilinear) that are most appropriate to that author's immutable nature? Whereas what are "corruptions" of that nature are due to other causes. Descartes seems to be argue for such a thesis in passages such as:

> For it follows of necessity, from the mere fact that he [God] continues thus to preserve it [quantity of motion] that there must be many changes in its parts which cannot, it seems to me, properly be attributed to the action of God because that action never changes, and which therefore I attribute to nature (CSM I, 92–93).

Descartes draws an analogy to human actions:

> Likewise, the theologians teach us that God is also the author of all our actions, in so far as they exist and in so far as they have some goodness, but it is the various dispositions of our wills that can render them evil. (CSM I, 97)

A clear advocacy of (P) or (Q) allows Descartes to escape the classification of proto-occasionalist. Unfortunately, there is also evidence that Descartes embraces (O). We have already noted those passages where Descartes makes it clear that God is the total and efficient cause of all things. But in his correspondence with Elizabeth, Descartes reinforces this claim and makes it difficult to find a place for finite causes.

> I must say at once that the reasons that prove that God exists and is the first and unchangeable cause of all effects that do not depend on human free will prove similarly, I think, that He is also the cause of all those that do so depend. For the only way to prove that He exists, is to consider Him as a supremely perfect being; and he would not be supremely perfect if anything could happen without coming entirely from Him. . . .

> The scholastic distinction between universal and particular causes is out of place here. The sun, although the universal cause of all flowers, is not the cause of the difference between tulips and roses; but that is because their pro-

duction depends also on some other particular causes which are not subordinated to the sun. But God is the universal cause of everything in such a way as to be also the total cause of everything; and so nothing can happen without His will. (CSM III, 272)

In these passages Descartes seems to make God the *sole* cause of everything. In so doing he seems to reject even the thesis stated above that God is just a universal cause who operates alongside particular causes. And even the earlier analogy with the will that suggests that God is the cause of what is good in the acts of will but finite minds are the cause of what is evil is not easily reconciled with the above passages that say that God is the total cause even of things which seem to result from acts of will by finite minds. These letters to Elizabeth go far beyond the claims of the continuous creation argument construed either as (P) or (Q). Perhaps, as Garber has suggested, they are just rhetoric intended to "console Elizabeth in her personal and familial troubles," but they certainly undermine any attempt to show that Descartes did not venture beyond (P) or (Q) (Garber 1992, 299 ff.).

The debate about Descartes's proto-occasionalism may never be settled. I tend to agree with Sleigh who notes that "Descartes' case is most difficult to determine" (among the three philosophers Malebranche, Leibniz, and Descartes) (Sleigh 1990, 172). If Descartes were a conscious occasionalist, one would expect him to recognize in some way that his causal language is a sham. If Descartes is truly a proto-occasionalist, there should not be so much evidence that he held (P) or (Q). Nor, for that matter, should he sound so much like an interactionist, unless we adopt the unflattering assumption that Descartes could not see a simple implication of his doctrine of continuous creation. The unsettled nature of this issue brings us to the final line of interpretation, namely, that Descartes's philosophy is simply lacking any coherent view about causation.

DID DESCARTES EVEN HAVE A THEORY OF CAUSATION?

There is a third line of interpretation which may well be the most popular, namely, that Descartes has no clearly defined metaphysical views about causation. Since he embraces no particular metaphysical view about causation, there can be no conflict between his theory of causation and his metaphysics. Since he has no particular view about causation, there is no question about whether he is or is not an occasionalist. Most who belong to this camp think that Descartes is an interactionist, that is, he believes *that* causal interaction occurs between bodies, between minds and bodies, and between God and created substances; he simply has no idea *how* these interactions occur.

Another feature of this interpretation is a certain impatience with the causal principle, a refusal to take this principle seriously. Obviously such a view is required since on the face of it, the causal principle is an attempt to answer the metaphysical problem of causation. Bernard Williams refers to the causal principle as "this piece of Scholastic metaphysics" and calls it an "unintuitive and barely comprehensible principle" (Williams 1978, 135). Anscombe and Geach suggest that formal and eminent inherence had "degenerated to mere jargon by Descartes' time" (Anscombe and Geach 1971, 81). Kenny labels the notion of eminent inherence as "obscure" and has nothing to say about formal inherence (Kenny 1968, 141). Wilson's insightful discussion of the "Third Meditation" finesses the entire issue of causation, although she does doubt that Descartes could defend his causal argument for the existence of God (1978, 100). Curley's discussion of the causal principle is more revealing of his frustration with the causal principle than anything else. Having noted the principle, Curley finds the concepts of formal reality and eminent reality obscure; he states twice in less than a page that there might be some principle of causation that could command his assent but Descartes's is not one of them (1978, 130–31).

Mark Bedau marshals an argument to the effect that Descartes is self-consciously committed to the view that there are causal interactions between distinct kinds of substances but does not know how such things interact (Bedau 1986, 485–86). Bedau cites the *Principles*:

> Now we understand very well how the different size, shape and motion of the particles of one body can produce various local motions in another body. But there is no way of understanding how these same attributes (size, shape and motion) can produce something else whose nature is quite different from their own. (CSM I, 285)

Bedau uses this claim to show that Descartes could not have been committed to the transference model defended by Radner and Broughton (Bedau 1986, 84). Bedau rightly points out that Descartes also believes that God interacts with created substances but Descartes does not know *how* God does this. If God's causal actions can be thought about in this way, why not treat mind-body interaction in the same way. Thus, Bedau concludes:

> Cartesian interaction is the conjunction of two claims about mind and body: that they interact and that each his its well-known Cartesian essence. I have not attempted to prove that Cartesian interaction is true, but I have tried to defend it in two respects. First, the mere fact that mind is essentially conscious and nonextended, and body extended and nonconscious, is not sufficient grounds for concluding that they do not interact. Second, our inability to conceive how they interact is not sufficient grounds for concluding that they do not interact. So the familiar objection to Cartesian interaction that

conscious mind and extended body could never interact is simply not well founded. (Bedau 1986, 495)

Bedau's points could be amplified, although he does not suggest such generalization, to argue that even if Descartes does not fully understand any causal interaction, he believes that they occur. And the messiness of Descartes's remarks about causation is not sufficient grounds to rule out that Descartes is an interactionist or that he has no right to believe in the causal interactions of created substances.

Although I argue that Descartes does hold more specific views about causation than those in this camp allow, I agree with what I take to be the gist of Bedau's argument, namely, fully grasping how causal interaction takes place need not preclude believing that it does take place, and Descartes was well aware of this fact. However, the passage from the *Principles* cited by Bedau does suggest that we do understand how causation between or among bodies can occur. Hence, those who disparage *any* theory of causation in Descartes are overstating the point. But the passage from the *Principles* makes it clear that whatever model of causation we apply to bodies acting on bodies, it is inappropriate as a model for mind-body interaction. Thus, scholars like Radner and Broughton, who attribute a transference model to Descartes based on what he says about the communication of motion or heat, are wrong from the start to try to extend this model to minds and bodies or, for that matter, to God and the material world.

Descartes does think he has a theory of causation for the interaction of bodies. That theory is probably some version of what O'Neill calls the atomistic corpuscular influx model wherein particles of matter with certain quantities of motion are given off by other bits of matter (the agent) and thereby cause changes in the motions of the recipient body (the patient). This is not a version of influx in which an accident or mode is transferred from one body to another but where bits of matter (corpuscles) are transferred from one body to another. In cases where the quantity of motion is lost, Descartes can always appeal to the subtle matter that fills the plenum and is found in bodies, solid and fluid (CSM I, 229 ff.). Examples of this influx causation abound in Descartes's scientific essays. It is a mode of causation that was adopted by his contemporaries Gassendi and Hobbes even though they, like Descartes, had no idea just how motion as force was redistributed among bits of matter. And therefore, like Descartes, they lack a complete answer to the metaphysical problem of causation.

CENTRAL THEMES

It is the concept of efficient causality which plays a crucial philosophical role for Descartes, and it is toward this key concept that Descartes and his critics and interpreters direct their attention. An efficient cause is something on which a thing depends, and it may be either total or less than total. Only in the total efficient cause does Descartes require a preexistent reality. God is Descartes's only example of a total efficient cause; a stone, the sun, or a builder are examples of less than total efficient causes. If God is the only example of a total efficient cause, then Descartes's famous causal principle has no application to efficient causation among created things. Certainly Descartes seems unencumbered by this principle—he allows a wide variety of causal interactions.

Descartes himself offers several observations about the metaphysics of efficient causation. Metaphysically, there *can* be similarity (sharing of properties) between cause and effect, but similarity is not a metaphysical requirement. An efficient cause is usually but not necessarily prior to its effect; they can be simultaneous. Perhaps most importantly, Descartes places a variety of ontological kinds in the role of efficient cause. First, and foremost, substances are efficient causes, for example, God, the builder, a body, a mind. Second, Descartes suggests that modes or attributes of substances are causes, God's willing is a cause, the motion of a body may be a cause, the heat of the sun; these are realities which inhere in substances and which are said to cause changes in other substances. Finally, there is the ontologically problematic force (moving force) of substances which may be the efficient cause of states in the same or other substances. Motion as divine impulse, power of God, or dynamic force in substances is ontologically awkward for Descartes; it does not belong to any of Descartes's recognized ontological categories, namely, substance, accident, or attribute.

In the next chapter we turn to Descartes's views on the epistemology of causation. Our discussion will put Descartes's theory of causation in a different light, a light that makes each of the previously mentioned lines of interpretation not so much wrong as they are incomplete. After we have discussed Descartes on the epistemology of causation, we shall conclude by arguing that Descartes should be classified as a concurrentist, that is, someone who holds that *both* God and created things collaborate in the production of change.

3.
Descartes: The Epistemology of Causation

PLACE IN THE DEBATE

As with his metaphysical treatments of causation, Descartes's views on causal explanation and how the causal structure of the world is known are foundational ideas in the modern debate about causation. Descartes's style and methods of proof become the most widely used and imitated methods of the modern period. Descartes's *Discourse on Method* (1637) inspired Hobbes to begin his own work on method and physics. And Le Grand consciously imitates Descartes's *Principles* in language, style, and method of proof. Spinoza views his *Ethics* as carrying out the synthetic task begun by Descartes.

But Descartes's views of causal explanation are influenced both by his scientific needs and by certain theological assumptions. Passages such as the following reveal that Descartes views science as dependent upon theology.

> I think that all those to whom God has given the use of... reason have an obligation to employ it principally in the endeavor to know him and to know themselves. That is the task with which I began my studies; and I can say that I would not have been able to discover the foundations of physics if I had not looked for them along that road. (CSM III, 22)

Descartes tries to use God in two specific ways. First, God is the guarantor of truth. The fact that God is not a deceiver guarantees the truth of clear and distinct ideas and the reliability of the senses. And these ideas ground the epistemology of science; it is the search for this certain foundation that inspires Descartes's most famous work, the *Meditations on First Philosophy*. Second, God is a source of substantive knowledge in science. The idea of God not only insures truth in science but also provides certain foundational principles of science; thus any proper scientific explanation that makes use of these principles makes at least implicit reference to God (Collins 1960; Garber 1992, 54–55). It is Descartes's second use of God that concerns us in this chapter.

In the previous chapter we saw that Descartes maintains that God is the total efficient case—perhaps the only total efficient cause of everything. This Scholastic, theological assumption found acceptance through Descartes in the philosophies of Spinoza, Le Grand, and Malebranche, although each imposes his own interpretation on it. If God is the total efficient cause of everything, two immediate issues arise. The first is how to apportion causal powers to created substances. Or, more importantly, can any causal powers be apportioned to created substances? We have already explored the ways in which Descartes's metaphysics of causation may suggest occasionalism or proto-occasionalism. The second and related issue is how to fit God into proper causal explanations. If God is a causal factor in every change and every phenomenon, then God must be part of any genuine scientific explanation. How Descartes responds to these two issues reveals much about his theory of causation, specifically his concurrentist solution and his theory of scientific explanation. And how others in this debate respond to Descartes's views is a useful way to approach their views on the epistemology of causation.

Because God is or may be part of every proper scientific explanation, this chapter explores two questions. The first is: what is the nature of God and how is that nature relevant to scientific understanding? The second is: what is scientific explanation and to what extent does it incorporate God?

THE EPISTEMOLOGY OF CAUSATION

Descartes's God is far and away one of the most powerful beings to stalk the pages of philosophy. God is, of course, all-powerful in the usual sense, that is, if God wills something to be, then it is (CSM II, 31; CSM III, 25). However, Descartes goes further; he does not even impose the usual modest restrictions on God's omnipotence; for example, he does not say that God can only will what is logically possible. Or to use language more familiar to Descartes, God might will to make two contradictory statements true. In his famous letter to Mesland, Descartes writes:

I turn to the difficulty of conceiving how God would have been acting freely and indifferently if he had made it false that the three angles of a triangle were equal to two right angles, or in general that contradictories could not be true together. It is easy to dispel this difficulty by considering that the power of God cannot have any limits, and that our mind is finite and so created as to be able to conceive as possible the things which he has wished to be in fact possible, but not be able to conceive as possible things which God could have made possible, but which he has nevertheless wished to make impossible. The first consideration shows us that God cannot have been determined to make it true that contradictories cannot be true together, and therefore that he could have done the opposite. The second consideration assures us that even if this be true, we should not try to comprehend it, since our nature is incapable of doing so. And even if God has willed that some truths should be necessary, this does not mean that he willed them necessarily; for it is one thing to will that they be necessary, and quite another to will this necessarily, or to be necessitated to will it. I agree that there are contradictions which are so evident that we cannot put them before our minds without judging them entirely impossible, like the one which you suggest: that God might have brought it about that his creatures were independent of him. But if we would know the immensity of his power we should not put these thoughts before our minds, nor should we conceive any precedence or priority between his intellect and his will; for the idea which we have of God teaches us that there is in him only a single activity, entirely simple and entirely pure. (CSM III, 235)

If we read this passage as asserting that Descartes's God can make any false sentence (including contradictions) true or any true sentence (including necessary truths) false then Descartes's God is indeed powerful, and this kind of omnipotence may indeed have some strange consequences (Wilson 1978, 123). For example, could God have made it true that everything he creates is independent of him? Could it be true that God both exists and does not exist? We might even speculate that if God is so powerful and evil, we could never discover any truth—conceptual or scientific. Such a God could make it seem that I must exist when I think or make it seem that an omnibenevolent perfect being is not a deceiver or make it seem that a being with all perfections must exist, when in fact these are contradictions.

There is another way of reading Descartes that is less troublesome. Instead of claiming that God is literally without limits in his power or that God literally can make contradictions true and necessary truths false, Descartes can be read as saying that our knowledge of God's power is so limited that we cannot and should not rule out what God can do based on what we can conceive. At the same time, we are allowed to infer that God can do something based on its conceivability to us. Consider the following excerpt, also from a letter to Mersenne:

> His power is beyond our grasp. In general we can assert that God can do everything that is within our grasp but not that he cannot do what is beyond our grasp. It would be rash [a presumption ("temerite")] to think that our imagination reaches as far as his power. (CSM III, 23)

What this passage and parts of the Mesland letter suggest is that there may indeed be limits to what God can do but that we are ignorant of them, and hence we should err on the side of allowing that God might do anything, even what is conceptually impossible. God has created our minds in such a way that some of what God can do is conceivable to us and without any idea of what he cannot do.

Whichever way we read Descartes, he is rejecting several tenets traditionally associated with rationalism. First, he refuses to acknowledge that what is inconceivable *to us* could not be logically possible. And second, he refuses to concede that God is limited by what is logically possible. Unlike most rationalists, then, Descartes embraces no absolute notion of what is conceivable (possible) and inconceivable (impossible). Finite minds presumably have limits as to what they can conceive and not conceive; these limitations are set by God. And these limitations allow us to divide propositions into necessary, merely possible, and contradictory. But such divisions are reflections only of our limitations, and these divisions are a poor guide as to what God can or cannot do (CSM III, 24–25, 235).

There are clear advantages in taking Descartes to be making an epistemological claim about our ignorance rather than a metaphysical claim about God's unlimited power. Because Descartes clearly thinks we are ignorant of God's capabilities, if he also makes the metaphysical claim that God's capabilities are unlimited, he seems to be stating epistemological nonsense, namely, that God's power is unlimited and that God's power is "incomprehensible" (CSM III, 25). If the second conjunct is true, we have no basis for asserting the first; and if the first conjunct is true, then the second conjunct would seem to be false. Thus, it is prudent, though textually risky, to read Descartes as an agnostic who thinks that we can know what is conceivable and inconceivable but can only infer from that some of what is possible for God and none of what is impossible. It may well be that for Descartes's God there are no truths that are true in all possible worlds—for all we know.

Thus, I shall state the first major thesis about God as follows:

> (G) We are unable to discern any limits on the power of the Divine will, and so should presume none.

A second major thesis about God is expressed in a letter to Mersenne:

> In God willing and knowing are a single thing in such a way that by the very fact of willing something he knows it and it is only for this reason that such a thing is true. (CSM III, 24)

Descartes repeats this claim in a later letter:

> In God willing, understanding and creating are all the same thing without one being prior to the other even conceptually. (CSM III, 26)

If Descartes is serious about this proposal, which he also includes in his letter to Mesland, it seems to follow that God cannot understand a world without creating it. If we assume, reasonably, that God understands all possible worlds, then it would seem to follow that all possible worlds are actual. Leibniz's distinction between what God can conceive and what God wills to exist is not defensible for Descartes. And as Descartes's occasionalist followers were able to argue, there is more than a hint of occasionalism in this doctrine—since God knows everything, God creates everything. Yet we have already seen that Descartes is no occasionalist. And in the "Fourth Meditation" he explains human error precisely in terms of a will that is able to operate independently of the understanding. It is hard to believe that the divine will could be any less free. However, I shall state Descartes's second thesis regarding the power of God:

> (W) In God willing a state of affairs and understanding (or knowing) it are one and the same.

The third thesis that is relevant to our discussion of causation is a counterpart to (G), but seems to follow directly from (W). (G) basically asserts that God's will is sufficient to bring about any state of affairs. The third thesis is that God's will is necessary to bring about any state of affairs. In the "Third Set of Objections and Replies" Descartes puts it thus:

> And such immense power is contained in this idea [of God] that we understand that, if God exists, it is a contradiction that anything else should exist which was not created by him. (CSM II, 132)

Elsewhere Descartes supports this thesis by claiming that everything comes *entirely* from God (CSM III, 272). And "there cannot be any class of entity that does not depend upon God" (CSM II, 294). The third thesis seems to follow in any case, given that God is all-knowing, that is, nothing can happen without God's knowing it, and given (W) that God's knowing and God's creating are one and the same, thus, it follows that nothing can happen without God's creating it or willing it. We shall articulate Descartes's third thesis as follows:

> (NG) No state of affairs exists unless God wills (understands) it.

Descartes makes little effort to justify these claims, except to assert that it is "blasphemy" to deny them (CSM III, 24). Such principles are theological axioms for Descartes. And they, like other foundational principles, are justified by the natural light of reason or by claiming that they derive from the clear and distinct idea of God.

At this point, then, we encounter a persistent central problem that, from the outset, haunts Descartes's remarks about causation. Given the above discussion, this problem can now be stated by a straightforward argument:

(1) By (G), God's will is sufficient for everything that happens.
(2) By (W), God's will is necessary for everything that happens.
(3) Any particular cause that is necessary for a particular effect is incompatible with (G).
(4) Any particular cause that is sufficient for a particular effect is incompatible with (W).
(5) Everything that is a cause is either necessary or sufficient for its effect.
(6) Hence, no particular cause can be a cause.
(7) Hence, God is the only true explanation of change.

In the previous chapter we examined other versions of the divine concursus argument, and these arguments, in the hands of Malebranche or Le Grand led to an occasionalist reading of Descartes. But differences in Descartes's principle of divine concursus led to interpretations that escaped a full-blown occasionalism. Here, if there is an escape it must be via a different route. Descartes's thesis about the power of God seems to lead to the conclusion of occasionalism stated in (6) and its epistemic corollary stated in (7). But before we can see if Descartes has a way out of (7), that is, a way to maintain both his theses about God and that particular things are true causes, we must examine, in some detail, his theory of causal explanation.

Throughout his writings Descartes links understanding something, explaining something, with providing an account of its causes. Thus, in typical fashion in the *Meteorology* he writes:

> This leads me to hope that if I here explain the nature of clouds . . . we will easily believe that it is similarly possible to find the causes of everything that is most admirable . . . . I shall try to portray the rainbow correctly, and to explain its colors in such a way that we can also understand the nature of all those which may be found in other objects. To this I shall add the cause of the colors we commonly see in the clouds and in the circles which surround the stars, and finally the cause of the suns, or moons, several of which sometimes appear together. (O, 264)

Descartes goes on to note that it is causes that "explain" effects whereas causes are "proven" from their effects (CSM III, 106–7). Stated in more contemporary terms, from the effect we can (inductively) infer *that* the cause occurred, from the cause we can (deductively) infer *why* the effect occurred, although as we shall see this contemporary terminology can be misleading in reading Descartes (compare Buchdahl 1969, 82 ff.). In the "Second Set of Replies" Descartes describes two kinds of scientific inference:

> As for the method of demonstration, this divides into two varieties: the first proceeds by analysis the second by synthesis.
>
> Analysis shows the true way by means of which the thing in question was discovered methodically and as it were a priori [prior in the order of discovery], so that if the reader is willing to follow it and give sufficient attention to all points, he will make the thing his own and understand it just as perfectly as if he had discovered it for himself. But this method contains nothing to compel the argumentative or inattentive reader; for if he fails to attend even the smallest point, he will not see the necessity of the conclusion. Moreover there are many truths which—although it is vital to be aware of them—this method often scarcely mentions, since they are transparently clear to anyone who gives them his attention.
>
> Synthesis, by contrast, employs a directly opposite method where the search is, as it were, a posteriori (though the proof itself is often more a priori than it is in the analytic method.[1] It demonstrates the conclusion clearly and employs a long series of definition, postulates, axioms, theorems and problems, so that if anyone denies one of the conclusions it can be shown at once that it is contained in what has gone before, and hence the reader, however argumentative or stubborn he may be, is compelled to give his assent. However this method is not as satisfying as the method of analysis, nor does it engage the minds of those who are eager to learn, since it does not show how the thing in question was discovered.
>
> It was synthesis alone that the ancient geometers usually employed in their writings. (CSM II, 110–11)

Roughly speaking, analysis proceeds from effects to their causes and is a nondeductive form of inference, while synthesis proceeds from causes to their effects and is a deductive form of inference. However, we must be careful in using terms like "deduction" and "induction" when describing Descartes's causal reasoning because as Gaukroger has noted:

> Descartes uses the Latin term *deducere* and *demonstrare* and their French equivalents *deduire* and *demontrer* with abandon, and they may mean explanation, proof, induction, or justification, depending on the context. (Gaukroger 1989, 49; compared Clarke 1982, 63–74)

What seems to be common to inferences (inductive or deductive) for Descartes is that when someone has a clear and distinct enough grasp of the propositions of the inference, then one will have an intuitive grasp of their connection (Gaukroger 1989, 50–51). Presumably the same thing happens in analysis, inference from effect to cause, and in synthesis, inference from cause to effect. But analysis and synthesis differ with respect to discovery, that is, analysis is a way of discovering causes from prior known effects, whereas synthesis—the geometrical method—conforms to what today would be pure deduction and nothing new comes out of the premises (causes). Thus, synthesis is not linked as closely to discovery, although Descartes is aware that we can uncover new things by way of deduction. In the end, analysis is reasoning inductively from effect to cause in order to discover new things; synthesis is reasoning deductively from cause to effect in order to explain the effect which is contained in the cause. And both proceed from an intuition of the connection among the propositions (compare Buchdahl 1969, 129; Gaukroger 1989, 71–75).

Because analysis uses conclusions (effects) to justify (causes) and the premises (causes) are used to explain the conclusions (effects), Descartes is concerned that he will be accused of circular reasoning, especially if one is not clear about the difference between explanation that something is the case and proving that something is the case.

> You say . . . that there is a vicious circle in proving effects from a cause, and then proving the cause by the same effects. I agree: but I do not agree that it is circular to explain effects by a cause, and then prove the cause by the effects; because there is a big difference between proving and explaining. I should add that the word "demonstrate" can be used to signify either. . . . (CSM III, 106; compare O, 61)

Descartes passionately contrasts his particular causal accounts in his physics with the causal accounts given by Scholastics who use as their causes "real qualities," "substantial forms," and "elements" as compared with Descartes's corporeal analysis of matter, which he believes has empirical warrant ("visible to the naked eye") (compare Buchdahl 1969, 85). He concludes:

> I hope this will be enough to convince anyone unbiased that the effects which I explain have no other causes than the ones from which I have deduced them. (CSM III, 107; compare O, 268)

Descartes regards his examples as exemplars of successful causal explanations:

> For instance from the oblong and inflexible shape of the particles of salt, I deduced the square shape of its grains, and many other things which are

obvious to the senses; I wanted to explain the latter by the former as effects by their cause. I did not want to prove things which are readily well enough known, but rather to demonstrate the cause by the effects a posteriori. . . . (CSM III, 77)

First, then, I must tell you that I hold that there is a certain quantity of motion in the whole of created matter, which never increases nor diminishes; and thus, when one body makes another body move, it loses as much of its own motion as it gives to the other. Thus, when a stone falls to earth from above, if it stops and does not rebound, I think that this is because it moves the earth, and thus transfer to it's motion. But if the earth which it moves contains a thousand times more matter, when it transfers its motion it gives it only a thousandth of its speed. (CSM III, 330)

The information from which we infer from cause to effect or from effect to cause is acquired in a variety of ways. Often in science we gain the most information about effects from observation and experiment (Garber 1993, 292 ff.).

The things which I say in the first chapters about the nature of light, and about the shape of the particles of salt and fresh water, are not my principles, as you seem to object, but rather conclusions which are proved by everything that comes after. Sizes, shapes, positions and motions are my *formal* object (in philosophers' jargon), and the physical objects which I explain are my *material* object. The principles or premises from which I derive these conclusions are only the axioms on which geometers base their demonstrations . . . but applied to various observational data which are known by the senses and indubitable. (CSM III, 77)

In other situations we may start with first causes and infer to effects; first causes are known not by the senses by way of clear and distinct ideas (intuitions):

We must start with the search for first causes or principles. These principles must satisfy two conditions. First, they must be so clear and so evident that the human mind cannot doubt their truth when it attentively concentrates on them; and, secondly, the knowledge of other things must depend on them in the sense that the principles must be capable of being known without knowledge of these other matters, but not vice versa. Next, in deducing from these principles the knowledge of things which depend on them, we must try to ensure that everything in the entire chain of deductions which we draw is very manifest. (CSM I, 180)

Descartes concludes that this second way of discovery is primarily open to God, who is "perfectly wise" and can complete these deductions (CSM I, 180).

In what may be the clearest statement of his views on scientific exploration, Descartes suggests in Part Six of the *Discourse* that human minds must be very cautious about trying to move from first causes to their effects (that way is filled with mistakes); he suggests instead that it is epistemically necessary for human minds to supply the "suppositions," or intermediate principles after the first principles, by analysis or reasoning from what is known to the senses (effects) back to their causes.

> Should anyone be shocked at first by some of the statements I make at the beginning of the Optics and the Meteorology because I call them "supposi-tions" and do not seem to care about proving them, let him have the patience to read the whole book attentively, and I trust that he will be satisfied. For I take my reasonings to be so closely interconnected that just as the last are proved by the first, which are their causes, so the first are proved by the last, which are their effects. . . . For as experience makes most of these effects quite certain, the causes from which I deduce them serve not so much to prove them as to explain them; indeed, quite to the contrary, it is the causes which are proved by the effects. And I have called them "suppositions" simply to make it known that I think I can deduce them from the primary truths I have expound-ed above; but I have deliberately avoided carrying out these deductions in order to prevent certain ingenious persons from taking the opportunity to construct, on what they believe to be my principles, some extravagant philosophy for which I shall be blamed. These persons imagine that they can learn in a single day what it has taken someone else twenty years to think out. . . . As to those who combine good sense with application [technology]—the only judges I wish to have—I am sure they will not be so partial to Latin that they will refuse to listen to my arguments because I expound them in the vernacular. (CSM I, 150–51)

The above passage reveals the ambiguity of Descartes's use of the terms "cause" and "effect," an ambiguity that slides between cause-as-thing and cause-as-proposition or premise in a proper scientific explanation. It is this ambiguity that allows Descartes to speak of the cause both as a set of premis-es from which the effect can be deduced and as a substance or shape, position, or size. In *The World* and the *Principles of Philosophy*, Descartes sometimes speaks, in the same paragraph, as if the laws of nature are causes and as if mat-ter or nature is a cause.

> By "nature" here I do not mean some goddess or any other sort of imaginary power. Rather, I am using this word to signify matter itself, in so far as I am considering it taken together with all the qualities I have attributed to it, and under the condition that God continues to preserve it in the same way that he created it. For it follows of necessity from the mere fact that he continues thus to preserve it, that there must be many changes in its parts which can-not, it seems to me, properly be attributed to the action of God, (because that action never changes), and which therefore I attribute to nature. The rules by which these changes take place I call the "laws of nature." (CSM, I, 92–93)

> From God's immutability we can also know certain rules or laws of nature, which are the secondary and particular causes of the various motions we see in particular bodies. (CSM 1, 240)

Of special note is the fact that Descartes's notion of *efficient cause* or *total efficient* cause is not immune to this ambiguity. Although Descartes identifies the builder, mud, the sun, parents, and God and their properties as efficient causes, he also uses these in their propositional form to derive effects; in the above passage he speaks of "the rules or laws of nature" as "secondary and particular causes." At one place, he urges that we start with God's attributes and draw conclusions "concerning those effects which are apparent to our senses (and we shall be assured that what we have once clearly and distinctly perceived to belong to the nature of these things has the perfection of being true [added to the French version])" (CSM I, 202). In Part Two of the *Principles*, Descartes attempts to demonstrate (explain) the laws of motion from the immutability of God (CSM II, 240). And we have already noted the passage where Descartes derives the shape of salt crystals from other propositions about salt.

Descartes's systematically ambiguous treatment of "cause" and "effect" is in part fueled by his goal of finding geometrical-type demonstrations of natural phenomena. Such demonstrations are in principle possible, and in places Descartes seem to embrace something like the principle of sufficient reason that was explicitly embraced by both Spinoza and Leibniz. To Mersenne he writes:

> I have become so rash to seek the cause of the position of each fixed star For although they seem very irregularly distributed in various places in the heavens, I do not doubt that there is a natural order among them which is regular and determinate. . . . For if we possessed it [the order], we could discover a priori all the different forms and essences of terrestrial bodies, whereas without it we have to content ourselves with guessing them a posteriori and from their effects. (CSM III, 38)

In an ideal world we would be able to start with first principles known by the light of nature and deduce their particular effects (compare Garber 1993). In a less than ideal world like this one, we start with effects and prove their causes. So the proof of suppositions or deductively prior hypotheses lies in the fact that they entail sensibly knowable phenomena. In fact, Descartes, for a rationalist, shows a remarkable distrust of simply starting with the most foundational principles and discovering science in what they entail. Overall, Descartes is remarkably sensible about the roles of different kinds of inference in scientific thinking. For example, he does not put absolute trust in deduction, even from clear and distinct ideas. Proper scientific deductions must at some point terminate with observable phenomena; and Descartes even seeks applications (technology) to support his scientific conclusions and regards the applicability of these conclusions as an ultimate test of his hypothesizing (CSM I, 150–51). In short, Descartes holds that a priori science which starts with first principles and leads to concrete conclusions about phenomena is a "dream" and probably unrealizable (CSMIII, 38). Even a deduction of observable phenomena from a set of premises does not ensure that the premises (causes) are true, although if a set of premises imply a number and variety of effects, they are more likely to be true (CSMIII, 107). And while Descartes does not assume the truth of every premise (cause) that entails a known effect, he is aware that sometimes false causes (suppositions) can be useful to science—his example is that of the epicycles used in cosmology (CSM III, 107). Finally, although Descartes generally recognizes that advances in knowledge come through analysis, he does acknowledge that we may discover new things through deductive processes, for example, new properties of triangles (CSM II, 256). Thus, while many of Descartes's scientific conclusions are simply wrong, and we might feel that Descartes's goal of a geometrically ordered science is unrealistic, Descartes's insights into method are generally sophisticated and surprisingly grounded in empirical knowledge (Clarke 1982, Garber 1993a).

Let me now try to put this summary of Descartes's views on explanation into a set of theses:

(T) There are true causal explanations which involve causes other than God (CSM III, 107).

(C) Causal explanation is revealed by explanatory deductions which proceed from (efficient) causes to their effects (CSM III, 106–7).

(O) Effects are better known through observation and experimentation (CSM I, 150–51).

(R) Causes are proven" because their effects are known (CSMI, 150).

(D) There is a pure deductive order which begins with clear and distinct ideas and terminates in observable effects, but that order to the extent to which it can be known is known after the effects are known and not prior (CSM I, 202).

Clearly (T), which asserts that created things are true causes, conflicts with (7) above that concludes that only God offers a true causal explanation. In the next section I shall argue that for Descartes both God and created things are true causes and that Descartes embraces a philosophical position called "concurrentism" according to which there are multiple causes for any effect; effects proceed from God and God's creations acting concurrently. I shall also argue that the historically relevant model for Descartes's concurrentism is the Thomistic model defended by Aquinas in *Summa contra Gentiles*, Book III. For

Aquinas, concurrentism is the view that "the same effect is ascribed to a natural cause and to God, not as though part were affected by God and part by the natural agent; but the whole effect proceeds from each" (ACP II, 130).

But before I discuss the relevance of the Thomistic model, it is important to note that Descartes himself frequently uses the language of concurrentism:

> I nowhere denied God's immediate concurrence in all things; indeed I explicitly affirmed it in my reply to the theologian [Caterus] (CSM III, 180)
> I must not complain that the forming of those acts of will or judgements in which I go wrong happens with God's concurrence. (C II, 42)

> . . . no creature can operate without the concurrence of God. . . . (CSM III, 182)

> It is a much more certain that nothing can exist without the concurrence of God than that there can be no sunlight without the sun. There is no doubt that if God withdrew his concurrence, everything which he has created would immediately go to nothing; because all things were nothing until God created them and lent them his concurrence. This does not mean that they should not be called substances, because when we call a created substance self-subsistent we do not rule out the divine concurrence which it needs in order to subsist. (CSM III, 193)

Many of Aquinas's remarks on causation bear a striking parallel to those of Descartes; the issues that Aquinas raises are so similar to those which concern Descartes that even their examples overlap. This is not to say that Descartes is a Thomist, but—for all his anti-Scholastic remarks—there is a tradition, and a highly relevant one, on which he draws in thinking about causation. How Descartes ultimately develops concurrentism is, I think, purely his own because he clearly rejects the hylomorphism of the Scholastics. However, he retains some Scholastic principles—the causal principle for one—a principle that Descartes notes in Aquinas and one that he believes "all metaphysicians [including Aquinas] affirm" (CSM II, 254; compare Garber 1992, 274–75).[2] Aquinas's causal principle states that for the realm of "inferior things," "like produces like" (ACP II, 126–27). Aquinas even cites one apparent objection to this principle, namely, that in spontaneous generation life seems to come from nonlife and rejects it for the same reasons that Descartes does, namely, mud, sun, and rain are not total causes (compare ACP II, 124).

> . . . the sun, the rain, and the earth are not adequate causes of animals [flies]. . . . Suppose someone does not discern any cause cooperating in the production of a fly which possesses all the degrees of perfection possessed by the fly; suppose further that he is not sure whether there is any additional cause beyond those which he does discern: it would be quite irrational for him to

take this as a basis for doubting something which . . . is manifest by the very light of nature. (CSM II, 96)

And like Descartes, Aquinas denies that although he holds this causal principle, that principle requires the transfer of an accident from cause to effect.

Again, it is absurd to say that a body is not active [a cause] because accidents do not pass from one subject to another. For when we say that a hot body gives heat, we do not mean that the identical heat which is in the heater passes into the heated body; by virtue of the heat in the heater, another heat, individually distinct, which previously had been in it potentially, becomes actual in the heated body. For the natural agent does not transmit its own form into another subject. . . . (ACP II, 128)

Compare this passage with Descartes's remarks to More:

And I say "the transfer" as opposed to the force or action which brings about the transfer, to show that motion is always in the moving body as opposed to the body which brings about the movement. The two are not normally distinguished with sufficient care; and I want to make it clear that the motion of something that moves is, like the lack of motion in a thing which is at rest, a mere mode of that thing and not itself a subsistent thing, just as shape is a mere mode of the thing which has shape. (CSM I, 233)

Consider next Descartes's remarks about the relationship between creation and preservation from the "Third Meditation":

The same power and action are needed to preserve anything at each individual moment of its duration as would be required to create that thing anew if it were not yet in existence. Hence the distinction between preservation and creation is only a conceptual one. (CSM II, 33)

Aquinas's version reads thus:

The cause of a thing must needs be the same as the cause of its preservation, because preservation is nothing else than its continued being. (ACP II, 116–17)

Significantly, Descartes and Aquinas, having embraced the distinction between the universal and primary cause and the particular and secondary cause, offer very similar arguments as to why particular and secondary causes must be efficacious (CSM I, 240; ACP II, 122).

For if no inferior cause, above all a body, is active, and if God works alone in all things, then since God is not changed through working in various things, no diversity will follow among the effects through the diversity of the things in which God works. Now this is evidently false to the senses. (ACP II, 125)

Descartes, too, doubts that there could be diversity and change without particular causes:

> . . . there must be many changes in its parts which cannot, it seems to me, properly be attributed to the action of God because that action never changes, and which therefore I attribute to nature. (CSM I, 92–93)

Finally, Aquinas, more than Descartes, directly confronts the central problem:

> Some find it difficult to understand how the effects of nature are ascribed to God and to the natural agent.
>
> For it would seem impossible that one action should proceed from two agents. Hence if the action productive of a natural effect proceeds from a natural body, it does not proceed from God. . . .
>
> Besides, if God produces the whole natural effect, nothing of the effect is left for the natural agent to produce. Therefore, it seems impossible that God produce the same effects as natural things.

And Aquinas answers this challenge by defending concurrentism:

> The whole effect proceeds from each yet in different ways just as the whole of one and the same effect is ascribed to the instrument, and again the while is ascribed to the principal agent. (ACP II, 130)

Descartes does not seem to be attracted to Aquinas's metaphor of God as builder and matter as his tools, although such a metaphor is certainly open to Descartes. It is unclear whether Descartes simply rejects this metaphor as inappropriate or whether he believes that he has a better way of describing divine concurrence (see CSM III, 272).

Let us now return to Descartes's remarks about causal explanations and see if we can find a way of talking about concurrence that conforms to that account (compare Clatterbaugh 1995). If Descartes thinks of causes as deductively ordered, which he does, then the claim that there must be at least as much reality in the cause as in the effect (otherwise something comes from nothing) means in part that deductive orders are nonampliative, that is, there is no more information in the conclusion of such an inference than is already contained in the premises. This understanding helps to remove one of the more puzzling things about Descartes's defense of his causal principle, namely, that he seems totally confounded that anyone would question such an *obvious* principle (CSM II, 96, 97). Descartes's refusal to think that the principle needs much defense is certainly consistent with his belief that deductive sequences do not need to he justified (compare CSM II, 111).

We can also make sense of what Descartes means by the total efficient cause, namely, that from which the conclusion can be (in principle) derived. In describing causes as premises in this way, we need not deny that causes are also things. But we do need to acknowledge that Descartes's causal principle is richer in meaning than the strictly metaphysical interpretations of the previous chapter allow. Thus, when Descartes talks about God and God's attributes as causes, he also has in mind a set of propositions about God and God's attributes that entail other propositions (effects) (CSM I, 202). When Descartes talks about matter as a cause, he has in mind a set of propositions, mostly geometrical, that entail other propositions, effects of the properties of matter (CSM III, 77).

As we have noted, throughout his writings Descartes identifies God as the total efficient cause of all things. In causal explanations God plays a role as a first principle of primary laws. But Descartes's possessive examples of causes also include a wide variety of other entities; he identifies particular substances, such as the sun or salt crystals, and a variety of properties of these substances, such as their shape or quantity of motion. Thus, it would seem that causal explanations of phenomena include both God-premises and created thing-premises. More specifically, Descartes holds that God is the first total efficient cause of the eternal truths—mathematical and metaphysical (C II, 294). God is also the total efficient cause of the laws of motion (C I, 202). Eternal truths and the laws of motion can be instantiated into descriptive laws (C III, 77). These instantiated descriptive laws can be tested experimentally and observationally in further localized instantiations. In such a hierarchy all premises are "causes" of entailed effects, and all substances referred to in these premises are cases of all changes referred to in the conclusions. In this way God, eternal truths, the laws of motion, and particular motions are all equally causes in Descartes's rich and comprehensive sense. They operate concurrently as do premises. Or, to put it another way, the crucial premise that a cause is either necessary or sufficient for an effect—premise (5) in the argument leading to (7)—must be rejected as a conception of causation. It makes no more sense to deny that a particular cause is a cause because God is a total cause than it makes to deny that a premise is a premise because the argument contains a first premise. Thus, in the conflict between (7) and (T), the concurrentist reading of Descartes on causation gives a reason why (7) is false and (T) is true, that is, why created things *are* explanatory causes.

There are a number of virtues of this interpretation. First, as we have noted, it makes sense of Descartes's frequent puzzlement that anyone should doubt his causal principle. On this reading part of what that principle says is that the premises of a deductive argument must contain at least as much information as the conclusion.

Second, we can use this interpretation of scientific explanation to understand what Descartes means when he says in the *Principles* that we understand better how one body can move another but we cannot understand how the mind can be moved by the body. He is simply reminding us that the explanatory deductions from cause to effect are more complete in the case of bodies acting on bodies than in the case of minds and bodies. After all, in the *Principles*, where Descartes makes this statement, he gives us the laws of motion and some of their consequences, which he thinks are observable. He is unable to prove any such deduction for laws governing the interaction of minds and bodies, but that does not mean he abandons the goal of providing such a deduction.

Third, it gives a sense to the question of what it means for God and created things to act concurrently to produce effects. It makes sense of a causal principle that is otherwise puzzling by taking seriously Descartes's equivocation of "cause" and "effect."

However, there are a number of philosophical concerns about this reading of Descartes, some of which will be raised in the next chapter since Malebranche, in particular, regards concurrentism as an unintelligible doctrine.

At the outset we might wonder why Descartes never produces such a deduction. It would be helpful to see an actual deductive hierarchy that begins with the idea of God and other clear and distinct truths and ends in an observational effect. Descartes promises such examples, but never provides one.

The answer to this concern may be that Descartes regards such deductions as possible only in principle—they are the ideal or "dream" of science. The links among God, eternal truths, laws of nature, and their instantiations are difficult, and human ingenuity allows for a multitude of false tracks. Furthermore, Descartes thinks he has provided substantial parts of such deductions. In his "Replies to the Second Set of Objections" he sets out the beginnings of such a dream. And in the *Principles* he tries to link God's nature to the principle of the laws of nature. In other scientific writings such as the *Optics* he believes he has deduced observable and experimental results from such laws.

A second concern is a Leibnizian perplexity as to how the eternal truths can be deduced from the attributes of God and at the same time be freely chosen. Descartes seems to hold to a pair of incompatible propositions, namely, that

God could have made the eternal truths other than the ones he created and that the eternal truths are deducible from God's nature. If the eternal truths are freely chosen, then they would not seem to follow from God's nature; something Descartes himself seems to see (AT 150, 152; compare Wilson 1978, 123). If the eternal truths follow from God's nature, then it would not seem that they could have been otherwise, unless God's nature could have been otherwise—something Descartes does not admit.

The easy way out of this objection is for Descartes to invoke his agnosticism and argue that the most we can claim is that we simply cannot understand how God could have made the eternal truths different; thus we cannot claim that the eternal truths could or could not have been different, only that we cannot understand how they could have been different. Of course, this answer is a weaker claim than the one Descartes sometimes makes.

A third concern is perhaps the most intractable. Have we not simply shifted the language of the persistent problem of Descartes's implicit occasionalism? Now that problem takes the form of asking whether some premises are necessary to the deduction and some are superfluous. If only the God-premise is necessary, then are not the premises about particular causes redundant, and is not Descartes an occasionalist after all? And if some of the premises are independent of God and necessary for the deduction, then does not God's power fail in its sufficiency? The occasionalist problem simply reemerges in new language.

There is no ready answer to this final concern. Gaukroger, in his discussion of Descartes's theory of inference, notes that in treating inference as an intuition where the mind grasps all at once the connections among the propositions "Descartes is . . . ruling out any attempt at analyzing inferential steps" (Gaukroger 1989, 51). If Gaukroger is right, then Descartes has no way of drawing the distinction between inferences that are pure deductions—each step follows directly from the previous step—and deductions which are not pure. And Descartes's inability to draw this distinction might well explain why his concurrentism is untroubled by our objection. But surely Gaukroger's claim is too strong. It is not clear why, even if Descartes thinks of arguments as grasped in a single intuition, he could not break out subarguments to determine if the second step is necessarily connected to the first and the third to the second. Descartes even talks this way when he distinguishes the first steps (laws of nature) which follow from the immutability of God. But Gaukroger's point may well explain why Descartes does not bother to break arguments into inferential steps—since he sees each as an intuitive whole. Descartes's theory of inference is more of an explanation of why he *does* not see the occasionalist implications of his own metaphysics rather than an explanation of why he *cannot* see them.

CENTRAL THEMES

In the previous chapter we noted three very different lines of interpretation concerning Descartes's remarks about causation, namely: (1) that Descartes is a failed interactionist, (2) that Descartes is really an occasionalist, and (3) that Descartes has no theory of causation.

Each camp highlights certain features of Descartes's overall metaphysical system, while ignoring others. Our conclusion in this chapter is that Descartes is an interactionist with a fairly sophisticated but still troublesome view of causation. He does give God a prominent place in every causal explanation. He does identify some causal sequences in which the cause and effect share the same kind of property (although he also identifies causal sequences in which they do not). He is clearer about how bodies interact with each other than about how minds and bodies interact. And he thinks about causation in a complex way that embraces both causes as things and causes as premises in scientific explanations.

The failed interactionist interpretation exploits Descartes's failure to say as much about mind-body interaction as he does about body-body interaction and wrongly attributes that failure to an overly rigid metaphysical account of causation. The occasionalist interpretation overemphasizes the power of God to the exclusion of particular causes and in ignoring Descartes's version of concurrentism finds no other way than occasionalism to explain God as a total efficient cause. And the third line of thought highlights the incompleteness of Descartes's account of causation but generally ignores the many claims that Descartes does make in response to both the metaphysical and epistemological problems of causation.

Descartes is both a scientist and a metaphysical theologian. If we read Descartes only as a scientist, we ignore the vital role that his thinking about God plays in how he constructs his science. And I know of no convincing argument that all Descartes's talk about God is a sham and should be ignored; the contrary seems more likely (Collins 1960, 55–69). Yet, if Descartes were a full-blown occasionalist, he would be a metaphysician without a science, since he believes that the goal of science is causal explanation in terms of real causes. Furthermore, I know of no convincing argument to show that Descartes's talk about causation is a sham and that his only cause is God. Since Descartes is both religious and a scientist, he sought a view compatible with the real causal efficacy of God and the real causal efficacy of created substances. Ordering causes into an explanatory hierarchy gives meaning to their concurrence. He still leaves God, in a sense, in first place.

Our look at Descartes's view on causation reveals two qualifications on some widely held beliefs about Descartes's philosophy. It is generally agreed that Descartes is both a rationalist and a mechanist. But the qualifications make these labels less appropriate.

Descartes is certainly a rationalist in that he accepts the ability of reason to arrive at fundamental truths. But this ability is qualified in two ways. First, the fundamental truths, even the necessary ones, could have been other than they are. God willed the current division into necessary, merely possible, and contradictory propositions, and God willed that we understand these categories in certain ways. Descartes abandons anything like a common set of absolute truths and contradictions that are available to both infinite and finite minds. Second, Descartes seems to think that rationalistic justifications are more ideal than real. His test of the truth of most suppositions is whether they conform to observation and experiment. He expresses deep distrust of a purely or mostly deductive pattern as a method of discovery. He thinks that the logic of discovery will always be inductive as will the justification of most of our suppositions. All of this, of course, requires a considerable confidence in our knowledge of empirical generalizations and particular objects. Through both of these qualifications Descartes departs from traditional rationalist strategies.

We have already argued that Descartes's failure to locate any dynamic force in bodies may well disqualify him as a *pure* classical mechanist. His matter is inert, and that very inertness makes it difficult for Descartes to explain the most basic push-pull motions of bodies without appealing either to a divine impulse or a divine intervention. Since his view is reductionist, that is, he tries to explain other properties of matter in terms of matter in motion, his whole account ceases to be explained simply in terms of matter in motion. Stated in another way, any causal explanation of a moving body will quickly include premises whose terms refer not to bodies and their properties but to minds, particularly God's will and the motive force of God's will.

In effect, Descartes creates a new theory of causation. It bears a little similarity to the Aristotelian/Scholastic theories that come before it, but more importantly it offers a number of claims about causation that come to be viewed as purely Cartesian. And it is around these claims that the causation debate in modern philosophy continues to develop.

4.
Classical Mechanism: Hobbes and Gassendi

PLACE IN THE DEBATE

We have already noted that Descartes published his *Discourse on Method* in 1637. Thomas Hobbes (1588-1679) received a copy of the *Discourse* in the same year from Sir Kenelm Digby. Descartes's thoughts on method inspired Hobbes to begin his own work on his major treatise on method and physics, *Elements of Philosophy*. The first section, *Concerning Body* (*De Corpore*), was published in 1655. Descartes completed the *Meditations* in the years 1638–40. In 1640, the same year in which Mersenne introduced Hobbes to Pierre Gassendi (1592–1655), he asked both men to prepare objections to Descartes's *Meditations*. The *Meditations* together with six sets of objections and Descartes's replies were then published in 1641. The third set of objections is Hobbes's and the fifth is Gassendi's. During the time in which they were preparing their objections, Hobbes and Gassendi became close friends and correspondents, exchanging views on various philosophical topics (Sarasohn 1985).

Hobbes had been developing a materialistic natural philosophy since the early 1630s, during which he published *A Short Tract on First Principles*, otherwise known as the *Little Treatise* (Brandt 1927, 143). Hobbes's mature reflections on causation, however, were not published until 1655 in *Concerning Body*. In that work, Hobbes defends a strict materialism that is corpuscular in a universe that is comprehensively lawful. Hobbes's friend and colleague

Pierre Gassendi meanwhile pursued his own reflections on causation and materialism, after abandoning his projected seven-part work on Aristotle in 1628 in favor of a study and rehabilitation of Epicurean atomism. Gassendi's atomism transformed the ancient atomism of Democritus and Epicurus by inserting God as the creator and maintainer of the atoms in the void. Motion, too, was a creation infused into atoms at the creation. Just when his *Physics* was almost finished in 1637, Gassendi lost his enthusiasm for atomism, fearing that he had wandered too close to the deterministic (atheistic) materialism of Hobbes (Sarasohn 1985, 368; compare Brundell 1987, 74). But in 1641 Gassendi revived his project and before his death in 1655 completed the *Syntagma Philosophicum*, which contains his mature physics; this work was not published until the 1658 edition of his complete works (Popkin 1967 VIII, 270).

Gassendi and Descartes agreed about many things; they were both advocates of the mechanical philosophy, and they rejected Aristotelian essences and occult properties. They disagreed about the existence of the void, the nature of matter, and the foundations of scientific knowledge (Osler 1994, 8–9; compare Garber 1988 for another view). Descartes was a superb mathematician; Gassendi's approach was more experimental than mathematical. For example, Gassendi published the modern law of inertia and supported it experimentally. Descartes and Gassendi also disagreed about the nature of causation. In the long run, Gassendi's views on causation prevail, although throughout much of the debate it is Descartes's view that is the focus of attention. The scientist-philosophers and certain later philosophers agree with Gassendi that a cause is that which is so identified in the best available scientific explanation, rather than that which is subject to a set of metaphysical conditions. Descartes's requirements that the cause is necessarily connected to the effect and that the cause has at least as much reality as its effect are abandoned in favor of a more pragmatic view of causation.

Descartes, Hobbes, and Gassendi were each advocates of classical (push-pull) mechanism, although Descartes's identification of force with divine will ultimately separates the metaphysics of his mechanism from that of Hobbes and Gassendi. Still, the mechanisms of all three thinkers share a set of anti-Scholastic requirements on causation in the material world, namely, they are opposed to Scholastic forms, natures, and real qualities. Charleton, a follower of Gassendi and admirer of Descartes, describes these requirements as a way to "lance and cleanse this cacoethical ulcer," that is, the hidden qualities of the Scholastics:

> (1) That every effect must have its cause, (2) that no cause can act but by motion; (3) that nothing can act upon a distant subject, or upon such whereun-

to it is not actually present, either by it self, or by some instrument . . . and consequently, that no body can move another, but by contact mediate, or immediate, i.e. by the mediation of some continued organ, and that a corporeal one too,
or by itself alone. (1654, 343)

HOBBES

Descartes divides the world into two kinds of substance, mind and matter, or
three if God is a distinct kind of immaterial substance. Descartes then faces
the difficulty of explaining how mind and matter or, for that matter, how God
and matter can causally interact. Hobbes, however, is a thorough going mate-
rialist who holds "for the *universe*, being the aggregate of all bodies, there is
no real part thereof that is not also *body*, nor anything properly a body that is
not also part of . . . the *universe*" (CU, 261). In the *Leviathan* Hobbes argues
that "incorporeal substance" is as much an oxymoron as incorporeal body"
(CU, 21). Thus, Hobbes's only division of substances is between natural and
artificial bodies (Sorell 1988, 515). Hobbes's corpuscular materialism reduces
the three major problems about causation to a single problem. Since minds are
corporeal and God is corporeal, all causal interactions seem to reduce to the
interactions among bodies; Hobbes's materialism would seem to effectively
delete the problems about how essentially different substances can interact.

However, Hobbes's simplification of *divine* causation to ordinary material
causation is not as straightforward as it seems. In the initial creation God still
creates the universe *ex nihilo*, and there is nothing in standard body-body
interaction to account for this special causation.[1] Thus, in his "Appendix to
Leviathan" Hobbes states:

> What ought to be believed when we use this word "creator"? that this world
> was made from nothing?

> Certainly from nothing, and not, as Aristotle thought, from preexisting matter.
> For it is expressly said in Sacred Scripture that all things were made from noth-
> ing. . . . God, however, who has not been made, either by another or by himself,
> cannot be changed or suffer a transformation, either by himself or by another;
> he is, rather, immutable . . . (CU, 500)

Hobbes's language in these passages leaves a double difficulty. First, if God
creates the universe out of nothing, then that kind of causation is inexplicable
in terms of the laws of motion, which are supposed to account for all change.
Second, Hobbes argues from Biblical stories that after the creation God used a
voice to speak to humans, and if God literally spoke, then God must be cor-

poreal. "Can it be properly said that God hath voice and language, when it cannot be properly said he hath a tongue or other organs, as a man?" (CU, 284). But how can an *immutable* God interact, with a mutable material object? Any physical interaction between God and man would seem to require some changes in the corporeal God. Thus, the second difficulty is that Hobbes's conception of an immutable God does not mesh with his doctrine that God is corporeal and acts through corporeal changes (motion).

In the Hobbesian ontology everything is either a body or an accident of a body (MO I, 75–76). Thus, apart from the perplexities surrounding divine causation, Hobbes must explicate causation in terms of these two categories, a project he undertakes in *Concerning Body*.

Hobbes introduces his concept of *body* as "that, which having no dependence upon our thought, is coincident or coextended with some part of space" (MO I, 102; C 53). An *accident* is "that faculty of any body, with which it works in us a conception of itself" (MO I, 103; C, 54). Accidents can be divided between those that are common to all bodies, for example, extension, and those that are common to only some, for example, rest, motion, color, and hardness (MO I, 104; C, 55). These definitions of "body" and "accident" approximate those of Descartes, who also treats body as that whose essence is extension and who suggests in the "Second Set of Replies" that accidents are that by which we perceive subjects. Hobbes's distinction between accidents common to all bodies and accidents common to only some bodies also suggests Descartes's distinction between attributes and accidents. Finally like Descartes, Hobbes rejects atoms; all bodies are divisible, no matter how small.

In speaking of accidents that are common to bodies, Hobbes does not necessarily violate his nominalism, that is, his claim that there are no general or universal things (CU, 25). Nor does he violate his claim that there are no accidents separate from particular bodies (MO I, 33). For an accident (extension) to be common to two bodies (a desk and a chair), it is sufficient, in Hobbes's view, to hold that in the separate sentences "This desk is extended" and "That chair is extended" the predicate refers to this desk in the first sentence and the same predicate refers to that chair in the second (MO I, 30–31). Hobbes never answers the metaphysical question of whether there could not be accidents that are numerically one and the same in different bodies. But he is emphatically clear that no accident can exist *separately* from a particular body (compare CSM II, 122–23).

Although bodies may act on other bodies, it is accidents that are properly termed "causes" and "effects":

> A Body is said to work upon or act, that is to say, do something to another body, when it either generates or destroys some accident in it: and the body

in which accidents are generated or destroyed is said to suffer, that is, to have something done to it by another body. . . . The accident, which is generated in the patient, is called the effect. (MO I, 120; C, 69–70)

CAUSE simply, or an entire cause, is the aggregate of all the accidents both of the agents how many soever they be, and of the patient, put together; which when they are all supposed to be present, it cannot be understood but that the effect is produced at the same instant; and if any one of them be wanting, it cannot be understood but that the effect is not produced. (MO I, 122; C, 71)

Hobbes's identification of accidents rather than substances (bodies) as causes goes against the Aristotelian/Scholastic traditions. Even in Descartes's writings causes are usually substances, although substances become causes by containing a reality or degree of perfection. Hobbes thereby also abandons a core assumption of influx theory, namely, that causes are substances (O'Neill 1993; compare 1995, 26). Consistent with his discussion of causes, effects too are treated as properties, for example, a quantity of motion that comes to exist in certain bodies. Hobbes makes this shift explicit:

Fire . . . does not warm, because it is a body, but because it is hot; nor does one body put forward another body because it is a body, but because it moved into the place of that other body. The cause, therefore, of all effects consists in certain accidents both in the agents and in the patients. . . . (MO I, 121; C, 70)

Hobbes's innovative language leads him to make drastic changes in the use of "efficient cause" and "material cause" (Doney 1973, 295). The efficient cause becomes the set of accidents in the agent, rather than the agent, and the material cause is the set of accidents in the patient—the entire cause being the set of accidents in both sets (MO I, 121; C, 71). It is clear that the entire cause must be sufficient to produce its effect and that each accident must be individually necessary to produce the effect:

An entire cause is always sufficient for the production of its effect, if the effect be at all possible. . . . But if it be not produced, and yet be possible, it is evident that something was wanting either in some agent, or in the patient . . . that is, that some accident was wanting which was requisite for its production. (MO I, 122; C, 71–72)

Hobbes further identifies "the power of the agent" and "the efficient cause," although at the same time he identifies the cause through the effect that it produces, whereas the *power* is "in respect of the same effect to be produced" (MO I, 127–28; C 76). In other words, "the cause is with respect to the past, power with respect to the future time" (MO I, 127–28, C, 76).

The fact that Hobbes speaks of power as relating to the future time should not be taken to suggest that causes occur temporally prior to their effects, although he wavers on this issue. In his definition of "cause" Hobbes makes it clear that cause and effect occur at "the same instant" (MO I, 122, 123; C, 71). Later, in the section on cause and effect Hobbes suggests that accidents that precede effects in time are contingent accidents, not causes (MO I, 126-27; C, 75). However, in the sections "On Method" in *De Corpore* Hobbes suggests that some accidents that are causes may precede their effects, although in the same passage he argues that if an accident is not present, the effect cannot occur (MO I, 77). Thus, for Hobbes, causes are generally instantaneous with their effects, although some prior accidents may be included in the entire cause. Hobbes offers no criteria to decide which prior accidents should be included and which should not; obviously there are an indefinite number of prior accidents such that if they did not occur the effect would not occur.

We have seen that Descartes's science is reductive with respect to certain properties (secondary) such as color, taste, and smell, and Hobbes, like Descartes, tends to see color, taste, and other qualities of sense as derivative from matter in motion.

> For the variety of all figures arises out of the variety of those motions by which they are made; and motion cannot be understood to have any other cause besides motion; nor has the variety of those things we perceive by sense, as of colours, sounds, savours, & c. any other cause than motion, residing partly in the objects that work upon our senses, and partly in ourselves, in such manner, as that it is manifestly some kind of motion, though we cannot, without ratiocination, come to know what kind. (MO I, 69–70; C, 22)

In other places, Hobbes is more cautious in talking about "secondary" properties, although he clearly entertains the hypothesis that they in some way reduce to matter in motion.

> And as for the opinion that some may have, that all other accidents are not in their bodies in the same manner that extension, motion, rest, or figure, are in the same; for example, that colour, heat, odour, virtue, vice, and the like, are otherwise in them, and, as they say, inherent; I desire they would suspend their judgment for the present, and expect at little, till it be found out by ratiocination, whether these very accidents are not also certain motions either of the mind or the perceiver, or of the bodies themselves which are perceived. (MO I, 104–5; C, 55)

It is difficult to see how Hobbes can avoid holding some form of reduction of secondary properties to primary properties whether the secondary ones are located only in the perceiver or partially in the perceiver and partially in the object of perception. When he speaks of change or mutation in things he is prepared to allow that all change is due to corpuscles in motion.

> . . . it is necessary that mutation can be nothing else but motion of the parts of that body which is changed. (MO 1, 26; C, 75)

> . . . mutation is motion . . . mutation, howsoever it be made, will consist in the motion of the parts, either of the body which is perceived, or of the sentient body, or of both. (MO I, 126, C, 75)

He is also clear that he holds the mechanist principle that nothing can cause motion except "a body contiguous and moved" (MO I, 125; C, 73). Thus, given his belief that all change is motion of corpuscles, it would seem that Hobbes must embrace a reduction of all accidents to motions; otherwise, how could accidents be the causes of other accidents?

Let us return now to Hobbes's definition of "cause" as *the total set of accidents (motions) in the agent and patient that are simultaneous with the effect and that are jointly sufficient and individually necessary to produce the effect.* Even at first glance this definition seems to have inadequacies.

In the first place it appears to be circular. The identity of the accidents that count as the cause is, in part, that they are accidents of the agent and the patient. But *agent* and *patient* are themselves used here as actor and recipient of action; in fact, Hobbes identifies the agent with what has the accidents making up the efficient cause and the patient with what has the accidents making up the material cause (MO I, 127–28; compare Leijenhorst 1996). But if the identity of accidents depends on the identities of agent and patient and these in turn depends upon the identity of causal accidents, then Hobbes's conception is clearly circular. And even if there is a way around this circularity, "agent" and "patient" are themselves terms understood as cause and recipient of causal action, which suggests we need a working notion of causation in order to understand Hobbes's conception of causation.

A second concern about Hobbes's metaphysics of causation is that it fails to answer the metaphysical problem of causation. The metaphysical problem of causation is to discover just what goes on at the metaphysical level during a genuine causal interaction. Hobbes tells us that all true interactions involve accidents and that these accidents must be present and that a change in the motion of the parts of agent and/or patient is required. What is not answered is: just how does one body bring about or produce a change in another body? Having reduced the problem of causal interaction to the interaction of bodies, Hobbes remains sketchy, to say the least, on the metaphysical details. More specifically, Hobbes does seem to hold some version of what O'Neill calls "the atomistic-corpuscular influx model" in which what is transferred from one body to another is a corporeal entity. Hobbes says as much when he notes that motion arises "when one body invades another body which is either at rest or in motion" (MO I, 71). But "invades" is itself a causal term, so we are left wondering just how that corporeal entity from the agent affects the motion of the patient (O'Neill 1992, 48 ff.; MO I, 203–17). Hobbes tells us in the *Leviathan* that "motion produceth nothing but motion" (CU, 7). But how does motion produce motion?

Hobbes's very definition of motion, "the continual privation of one place, and acquisition of another," favors descriptive laws, like those of Descartes; they tell us what happens when bodies possessing a certain motion or rest come into contact with other bodies also so modified (MO I, 204). For example, "whatsoever is at rest will always be at rest, unless there be some other body besides it, which by getting into its place suffers it no longer to remain at rest" (MO I, 205). Or in the case of two bodies of equal magnitude the swifter moving body can do greater work (MO I, 217). But nowhere does Hobbes speculate about the motive force that produces the change of place or how this force metaphysically manifests itself in different parts of matter.

The wording of Hobbes's laws of motion, in contrast with those of Descartes, does not use the language of communication or transfer of motion. Hobbes suggests that bodies may change direction or speed because they are pressed or pushed by other bodies. In some places Hobbes suggests that a pressed body will return to its original shape if the pressing body is removed (MO I, 343–44; C, 100). In other places he talks about weak and strong "endeavours" that may compete but when the hindrance to one endeavour is removed, it will resume (MO I, 345; C, 104). These claims are empirically suspect, and they seem to suggest a conservation principle by which each body has a set amount of motive force that it never loses and the motions of the body never change, except temporarily, under the influence of a stronger endeavor. Such a view, if that is what Hobbes is offering, has the advantage of defusing the idea that motion is the transfer of an accident, but it requires an account of what happens internally to a body whose endeavor is thwarted by a stronger endeavor that allows that body to cease and then resume its earlier state. In fact, such an account is not forthcoming from Hobbes except to repeat the story. Bodies are just aggregates of other bodies (CU, 260–61). Macroscopic mechanisms move as they do because their endeavor is the sum of the combined endeavors of corpuscles or internal parts that they contain or acquire as physical influxes (MO I, 335–37, 345–47). And since the internal parts themselves are moved in the same way, Watson argues that mechanisms like Hobbes's are committed to endless causal accounts of microscopic motions (1993, 86). Another way to state Watson's claim is that

Hobbes's mechanism only puts off the metaphysical problem of causation; it does not attempt to answer it.

Hobbes's claim that entire causes are sufficient and that each component accident is necessary—otherwise the cause would not be entire—does not of itself make Hobbes's view necessitarian, although his belief that the universe is comprehensively lawful may well make his view deterministic. Hobbes probably accepts (D) without being committed to (N):

> (D) Every change of accident has an entire cause. [(D) is simply one principle of mechanism.]

> (N) If C is a true causal statement, then C is a necessarily true.

However, as Brandt has argued, Hobbes seems to take the additional step of embracing (N) along with (D) (1927, 266; compare Sorell 1986, 94):

> A necessary cause is defined to be that, which being supposed, the effect cannot but follow. . . . It may be shewn, that whatsoever effects are hereafter to be produced, shall have a necessary cause; so that all the effects that have been, or shall he produced, have their necessity in things antecedent. (MO I, 123; C 72).

Hobbes's language in this passage is such that we may wonder if we are here again encountering an equivocation that allows causes to be both accidents of bodies and premises in scientific explanations, which Hobbes takes to be deductive. Brandt, for example, notes that the language by which Hobbes talks about the premise-conclusion relationship is strikingly similar to that used to describe the cause-effect relationship (Brandt 1927, 275). Thus, in Part I of *De Corpore* Hobbes defines the logical relationship as follows:

> A proposition is said to follow from two other propositions when, these being granted to be true, it cannot be denied but the other is true also. For example, let these two propositions, *every man is a living creature*, and *every living creature is a body*, be supposed true. . . . Therefore, if these be understood to be true, it cannot be understood . . . that *every man is a body* is false, this proposition [*every man is a body*] will be said to follow from those two, or to be necessarily inferred from them. (MOI, 42)

Similarly, when Hobbes talks about cause-effect relationships, he argues that once we have a characterization of the cause *we cannot but understand* that the effect is produced (MO I, 123; C, 72). In fact, Hobbes makes it a feature of a *necessary* as opposed to a *contingent* proposition that once the subject is named, one cannot but conceive of the predicate (MO I, 37).

Although Hobbes suggests that cause-effect claims are necessary in precisely the same way that premise-conclusion claims are necessary, it does not follow that Hobbes confuses the two. Indeed much of our discussion of the epistemology of causation will focus on the question of how Hobbes understands these two relationships.

Hobbes's entire epistemology revolves around his basic concept of causation. He defines philosophy as knowledge acquired by reason (ratiocination) of effects from their causes or knowledge of causes through their effects (MO I, 65–66; MO I, 3; C, 18–19; C, 6). Descartes, similarly, embraces both forms of knowledge in his *Discourse on Method* wherein he describes explaining effects through their causes and establishing causes through their effects (O, 60–61). Even when Hobbes speaks of primary universal propositions that are "manifest of themselves," these propositions are identified as causes (MO I, 69, 81; C, 22; C, 32–33). Similarly, the goal of method is for Hobbes finding "the shortest way of finding out effects by their known causes, or of causes by their known effects" (MO I, 66; C, 18).

Descartes's distinction between analysis and synthesis also appears in Hobbes; generally, *synthesis* is reasoning (deductively) from cause to effect; *analysis* proceeds from effects to their causes (CSM II, 110; O, 52–53, xviii-xxvii). Indeed, what is striking about Hobbes's account is that causal inferences are the only way to gain knowledge.

Synthesis (true science) for Hobbes is deductive reasoning from universal principles to other principles—from cause to effect (MO I, 66, 70-71; C, 18, 22–23; Brandt 1927, 243). Hobbes lists a number of first principles, many of which are simply definitions of key terms such as "motion," "line," "body," and "place" (MO I, 69–71; C, 22–24). Having defined the key terms, "it remains, that we enquire what motion begets such and such effects; as, what motion makes a straight line, and what a circular; what motion thrusts, what draws . . ." (MO I, 71; C, 23). Sorell notes that Hobbes's first principles, unlike Descartes's, are "preliminary to explanation proper" a lexicon of general terms (Sorell 19986, 58-59, 61–62).

Much of *De Corpore* is synthesis, especially Part III, Chapter XV, on motion and endeavor (MO I, 203–17; C, 95–105; compare Brandt 1927, 243). For example, having defined "motion" as "the continual privation of one place, and acquisition of another" and "impetus" as the "velocity of the body moved," Hobbes observes that if the body moved is a straight line, not a point, then the plane "described by its motion" will be greater or less in proportion to its impetus (MO I, 207–8; C, 98–99). In effect, Hobbes's physics is geometrical physics—the motions of bodies described in purely geometrical terms.

Analysis for Hobbes is the process of looking at the effect, often empirically known, and arriving at universal or general principles (MO I, 68–69; C, 21). To use Hobbes's example, a singular thing, say, a square object, has *general causes*, the universal notions of plane, equal-sidedness, etc., which are needed to have the idea of a square, and *particular causes*, the accidents of the artist or printer that produced the square. Thus, part of what Hobbes counts as analysis is conceptual analysis, that is, breaking out the universal notions that are elements in the concept of a particular thing. The other part of analysis is the discovery of the particular causes of a particular object, taking the accidents singly and determining if they are necessary to the effect (MO I, 78–79; C, 28–29). In Hobbes's words in *De Corpore*, Chapter VI, "On Method":

> But to those that search after science . . . which consists in the knowledge of the causes of all things, . . . it is necessary that they know the causes of universal things, or of such accidents as are common to all bodies . . . before they can know the causes of singular things, that is, of those accidents by which one thing is distinguished by another. (MO I, 68; C, 21)

Thus, Hobbes's notion of analysis is a combination of empirical induction—finding the particular causes—and conceptual analysis—finding the general and universal causes.

In most cases, when we look for causes, we combine both analysis and synthesis. Synthesis often begins with definitions or first causes, and analysis is used to arrive at intermediate causes of particular events. This combination produces a deductive sequence that is science or knowledge MO I, 79–81 C 31–32; compare CU< 22–27).

Given the above discussion, it might seem that Hobbes is guilty, as was Descartes, of conflating "cause" with "premise" and "effect" with "conclusion." However, Hobbes's various discussions of these notions suggest that he is prepared to draw a distinction between real efficient cause (accidents) and propositions in causal explanations:

> Now, seeing none but a true proposition will follow from true, and that the understanding of two propositions to be true, is the cause of understanding that all to be true which is deduced from them; the two antecedent propositions are commonly called the causes of the inferred proposition, or conclusion. And from hence it is that logicians say, the premises are causes of the conclusion; which may pass, though it be not properly spoken; for though understanding be the cause of understanding, yet speech is not the cause of speech. But when they say the cause of the properties of any thing, is the thing itself, they speak absurdly. . . . But seeing the figure does not itself make its angles, and therefore cannot be said to be the efficient-cause, they call it the formal-cause; whereas indeed it is no cause at all; nor does the property of any figure follow the figure, but has its being at the same time with it; only the knowledge of the figure goes before the knowledge of the properties; and one knowledge is truly the cause of another knowledge. (MO I, 43–44)

In reasoning Hobbes distinguishes the propositions (speech or letters) that make up a syllogism from the thoughts or knowledge that are associated with these propositions (MO I, 49–50). Both of these entities are distinct from the bodies and accidents about which one is trying to reason. Propositions are never causes of other propositions, although logicians talk this way. Thoughts or knowledge are causes of other thoughts or knowledge. Deduction occurs for Hobbes when the mind *cannot but move* from one thought to another (MO I, 42). Thus, Hobbes's notion of inference seems to involve his notion of cause: in deductive inference one bit of knowledge *causes* another bit of knowledge, every bit of knowledge being an accident of a corporeal mind. Thus, inference becomes a special kind of causal interaction, namely, one that has knowledge or understanding as cause and effect. But there are difficulties with this view.

In the first place, such an explication fails to capture in an adequate way the nature of logical necessity. We have already seen that the necessity in causation is explained in the same terms as the necessity in deduction; thus causation can hardly capture logical necessity for Hobbes except in a circular manner.

Second, even if we grant that in deductive inferences one bit of knowledge causes another bit of knowledge, not all "reasonings" are certain or deductive. Hobbes admits as much in the *Leviathan* where he notes that some science is certain and infallible and some is probable but uncertain (CU, 26–27; compare Brandt 1927, 221). In the *Elements*, Chapter VI, section 1, Hobbes distinguishes two kinds of knowledge: knowledge that is truly science, which involves knowledge of causes and is properly *science*, and knowledge that is *history*, which depends upon sense, imagination, and memory (MO I, 3, 10–11; 65–66; compare CU, 25, and Sorell 1986, 45–54). Brandt's translation of the relevant parts of Chapter VI, section 1, of *De Corpore* is:

> There be two sorts of knowledge, whereof the one is nothing else but sense, or knowledge original, and remembrance of the same; the other is called science or knowledge of the truth of propositions, and how things are called, and is derived from understanding . . . and of the former, the register we keep in books, is called history: but the registers of the latter are called the sciences. (Brandt 1927, 221)

Thus, Hobbes needs another way to characterize the relationship between two bits of knowledge where the inference is *not* deductive. In fact, Hobbes has a candidate for this connection; it is the relationship between a sign and a thing signified or antecedent and consequent:

> A sign is the event antecedent of the consequent, and contrarily, the consequent of the antecedent, when the like consequences have been observed

before; and the oftener they have been observed, the less uncertain is the sign. (CU, 14; compare MO I, 79–80; C, 31)

It would seem, then, that some bits of knowledge could be associated with other bits of knowledge by the repeated experience of observation and memory. Hobbes can, consistent with his view of signs, treat these bits of knowledge not as causes of each other but as associations learned from experience, in much the same manner as "a thick cloud is a sign of rain to follow, and rain a sign that a cloud has gone before" (MO I, 14–15). In his discussion of signs Hobbes is careful to avoid using the terms "cause" and "effect" (Brandt 1927, 270–71). But our distinction between sign/signified and cause/effect means that for Hobbes the distinction between science and history not only describes the content of the two but also how the bits of thought are connected. When one thought *causes* another—for example, knowledge of the nature of triangle causes me to know that all triangles have interior angles equal to two right angles—that knowledge is deductive; it is *science*. When one thought is habitually associated with another—perhaps some third bit of knowledge causes both—then we have probable or uncertain reasoning grounded in memory of associations; that is *history*.

There is an obvious similarity between Hobbes's wording about signs and Hume's description of a cause as an event that is so regularly associated with another event that when the first occurs we are led to think of the second. But Hobbes is clear that sign/signified is not a causal relationship. It may be a flaw of his whole discussion of causation that only necessarily related accidents can be causal, but then Hobbes's view can hardly be an anticipation of Hume who denies this very necessary connection. That some events are only signs of others is, in Hobbes's view, the very reason we should not treat them as causes. Thus, the fact that we can, indeed we must, reason from cause to effect should not be confused with the habit we have in some cases of jumping from one event to another.

Descartes's hostility to Hobbes (that Englishman) is well known, as is Hobbes's view that Descartes in certain respects remains too close to the Scholastic philosophy (CSMII, 122; CSM III, 178). Brandt attributes the strained relations between the two not to philosophical differences but to philosophical agreement and the question of who thought of it first.

> The enmity that sprang up between Descartes and Hobbes during their exchange of correspondence in 1641 is not—strange to say—due to their being at variance in philosophical matters, but precisely because they were of one mind. The points where they were at variance (the determination of motion, the physical cause of the rebound of bodies, the transmission of light etc.) they discuss calmly, but the ideas about which they agree (*materia sub-*

tilis and the subjectivity of sensible qualities) arouse their ire, for concealed
behind this agreement there lies the question of priority. (1927, 141–42)

Sorell also notes, "Despite their fallings out in 1641 and 1648, Hobbes and
Descartes did not disagree fundamentally in their approach to questions in
natural science" (Sorell 1988, 515). At the same time, Sorell notes that there
are differences in their respective views of the foundations of science.
Descartes, for example, seriously believes that God's attributes, especially
God's immutability, is a first premise in causal explanation and a first cause in
the metaphysics of causation. God's causal powers are also unlimited and special since God contains more formal perfection than any other entity. Hobbes,
while he agrees that there must be first principles or self-evident definitions
before scientific explanation can proceed, explicitly excludes God from first
principles:

> The subject of Philosophy . . . is every body of which we can conceive any
> generation . . . that is to say, every body of whose generation or properties we
> can have any knowledge. . . . And . . . where there is no generation or prop-
> erty, there is no philosophy. Therefore, it excludes Theology, I mean the doc-
> trine of God, eternal, ingenerable, incomprehensive, and in whom there is
> nothing either to divide nor compound, nor any generation to be conceived.
> (MO I, 10)

In the context of the causation debate there are once again significant differences and special similarities between Hobbes and Descartes. Burn argues:

> Hobbes's combination of materialism and nominalism . . . prepared him to
> proclaim quite frankly and without the qualifications and exceptions in
> Galileo and Descartes the doctrine of causality which has become accepted
> more and more fully and clearly in modern times. . . . Hobbes insists very
> strongly on interpreting causality always in terms of particular motions of
> particular bodies. The vast, hidden forces which were for Galileo the prima-
> ry or ultimate causes of effects, disappear in Hobbes. (Burtt 1925, 125)

Burtt's view of Hobbes on causation is right in asserting that Hobbes seems
closer to a modern notion of causation, but Burtt is wrong to assert that primary or ultimate causes totally disappear in Hobbes. Both Descartes and
Hobbes cite particular causes for particular effects, and both Descartes and
Hobbes cite universal causes and principles for general effects. Some among
the general causes are self-evident, or as Hobbes observes, "The highest causes, and most universal in every kind, are known by themselves" (MO I, 69).
Indeed, how can a deductive system which proceeds from knowledge of the
general to knowledge of the particular do without primary causes? In his dis-

cussion of abstract names, Hobbes is clearly aware of the need to transcend talk about individual bodies in favor of talk about the accidents that they have in common and that are lawfully connected:

> Now in all matters that concern this life, but chiefly in philosophy, there is both great use and great abuse of *abstract names*; and the use consists in this, that without them we cannot, for the most part, either reason or compute the properties of bodies; for when we would multiply, divide, add, or subtract heat, light, or motion, if we should double or add them together by concrete names, saying (for example) hot is double to hot, light double to light.. . we should not double the properties, but the bodies themselves that are hot, light, moved, & c. (MO I, 33)

At the same time, Burtt is correct in noting that Hobbes is closer to a more modern notion of causation if this closeness amounts to distancing his theory of causation from that of the Scholastics. In the first place, Descartes insists, but Hobbes does not, that the total efficient cause must contain, formally or eminently, the reality which is formally in the effect. We have already reviewed the struggles over Descartes's causal principle and noted that at least the language of this principle calls to mind Scholastic theories of causation. Descartes's dualism also makes his theory complicated because he is unable to explain how minds act on bodies or bodies act on minds. How God acts on the material world is equally mysterious for Descartes, especially in light of Descartes's view that somehow God and created things act concurrently in the production of change. Hobbes, in contrast, frees his view of causation from principles like the causal principle, and he makes everything material; thus, Hobbes comes as close as possible to a strictly mechanistic view of causation, by which I mean that he conceives of macroevents as governed by a push-pull form of causation and views the microworld as alike in kind to this macroworld.

Still, Hobbes's discussion of what happens metaphysically in causal interactions is far from clear. How God creates a material world out of nothing is a mystery. And even though God is not part of the explanation of change, God does interact with the material world. And how God, a material being, interacts with the material world without changing is left unexplained. Perhaps most importantly, Hobbes never attempts to explain how motion causes motion; he limits himself to describing the behavior of bodies in motion and at rest. Thus, while Hobbes encounters fewer metaphysical perplexities because of his thoroughgoing materialism, he essentially abandons much of the metaphysical task of showing how causation works in favor of the scientific task of listing the necessary accidents that accompany various changes.

GASSENDI

Gassendi's views on causation appear from the outset to be filled with paradox. On the one hand, Gassendi seriously pursues scientific understanding and scientific explanation—he keeps current on the science of his time and even replicates some experiments, for example, those used to determine that the height of a column of mercury varied inversely with its altitude (Osler 1994, 186). On the other hand, as an admirer of the ancient skeptics, Gassendi often seems to deny that we can have knowledge of the true causes of things:

> The occasion arises only too frequently in the physical sciences to declare that we are fortunate if we attain not what is true but what is probable. As you see we feel that in such an incapacitated state it should be considered a great gain if we can rise to the point where we may glimpse not the truth itself, . . . but some slight image of it, or even its shadow. For indeed nothing would be more beautiful . . . than to know fully the things that nature had kept in her depths or her farthest recesses; but though we may wish for that. we are being quite absurd as when we yearn to fly like the birds or to stay young forever. . . . (G, 327)

To continue with the paradoxes, on the one hand, Gassendi wants to have a science of appearances; on the other hand, Gassendi defends a metaphysical structure, atomism, that is nonempirical and for which many of his arguments are historical and conceptual rather than empirical. On the one hand, Gassendi denies that there is any causation except efficient causation; on the other hand in his correspondence with Descartes he defends final causes as contributing to our understanding of natural things (CSM II, 215).

These paradoxes have contributed to the view that Gassendi's *Syntagma Philosophicum* is "an unreadable compilation of everything ever said on the topics discussed. . . . The work grew like Topsy, and was published in its ultimate form only as a posthumous work, when the author was finally beyond the possibility of adding and patching" (Westfall 1971. 39; compare Brett 1908). And Gassendi is frequently omitted—probably for such reasons—from historical accounts of the mechanical philosophy before the 1980s. However, in the late 1980s Gassendi was rediscovered as a major figure of modern philosophy, a writer whose major work offers a systematic and coherent view of science (Joy 1987; Brundell 1987; Lennon 1993a; Sorell 1993; Osler 1994).

Gassendi's skepticism leads him to avoid prolonged discussions of the metaphysics of causation and when he does discuss the issue, it is often to criticize the views of others, especially Descartes and the Scholastics.

In the "Fifth Set of Objections" to Descartes's *Meditations* Gassendi clearly rejects Descartes's causal principle. Gassendi interprets this principle as requiring either that there is a likeness between the total efficient cause and its effect or that the effect somehow preexists in the total efficient cause.

> An efficient cause is something external to the effect and often of a quite different nature. Although an effect is said to get its reality from its efficient cause, it does not follow that the efficient cause necessarily has this reality in itself; it may have borrowed it from elsewhere. This is transparently clear if we consider effects produced by some skill. Although a house gets all its reality from the builder, the builder does not have this reality in himself—he simply takes it from some other source and passes it on to the house. The sun does the same when it transforms inferior matter in various ways so as to produce various animals. . . . Your objection that the effect must be contained in the cause "either formally or eminently" proves nothing more than that an effect sometimes has a form which resembles the form of its cause, while sometimes it has a dissimilar and imperfect form. . . . But it does not follow that even an eminent cause bestows on the effect some of its essence (that is, that which it contains formally), or that it shares its form with the effect. (CSM II, 201)

Gassendi's insight in this objection is that while it is true that the cause sometimes resembles the effect, resemblance is not a metaphysically necessary condition between cause and effect. More specifically, the cause neither needs to be of the same essence as the effect, which Foucher assumed to be Descartes's view, nor needs to contain the same accidents as the effect—Radner's interpretation of Descartes—although in some cases it may share accidents or essences with its effect. Gassendi is at least suggesting that if Descartes's causal principle is a close relative of the Scholastic influx model that requires a transmission of either an accidental or essential property from cause to effect, then Descartes is mistaken about the nature of causation (Lindberg 1983, 45).

What is significant in Gassendi's argument is that he is explicitly rejecting any theory of preexistence or likeness between cause and effect. And given that he is an atomist who holds that atoms produce qualities they do not themselves possess and that atoms, which are indivisible, may produce matter which is divisible, it is not surprising that Gassendi should reject what he perceives as claims of likeness between cause and effect. However, as we shall see, Gassendi, like Hobbes, builds a version of a likeness principle into his science by insisting that among secondary causes, only motion can produce motion.

Descartes's response to Gassendi does not directly challenge Gassendi's counterexample—in part this may be because Descartes himself does not insist on a likeness between cause and effect. Instead, Descartes first argues that Gassendi himself concedes that the form or reality must preexist in the material cause, an idea which Descartes rejects because he holds that it preexists in the efficient cause (CSM II, 252). In fact, Descartes is mistaken; what Gassendi suggests is that a builder—the efficient cause—*may* borrow the properties of a house from the materials that are used. This claim does not commit Gassendi to the view that the properties preexist in the matter, although they might. Descartes also argues that Gassendi reaches the same conclusion that Descartes does. What Descartes means by this claim is unclear, but Gassendi is certainly prepared to concede that except for the initial creation, something does not come from nothing, which Descartes takes to be the main content of his causal principle (G, 398–408; CSM II, 97).

Gassendi displays a thorough familiarity with the classical distinctions of formal, final, material, and efficient causation. Formal causes are rejected by Gassendi because he views them as "incorporeal" efficient causes whose principle of action is a mystery and "mere verbiage" (G, 415–16; compare Brundell 1987, 125). Final causes are defended by Gassendi only in the sense that from God's creation, "the excellent works of this universe," one can make inferences to "God's existence, power and goodness" (G, 208–9). God's purposes are hardly the final causes of Aristotle or the Aristotelian Scholastics. And Gassendi makes no use of God's purposes in scientific explanations.

Gassendi's discussion of the distinction between material and efficient cause is original. He construes the debate about material cause versus efficient cause as a question as to "whether all matter is active" and he tends to side with the view that there is no passive matter, although "nothing prevents us from supposing either that some atoms are inert or that they are not all equally mobile" (G, 417, 418). Thus, the distinction between material and efficient cause becomes the difference between atoms that are more active (contain more motion) in the production of their effects and atoms that are more passive in their causal role. And he tends to see the activity of the efficient cause as producing new accidents or modes in the material cause (patient):

> To explain the matter more clearly, whenever a craftsman is the cause of something, a house for example, as he works toward that end, or builds, he is a being and a body; but what he makes or what results from his construction is not stone, not quicklime, not plaster, not wood, nor any being, or body, at all that had been a body before, but is only a mode, form, or arrangement added to such preexisting bodies by which means an assemblage of them arranged in this fashion earns the name house. But others did not distinguish cause and matter in this way....(G, 410–11)

The idea of more active bits of matter producing organization in less active bits of matter—the way a general might collect an army—fits well with Gassendi's view of how things come to be from atoms that are both matter and artisan but some are more artisan while other are more matter (G, 418–19). In the end, material and efficient causation are "different in thought, but not in fact and substance" (G, 411). Perhaps a better way to put the distinction is that material and efficient causes are different only in degree not in kind.

Gassendi's distinction is made possible in part because he takes up explicitly a doctrine suggested by Hobbes, namely, that the motive force of an atom is a constant in each atom that can only be held back or augmented through collisions with other bodies. Gassendi seems to adopt such a view explicitly:

> One thing may be legitimately assumed, namely that however much mobility may have been implanted in the atom, it continues to be the same always, so that atoms may indeed be restrained until they do not move, but not to the point that they do not strain and endeavor to disentangle themselves and renew their motion. (G, 417).

Thus, Gassendi, like Hobbes, apparently avoids discussing the problem of the transfer of motion. Unlike Descartes, who seems to imagine a "force" as moving from body to body, Gassendi imagines bodies with a fixed amount of force constraining one another or pushing one another, each trying to restore itself to some initial state. But like Hobbes's, this view requires some account of what happens to the "force" when the body is constrained or pushed and how that "force" restores itself in unconstrained situations. Gassendi offers no speculations on these matters.

In his positive view on causation, Gassendi, like Hobbes, is attracted to a physical influx model of causal interaction. Aquinas notes in the *Summa Theologica* that the atomist Democritus "claimed that every operation [*actionem*] is by way of an influx [*influxionem*] of atoms" (as in O'Neill 1992, 38). Gassendi certainly seems to embrace this atomistic view with regard to the corporeal world. He notes:

> . . . it must be concluded first that the internal principle of action that works in second causes is not some incorporeal substance, but a corporeal one (G, 412)

> . . . that the principle of action in bodies must be corporeal can be inferred from the fact that since corporeal actions are physical, they cannot be induced by any principle except a physical and corporeal one. (G, 412–13)

In his discussion of causes in the *Syntagma* Gassendi identifies "real" causation with "physical" causation (G, 414).

Atoms are the ultimate indivisible elements of matter; atoms also exist independently of one another, though not of God. Gassendi's atomistic thesis, then, is both a physical and a metaphysical one (compare Lennon 1993a, 138–39). He "praised the Epicurean/Stoic rejection of a distinction between physics and metaphysics" (Brundell 1987, 71). Atoms, as we have noted, are both material and efficient causes; they are the agents, "imbued" with motion, that cause other atoms (matter) to move or rest (G, 41; compare Brundell 1987, 119–21). Atoms, for Gassendi, have the qualities of size, shape, and weight or motion (G, 424). Atoms also have impenetrability (solidity) which allows them to impart motion to other atoms, roll about, and knock into other atoms (G, 400–401; compare Osler 1994, 191). Atoms collect into "molecules," gaining size until they "can be observed" (G, 422). Other qualities such as color, warmth, and taste are due to the combinations of atoms and how they impinge on the senses (G, 424). In one passage, Gassendi presents his reductionistic explanation of how atoms, which do not "possess" heat as a property, can produce the sensation or quality of heat:

> Touch both of these, namely vitriol [sulfuric acid] and tartar, with your finger, and neither appears to be warm. Mix a few drops of the second with a certain amount of the first, and you will see the whole thing boil over and get extremely hot. How can this be when there is nothing new in the admixture that was not in the separate components? But here, on the contrary, it is obvious that the arrangement of the parts and their position has not been changed. A mutual severing and intermixture has taken place; then some air was absorbed causing the liquid to grow thinner, to foam, and turn spongy; then once the particles that had been compact had been separated and dissociated, the barbs of the corpuscles turn outward and when they strike the senses, they smart and produce in them the sensation, or quality, that we call heat. (G, 429)

In a similar way Gassendi imagines that gravity or resistance to motion is due to "many little cables" that interlock and hold a thing [a stone, for example] entangled. Thus, when "a greater force intervenes to move these deflections and crisscrosses and force the bonds to be made at a point further away, the stone will never be picked up from the ground" (G, 137–38) 137–38). He offers a similar account of magnetic attraction because "a body cannot attract another unless it transmits something by which it draws the other body to itself" (G, 133). Thus, we have a sense of "the universal machine of the world" as a set of interlocking chains of atoms that push and pull one another according to specific laws of motion (G, 412). Here, Gassendi's push-pull mechanism appears even more hard-core than that of Descartes, who attributed the effects of gravity to centrifugal force generated by invisible aether (Westfall 1971b, 305).

Gassendi agrees with Descartes that motion is not something intrinsic to atoms; they are activated (*actuosas*) "from the power of moving and acting which God instilled in them at their very creation, and which functions with his assent, for he compels all things just as he conserves all things" (G, 99).

Thus, for Gassendi, like Descartes, God plays a continuous causal role in the creation. Motion, however, is not as much of an embarrassment in Gassendi's metaphysics since it is a quality he readily attributes to atoms, although he denies that it is an "inherent" quality.

Gassendi does, however, face a different problem in his account of motive force than corpuscularians like Descartes and Hobbes. We have already noted that if matter is infinitely divisible and each motion of an aggregate must somehow be the sum of the motions of the parts, then one can plausibly argue that an aggregate starts to move, for example, because new particles with greater activity have been added to it. These particles in turn get their motion in the same way and so on ad infinitum. And while this account is of dubious scientific merit, it works better for complexes of atoms than for atoms themselves. If motion is caused by the motions of still-lesser bodies being added to (or subtracted from) the moved body this account does not work for atoms themselves since one cannot add parts to or subtract parts from an atom. In Gassendi's analysis each aggregate is finitely divisible into atoms; thus there seems to be a second level of interaction between atoms that cannot work through a physical entity being added to or subtracted from another body. Atoms, by definition, do not admit of such physical influence. Thus, Gassendi must ground change of motion in atoms in different terms than he explains changes in motions in aggregates. Unfortunately, Gassendi says little that would explain the change in motion of individual atoms moving in the void.

Ultimately, Gassendi concedes a causal role to God. With respect to causation in the physical world, God preserves the physical atoms that do create change; this view is not dissimilar to Descartes's concurrentism, because like Descartes, Gassendi supposes that created things are always dependent upon God.

> It would also seem appropriate to mention universal causes which concur with several particular causes to produce their effect, and which are sometimes called equivocal because they produce effects of a nature different from theirs, for example God produces man, or the sun produces a frog, in contrast to particular causes, which are called univocal because they yield effects of their own nature, for example a man produces a man or a frog produces a frog. One should also mention concomitant causes, or co-effective causes, as these universal causes are sometimes known; for particular causes are so dependent upon them that they cannot function without them and are usually said to be subordinate to them in essence (as God works within all second causes, and as the sun is also thought to act upon all things beneath it). (G, 423)

Of course, Gassendi's analogy is not wholly accurate. God's causal action is not at all like the causal actions of the sun. God does not emanate chains of atoms in the same way the sun does; unlike Hobbes, Gassendi denies that God is material (G, 412). Cassendi, a Catholic priest of orthodox belief, holds the more traditional view that God acts by command or will (G, 413; compare Brundell 1987, 75).

At one point, Gassendi notes that God is the only cause that is not included under the category "second causes" (atoms in motion) (G, 409). However, in conflict with this claim, Gassendi elsewhere introduces a second entity, "the intellect," that is capable of causing thoughts and other incorporeal states in the mind, while he reserves for the "sentient," "animate" (corporeal) parts of the soul the ability to move the body and allow the senses to work (G, 413). Of the two kinds of nonmaterial causation, God and the intellect, the first is an article of faith for Gassendi and the second suggests that he holds a kind of correspondence or occasionalism between mind and body that avoids the problems of Cartesian interactionism. Gassendi clearly holds, for example, that minds cannot act on bodies and bodies can only act on other bodies. Even ideas (caused by) material things must be extended given Gassendi's rigid dichotomy between physical causation and nonphysical causation (CSMII, 234). Gassendi finds causal interaction between mind and body unintelligible (CSM II, 239; G, 414). He suggests separate spheres for the actions for the intellectual and corporeal components of the soul:

> As for the fact that the human soul acts upon its own body and moves it despite the fact that the soul is incorporeal, we shall say in its place that the human soul, insofar as it is the intellect, or mind, and so incorporeal, does not stimulate actions except for intellectual, or mental, and incorporeal ones, and insofar as it is sentient, animate, and endowed with the power of moving bodies, and so is corporeal, does stimulate corporeal actions and moves its own body sometimes and sometimes also a foreign body by its intervention. (G, 413)

Of the three central problems, Gassendi leaves God's actions a matter of conservation; he denies mind-body interaction (which is the same as incorporeal-corporeal interaction), and he argues that body-body interaction takes place only through physical contact between the surfaces of atoms (compare Osler 1994, 188).

In the end, Gassendi's positive view of causation offers very little by way of metaphysical analysis. He relies on our commonsense notion of pushing, pulling, and interlocking (of atoms) with hooks. But how one or several atom(s) can transmit motion to another through contact (pushing or pulling) is left unresolved as is how an individual atom can change its motion. Gassendi, contrary to Hobbes, makes causes particular things, rather than accidents or sets of accidents, although he aligns himself with those who hold that effects are accidents, not particular things (G, 410). Gassendi rejects any claim of similarity between cause and effect, except that motion produces motion. He twists the distinction between material cause and efficient cause into the distinction between more passive and more active atoms. Ultimately, second causes for Gassendi are atoms, entities unlike, though not totally unlike, familiar material objects in the sensible world. The dominating question in the remainder of this chapter is how, given Gassendi's commitment to a science of appearances, he justifies his claim that insensible atoms are the causes of the sensible world.

Gassendi's views on scientific knowledge also seem to be paradoxical. On the one hand he thinks that the purpose of logic ("soundly conducted thinking") is to arrive at the truth (G, 284). On the other hand, he is acutely aware of the skeptical arguments against the possibility of knowing the truth. Thus, at one place Gassendi considers it "a great gain if we can rise to the point where we may "glimpse not the truth itself . . . but some slight image of it, or even its shadow" (G, 327). Gassendi is prepared to settle for probability, "neighbor enough of truth" (Osler 1994, 110). However, when articulating his hopes for science, Gassendi seems to set skepticism aside and argue that truth can be achieved in the sciences; we can determine cause and effect relationships, though we will never have the kind of certainty that Aristotle, the Stoics, Plato, or even Descartes thought possible (G, 284–326; G, 157–223). Ultimately, Gassendi constructs his own theory of knowledge, which is very much at odds with the foundationalism of Descartes or Hobbes.

All knowledge, Gassendi holds, begins with the senses (G, 333). The senses escape skeptical doubt in the sense that skeptics do not doubt "appearances . . .[and] they do not dispute the fact that people can make statements and draw conclusions concerning the kind of appearances they perceive" (G, 329). Skeptical doubt applies to what may be "under the appearances" (G, 329). But at the same time, Gassendi views appearances as "signs" of the causes that underlie them. Accordingly, we apply our reason to the signs and make judgments about the underlying thing. "Reason . . . is superior to the senses [and] can correct the perception of the senses so that it will not accept a sign from the senses unless it has been corrected and then it deliberates, or reaches its judgement of the thing" (G, 333).

With respect to the certainty of knowledge, Gassendi actually turns Descartes and Hobbes around. He believes that effects (appearances) are more certain than their causes and, therefore, provide a better foundation for knowledge. To this extent Gassendi's epistemology is clearly empiricist rather than rationalist.

> An *a priori* proof is from causes and from more or less universal statements; an *a posteriori* proof is from effect and from less universal statements. But

since the inquiry after causes follows upon the observation of effects, aren't effects better known than causes? Are not individual or less universal facts better known than universal ones since the second are derived by induction from the first, which are already known? Therefore, a proof that is *a posteriori* is better known, or proceeds from better known facts, than one that is *a priori*—hence is more certain, or proceeds from more certain facts. Certainty in fact comes from a greater or more evident knowledge. . . . (G, 84).

When Gassendi constructs a science of appearances, he is trying not simply to establish regularities among appearance but to construct a theory of "the thing lying hidden unperceived by the senses" (G, 333). Appearances for Gassendi, then, are signs, and signs may be of one of two kinds, namely, *empirical* and *indicative* (G 332). Empirical signs are signs of what may later be observed, where we do have a regularity among appearances: smoke is an empirical sign of fire; or with the development of a microscope, welts are an empirical sign of mites; or with the development of the telescope, millions of individual stars are revealed as causes of (the appearance of) the Milky Way (G, 332, 334–35). In more contemporary language, empirical signs may be caused by that which is only technologically impossible to observe. Indicative signs are appearances caused by "things naturally hidden," things that are unobservable (in principle). Atoms are among naturally hidden things as are pores in the skin or in glass, humors, and even the soul of a body (G, 332–36). Obviously, Gassendi's observable/unobservable distinction is not rigid, since entities such as pores of the skin or even atoms may at some point become observable.

In *Exercises Against the Aristotelians* Gassendi hints that scientific explanations are noninferential. To explain something is simply to state its causes. Using the example of why every man is capable of laughing, Gassendi writes:

> If a man wants to know, or what amounts to the same thing, to prove to himself that every man is capable of laughing, will you tell him "Every rational being is capable of laughing. Every man is rational. Therefore, every man is capable of laughing"? I would not use that syllogistic form; but yet if I said "Every man is capable of laughing because he is rational," wouldn't I be giving him the same cause as you, but in fewer words, and without any beating around the bush? Surely that little causal conjunction "because" expresses more clearly what way being rational is the cause of being capable of laughing than all your reasoning. (G, 82–83).

In these passages, Gassendi seems to suggest more than that we can offer abbreviated syllogisms. He may be suggesting a point made by contemporary philosophers of science, namely, once you give the causes for a phenomenon it is not necessary—indeed, it is redundant to offer covering laws or covering generalizations from which one deduces a statement describing the phenomenon (compare Miller 1987, 60 ff.). Or as Gassendi might put it, the best way to prove to someone why something is the case is to describe its cause.

Whether Gassendi is right in his classifications of things hidden or not hidden is less important than the argument by which he seeks to justify his claims of their existence. His argument is that we need to posit certain causes, hidden things, because they provide the best (noninferential) explanation of why the appearances are as they are. Thus, he repeatedly argues:

> [The appearance] is of such a nature that it could not exist unless the thing [hidden thing] exists, and therefore whenever it exists, the thing also exists. An illustration of this is sweat as it indicates the existence of pores in the skin, for pores cannot be seen; still sweat is of such a nature that it would not appear upon the skin unless pores existed through which it could pass from inside to the outside. . . . (G, 332)

> By an analogous line of reasoning we concluded in another instance that light rays are corporeal and that glass is permeated with pores since part of the rays landing on the glass are reflected and part pass through and it is logical that only those which strike solid, corporeal parts of the glass are reflected, and those which fall upon the empty parts and interspersed holes pass through. (G, 334)

> It is asked if there is any truth; the answer is that there is; and in order to forestall any subterfuge, one must then say what kind of truth it is, for instance that there are pores in the skin. The question comes whether this is claimed with or without proof. The answer is proof, namely the one given above. But is this proof true or false? The answer is that it is true. . . . And this is demonstrated fully, not from the fact that there are pores, but from the fact that if there were not, two bodies would have to be in the same place at the same time. (G, 346–47)

> The moon constantly changes its quarter according to its relationship to the sun by which it is illuminated. Using this change as a sensible sign we have occasion to prove that the moon, which otherwise appears to be a flat disc, is a globe, or spherical, because it would not undergo such change unless it were spherical and because it must undergo it as long as it is spherical. (G, 339)

Gassendi even offers a similar argument for the existence of God and God's true nature; it is an argument to a craftsman based on appearances (G, 337). "Hidden" things include pores, the shape of the moon, and atoms, the ultimate causes of *all* appearances are atoms, their arrangements, and their properties (G, 422–423).

> It may therefore be said that the prime cause of motion in natural things is the atoms, for they provide motion for all things when they move themselves

through their own agency and in accord with the power they received from their author in the beginning; and they are consequently the origin, and principle, and in nature. (G, 422)

Gassendi's view is often causally reductive or what O'Neill calls a structural explanation, that is, the properties of a sensible object are explained "when the relations among the elementary parts of these objects is given" (1983, 28). What is significant about Gassendi's argument, however, is that it suggests a new way of talking about causes, namely, the cause of a change is that entity that best explains the change where "best explains" is understood as that which conforms to a set of explanatory standards relating to simplicity, consistency, and explanatory depth. Such a view of explanation will emerge as the dominant view among scientist-philosophers such as Newton and Boyle.

Anyone familiar with the contemporary debates between realists and anti-realists with respect to theoretical entities (hidden things) is aware that there are often alternative explanations of the same phenomenon and that each explanation depends upon a host of auxiliary assumptions. Gassendi seems to be aware that his "best explanations" depend upon accepting a set of universal principles drawn from logic, common sense, and philosophy which must be defended if the explanation is to be the best. In some cases these are defended simply because they are clear (and distinct) and cannot reasonably be denied.

Next, it is permissible to say that proof does not count and is not necessary when things are so clear that merely stating them convinces us of them, as is the case not only with specific things that are obvious to the senses and established by experience, but also with general statements against which no counter argument can be brought forth, such as the axioms to which mathematical demonstrations can be reduced like "the whole is greater than its parts." (G, 347–48)

The worth of such statements is that they help to provide a satisfactory explanation. Of course, scientists cannot always produce a satisfactory best explanation; there are some things that may remain forever hidden (G, 336).

In the particular case of atoms and their nature, Gassendi defends this theory of matter because "it does not do a bad job of explaining how composition and resolution into the primary elemental particles is accomplished, and for what reason a thing is solid or corporeal, how it becomes large or small, rarefied or dense, soft or hard, sharp or blunt, and so forth" (G, 339). The atomic theory of matter also has "the advantage that it accounts for the innermost source and root, as it were, from which all movement and all activity arise in cases as second causes" (G, 400). Other theories fail to measure up to

Gassendi's implicit explanatory standards (G, 399–400). Unfortunately, Gassendi does not offer a clear set of criteria for the best explanation much beyond his claim that the senses produce signs which can be read by careful use of reason to reach probability, although he provides many examples of what are presumably the best explanations (Egan 1984, 79-94). His account of proper scientific thinking is coincident with his account of clear thinking, that is, clear thinking is "forming clear ideas, stating propositions clearly, making clear deductions, and organizing thought clearly" (G, 351). Gassendi's model for (clear) scientific thinking is, of course, Epicurus (G, 359).

Since Gassendi tends to view other philosophical accounts of motion and change as competing explanations or as efforts to show that atomism fails as a best explanation, he must take on the task of showing his account is superior to the critics. Hence, Westfall's criticism of Gassendi as someone who repeats everything ever said on a particular subject is in some sense right. And Westfall is certainly correct in another sense; Gassendi's defense of his own view requires that he take on the historical arguments, for example, Sextus Empiricias's arguments against epicurus concerning the existence of atoms and the void (Joy 1987, 165–94). And Joy is probably right that Gassendi needs a historical argument to buttress his case because—in spite of his avowed empiricism—it is empirically weak. And Gassendi is also confronted by alternative accounts in his own time, for example, by a Cartesian, nonatomistic corpuscular physics. Thus, Gassendi's scientific explanations and their concomitant view of causation tend to be inserted into a larger context that weighs the many historical arguments surrounding each issue, unlike the later scientist-philosophers who appeal directly to experience and experiment to justify their causal claims (Joy 1987, 165; Osler 1994, 189; compare Lennon 1993a, 139).

In his metaphysics of causation Gassendi relies on physical causes operating according to an intuitive notion of pushing and pulling. And in his classical mechanism Gassendi agrees with Hobbes and to some extent with Descartes. Like Descartes, he identifies certain causal domains for immaterial entities like the intellect and God, but unlike Descartes he does not try to argue for causal interaction between material and immaterial domains. Ultimately, Gassendi has little to say about what goes on metaphysically when one atom causes another to move or rest, although it is clear that he rejects the model and/or the language of a property (motive force) being communicated from one to another. Throughout most of his writing, Gassendi reinforces the view that efficient causation is the only causation of consequence in scientific explanations.

Gassendi is never as bold as Hobbes in identifying philosophical knowledge with knowledge of causes and effects. But he clearly thinks that such knowledge is the goal of science. Like Hobbes, he recognizes the importance of universal principles, but he establishes such principles by induction from appearances which are more evident (G, 84; Osler 1994, 113). Gassendi is also a voluntarist, that is, God has absolute freedom to create the world as he chooses, consistent with the laws of logic. In the *Syntagma* Gassendi writes: "There is nothing in the universe that God cannot destroy, nothing that he cannot produce; nothing that he cannot change, even into its opposite qualities" (*Opera Omnia* I, 308; as in Osler 1994, 53) Thus, although knowledge of cause and effect involve each other, there is no indication of the necessitarianism of Hobbes in Gassendi's view of causation.

In the end, Gassendi is probably a metaphysical realist and an epistemological antirealist. That is, he believes that atoms exist, but he cannot say that the hypothesis that atoms exist is intended to be literally true, only that it is intended to be probable. The certainty that grounds Hobbes's geometrical physics and Descartes's metaphysical physics is missing.

CENTRAL THEMES

Hobbes and Gassendi both deny the value of any explanations other than those in terms of efficient causation. And both offer new understandings of the notion of efficient cause: for Hobbes, it is the total set of accidents in the agent; for Gassendi, it is the atoms and sets of atoms with the greatest activity. Both are clear that causes are not propositions in scientific explanations. And causal interactions are understood by both philosophers as the crudest sort of (instantaneous) push-pull mechanisms (compare Lennon 1993a, 13).

Neither Hobbes nor Gassendi commits to the view that causation involves a transfer or communication of some aspect of the cause to the effect; such a view would make no sense given that Hobbes's causes are strictly nothing but sets of accidents. And in Gassendi such a principle makes no sense because each atom or set of atoms has once and for all time the amount of "force" or "energy" that it will ever have. In body-body interaction, both Hobbes and Gassendi avoid the metaphysical problem of causation by relying on basic intuitions about solid bodies that can push and pull each other. Indeed, the microworld for both is very much like the sensible world except that the latter is larger and, in Gassendi's case, divisible. Hobbes avoids mind-body problems by making minds corporeal; Gassendi keeps the division between mind and body but disallows any causal interaction between them.

Hobbes's scientific explanations are properly deductive sequences of laws and particular conditions beginning with axioms or first principles, most of which are definitions. Gassendi seems to reject the idea of explanations as inferential in favor of the view of explanations as causal statements of the form "A because of B." For Hobbes, cause and effect are necessarily linked by a necessity akin to logical necessity, although Hobbes's notion of cause and effect is metaphysically prior to his notion of logical necessity. Gassendi, a voluntarist, rejects any hint of necessitarianism.

God is the total efficient cause of everything for Hobbes, Gassendi, and Descartes. But Hobbes's God is largely a first cause who plays no role in scientific explanation; Gassendi's God is a free creator who maintains the world but who need not be brought in as a necessary element in scientific explanations (Osler 1994, 229). Gassendi clearly allows that God's nature can be inferred from the excellence of God's work. Of the three "mechanists" thus far examined, only Descartes finds direct scientific content (first principles) in the nature of God.

5.
The Temptation of Occasionalism: Le Grand and Malebranche

PLACE IN THE DEBATE

Occasionalism is one answer to the metaphysical problem of causation. Simply stated, it is the doctrine that "causal efficacy belongs to God instead of to creatures" (Radner 1993, 351). Stated in this generalized way, it appears as if occasionalism is an all-or-nothing view; in fact, as we saw in our discussion of Descartes, there can be degrees of occasionalism (partial occasionalism) wherein causal efficacy might be denied to bodies, while minds are treated as having causal efficacy (Nadler 1993c). For the occasionalist, God's will acts directly on the world to produce change and motion. God's actions, however, are not random; God also selects and obeys laws of nature. When two states are associated lawfully, for example, cold temperature and the freezing of water, the cold temperature is not the cause of water freezing but the occasion on which water freezes. Since occasionalists use occasions—rather than the real causes in the explanations of change, occasionalist scientific explanations look precisely the same as their interactionist counterparts, except that occasions are not the true causes of why things happen as they do.

Descartes and Gassendi offered concurrentist theories of causation, that is, causal efficacy is ascribed both to God *and* to created substances. Hobbes is a deist, that is, with the exception of miracles, the different states of the world after creation are caused by God's creations (second or material causes). Occasionalism is a rejection of both concurrentism and deism for the same reason, namely, both attribute some causal efficacy to things other than God.

We have already seen that the mechanisms that emerged in the first half of the 1600s are vulnerable to various difficulties. Most notorious was the problem of how to explain, within dualism, the apparent interaction between mind and body or between bodies and minds. Mechanism offers a model for interactions only between material things, thus, dualists, like Descartes, who are also mechanists face a very skeptical reception when they speak of the interactions of mind and body. But even at the level of material things, mechanism is unsatisfactory. We have already noted the fact that although the mechanisms of Descartes, Gassendi, and Hobbes reduced all physical change to matter in motion, they offer only vague hints at how these material interactions occur. Descartes seems to hold, and then deny, that they occur when motive force is transferred or communicated from one body to another. Gassendi suggests that each atom conserves its force, but somehow the speed, direction, and movement of macroscopic bodies results from these atomistic forces in combination and constraint. Hobbes also hints at such a view, but he seems more inclined to view nature as a wrestling match among weaker and stronger endeavors. Thus, mechanism leaves the fundamental metaphysical problem of how motion is distributed unsolved.

The origins of occasionalism in the modern period are somewhat obscure. It is an issue for specialists to track the various ways in which occasionalists influenced one another. It is generally agreed that occasionalism emerged in the middle of the 1660s. Louis de La Forge (1632–66), Geraud de Cordemoy (1626–84), and Arnold Geulincx (1624–69) are often identified as founders of modern occasionalism (Doney 1967b; McCracken 1983; Radner 1993, Nadler 1993b, 351; Nadler 1993b, 1993c).

The 1660s saw a series of followers of Descartes who pursued an occasionalist course. Louis La Forge's *Traite de L'espit de l'homme*, which first appeared in 1665, shortly before his death, and Geraud de Cordemoy's *Le discernement de L'ame et du corps* (1666) serve as important first steps toward Cartesian occasionalism. Cordemoy, more than La Forge, was concerned with reconciling his views with those of Descartes, although Cordemoy has the distinction of being the only Cartesian atomist. Both offer a series of arguments based on Descartes's ontologically impoverished concept of matter. Their arguments amount to a demonstration that there is nothing in matter—whose essence is extension—that could possibly account for its movement and quantity of motion. Thus, La Forge argues that the clear and distinct concept of matter shows that it has only the properties of extension and mobility and even if the motive force were a mode of a body it could not be transferred from one body to another (Lennon 1980, 810–11; Nadler 1993c, 61–63). It is a matter of dispute whether La Forge extended his occasionalism to mind-body interactions (Watson 1987a; Nadler 1993c). Cordemoy, particularly, went on to embrace a full-blown occasionalism in which God is the only true cause. Both authors were known to Malebranche and Le Grand. Malebranche probably read Descartes's *Treatise on Man* with remarks by La Forge.

Arnold Geulincx developed an independent version of occasionalism in the 1660s premised on the belief that a true cause must be a knowing agent, one which knows how its action affects things. His argument begins with a self-evident principle: "*Quod nescis quomodo fiat, id non facis*—If you do not know how it is done, you do not do it" (Radner 1993, 359). This condition immediately rules out body-body interaction and body-mind interaction. It also rules out finite mind-body interaction since finite minds do not know how they affect bodies—hence they do not affect them. Neither Malebranche nor Le Grand refer to Geulincx, and it is unlikely that Geulincx knew of the works of La Forge or Cordemoy (Doney 1967; Radner 1993).

By the 1670s some philosophers were arguing that occasionalism was simply the way of Cartesianism. In 1672 an anonymous letter—probably written by the Jesuit A. Rochon—appeared. In this letter was the claim that "all Cartesians agree that God alone is able to cause motion" (Lennon 1980, 810; Gilson 1937, 210). We have argued that Descartes is certainly not an occasionalist, although we have also noted that his views do contain doctrines that appear to some to suggest occasionalism. The relationship of later occasionalists to the views of Descartes is complex. In this chapter I examine two occasionalists, Anthony Le Grand (1620–1699) and Nicholas Malebranche (1638–1715). Both of these philosophers espouse a full-blown occasionalism. Malebranche is the better known today, although Le Grand was widely read as an expositor of Descartes (Watson 1967, 70). Malebranche consciously goes beyond Descartes's positions and arguments, although he treats Descartes with great respect; Le Grand is conscientious about treading carefully in Descartes's steps. Much of his writing is a paraphrase of Descartes's.

Le Grand sees himself as spelling out the "clear and distinct" consequences of Descartes's principles in his *Philosophia veterum e mente Renati Descartes more scholastico breviter digesta* (1671) and *Institutio philosophiae secundum principia Renati Descartes* (1672). These works were translated and modified into *An Entire Body of Philosophy according to the Principles of the Famous Renate Des Cartes*, in 1694 (Sorley 1965, 336). This ambitious work is divided into three books: *The Institution, The History of Nature,* and *A Dissertation of the Want of Sense and Knowledge*; the English translation was carried out by R. Blome under Le Grand's supervision. The work is exhaustive in its presentation of Cartesian theology, metaphysics, physics, and ethics. It allows the reader to clearly follow a transformation of Descartes's concurrentist interactionism into a full-blown occasionalist metaphysics.

Le Grand's admiration of Descartes and his claim not to go beyond Descartes's ideas is explicit in his "Preface":

> He was of such a singular Genius, that he alone discovered more philosophical truths, than ever were discovered in all foregoing ages. We do not go about here to give any instances of his philosophical sentiments, since this whole work contains noting else, but his opinions, or what may clearly and distinctly be deduced from them. (LG Preface, Section II)

Yet, as we shall see, Le Grand does depart from Descartes, especially on crucial issues of causation. He takes Descartes's views on divine concursus and divine power, and even Descartes's argument from divine concursus, to be evidence that Descartes is truly an occasionalist.

Malebranche is, for the contemporary student of modern philosophy, the paradigm of an occasionalist. He is the occasionalist against whom Leibniz offers his theory of preestablished harmony, from whom Berkeley carefully distances himself, and who influences Hume to identify causes and occasions. It is his philosophy that is ridiculed by the Newtonians and scientists of the Enlightenment, although there is respect for his work in mechanics (Hankins 1967). Although Malebranche regards himself as a Cartesian and he prefers to read Descartes as an occasionalist, his arguments for occasionalism are often strikingly original. Malebranche's major work on occasionalism, *De la Recherche de la verite* (*Search after Truth*) appeared in two volumes in 1674 and 1675. Malebranche's other major occasionalist writings, *Traite de la nature et de la grace* (1680) (*Treatise on Nature and Grace*) and *Entretiens sur la metaphysique et sur la religion* (1688) (*Dialogues on Metaphysics and on Religion*) embroiled him in enough controversy about his views that his "Elucidations," published with the *Search*, became a fourth major defense of his occasionalism (LO, 530 ff.).

LE GRAND

The notion of cause is not problematic to Le Grand; it is "self-sufficiently known to all" (LG I, I, 9, 20). Having said as much, Le Grand offers up a fairly complex system in which he distinguishes five kinds of causation: (1) material cause, "that out of which things are made or formed, as Wax is the matter of which tapers are made"; (2) formal cause, "as the soul is the form of man"; (3) efficient cause, "that which produces another thing"; (4) the final cause, "the end for which any thing is, as when a man applies himself to his studies, in order to the attaining of learning"; and (5) the exemplary cause, "the form which a man proposeth to himself in going about to make a work . . . so he who is the object of the eyes or mind of the painter, is the exemplary cause of his own effigies or likeness" (LG I, I, 9, 20–21).

Seemingly within these broad categories Le Grand also distinguishes a wide variety of causes such as "proper causes" (the sun is the proper cause of light), "near causes" (the father is the near cause of the son), "accidental causes" (the sun is the accidental cause of heat stroke in a sick man), "natural causes," which do not have foreknowledge of their effects, and "intellectual causes," which do have foreknowledge of their effects (LG I, I, 9, 20–21). The sun and fire are examples of natural causes and human agents of intellectual causes. Thus, a casual reading of Le Grand would suggest that he is anything but an occasionalist; he seems to find causal agency everywhere. And in contrast to Descartes's focus on efficient causation, Le Grand appears to be an elaborate Scholastic.

Le Grand spells out a series of necessary conditions which must apply in the case of causation each of which seems to apply to all five types of causation. Two of these conditions play central roles in his discussions of the metaphysics of causation.

First, there is the priority principle that causes are prior to their effects. Their priority is, however, divided between priority of nature and priority of time. Only the priority of nature is a necessary condition for cause and effect; this priority amounts to little more than the fact that effects are dependent on their causes. Le Grand concedes, as does Hobbes and Descartes, that causes may or may not be temporally prior to their effects (LG I, I, 22, 49–50). From this first condition Le Grand infers that "nothing can be a cause of itself" because nothing can be prior to itself (LG I, I, 22, 50). Here he, like Descartes, makes an exception since he regards God as the formal cause of himself (LG II, I, 55).

Second, there is the preexistence condition (his version of Descartes's causal principle) that "a cause cannot give that which it hath not" (LG I, I, 22, 50). Le Grand's explanation of what I have called the "preexistence condition" is sketchy at best. He repeats the condition by saying, "for a cause gives something to another thing, but it cannot give that which itself wants" (LG I, I, 22, 50). A little later he suggests that the kettle is hot because the fire is more hot, but warns that a person is not satiated by meat because the meat is satiated (LG I, I, 22, 50). From his other statements of Descartes's causal principle it is clear that Le Grand also allows for some kind of eminent containment:

> There is nothing found in any effect, which is not formally or eminently contain'd in its cause. A thing is said to be formally in its cause; when it is such there as we perceive; but eminently, when the cause can supply its stead. Thus, fire when it produceth heat in the body, is said to contain it formally, because it hath the very same thing in itself, which it hath produc'd in the body; but the sun and the earth, when they produce fruits, do not comprehend the thing caused by them formally, but eminently only. This notion is the first of all others, and is as evident, as that nothing can be made out of nothing: For should we admit that something is contained in the effect, which is not contained in the cause, we must own that something may proceed from nothing. (LG I, II, II, 56; compare CSM II, 96)

It is a general principle of the modern causation debate that the more metaphysical conditions that are put on causation, the fewer the situations in which true causation is likely to be found. Thus, occasionalists tend to offer the most elaborate metaphysical accounts of causation, from which they infer that very few things—perhaps only God—qualify as causes. Le Grand certainly argues to the conclusion that only God is a cause, and his complex analysis of causation that is grounded in Cartesian metaphysics plays a critical role in the argument. Although there appear to be separate arguments in Le Grand's writings, they should not be treated as standing alone; instead, they constitute a web of argument that leads to a common conclusion, namely, that only God is causally efficacious. We shall now examine the four most important arguments.

The No-Real-Accidents Argument

There is an obvious interpretation of Le Grand's principle that a cause cannot give that which it has not. Thus, at least for situations like kettles and fires, it is plausible to argue that the fire, which has the accident or mode of heat, can give the kettle that accident or some portion of it, if the two are brought into contact. As we have noted, according to the transference model, causal interaction occurs when an accident or mode is transferred, communicated, or passed, from one substance to another—one view of causation that Le Grand finds in the causation debate and that he seeks to discredit. Some Scholastics and even some Cartesians, Le Grand believes, subscribed to this answer to the metaphysical problem of causation (LG I, IV, 8, 104-105; LG I, IV, 117). Le Grand is also aware that Descartes himself talks about the communication of motion from one substance to another (LG I, IV, 14, 117). However, Le Grand argues that this theory of causation presupposes that there can be real accidents, that is, accidents that can survive separation from the substance which they modify (LG I, IV, 8, 104). And Le Grand is at pains to argue that Descartes who speaks of the communication of properties also denies the existence of real accidents and therefore should not be read literally.

Le Grand's rejection of real accidents is largely definitional. He defines modes or accidents as an "inbeing" which determines a particular substance to a "such like" (LG I, I, 6, 14). Since an accident is conceived of as nothing but a determination of a particular substance, it cannot exist without that subject (LG I, IV, 8, 104–106). He states this stipulation in a number of ways—there is no "real distinction" between a substance and its accidents; the essence of an accident is to be in another and a thing cannot "be clearly and distinctly conceived without its essence" (LG I, I, 6, 14). From which Le Grand concludes:

> . . . an accident or mode cannot exist without its subject, nor pass from one subject into another: for if that could be, it would follow, that when it was in the first substance it did not absolutely depend on it, which implies a contradiction. (LG I, IV, 8, 106)

From the fact that each accident is tied to a particular subject it follows that causal interactions—the usual example is motion—must not suppose that an accident is removed from one subject and becomes resident in another (LG I, V, 7, 143). Thus, when Descartes speaks of the communication of motion from one body to another, he should not be taken literally.

> The second or particular cause [the first is God] is the meeting of bodies, by which means it happens, that this divine action, which motion, exerts itself sometimes in these, sometimes in other bodies: whence the difficulty which ariseth from the communication of motion may be easily solved; for tho' motion, as being only the mode of a body cannot remove from one subject to another, which Regius unwarily asserts; yet the agitating force, being no mode of a body, may by removing shew itself sometimes in this, sometimes in the other body.

> Whensoever therefore Des Cartes speaks of the communication of motion, he is to be understood "as speaking" of that power, which preserves natural things [the will of God]. (LG I IV, 15, 117)

Le Grand's argument is revealing of the odd place of motive force in Descartes; in fact, Le Grand seems to contradict himself when he introduces the notion of a motive force ("agitating force") as that which is neither a mode (accident), essence (attribute), or substance—contrary to his premise that every creation is either a substance, or an accident (LG I, I, 6–7, 14–15; LG I, IV, 15, 117). Thus, the agitating force stands outside of the Cartesian ontological categories and serves the same role as "the something" that gets transferred from substance to substance. Here, Le Grand comes close to subverting his own occasionalism by allowing a transfer model of causation even though it makes use of an ontologically odd entity. However, Le Grand is quick to identify the "agitating force" or "moving force" with the will of God (LG I, IV, 16, 119). Thus, he explicitly adopts the view that Hatfield attributes to Descartes, namely, the motive force (*vis movens*) is God's will (1979).

In a second line of attack against real accidents Le Grand argues that real accidents are deemed necessary in order to explain perception, that is, how the senses are affected by bodies. Presumably, the bodies give off a sensible species or sensible mode which is picked up by the senses (LG I, IV, 8, 104). But Le Grand argues that he can explain sensation equally well by appealing only to matter in motion, without the apparatus of real accidents.

> But they will say that real accidents are to he admitted in order to the explain-ing of sensation: But neither is there any necessity for this; since nothing is requir'd to the moving of our senses, besides the variously disposed superfi-cies of objects; For we may easily understand how from the different magni-tude, figure and motion of the particles of one substance, divers local motions may be produc'd in another. (LG I, II, 8, 104)

This argument, however, seems inconclusive. For Le Grand to argue that he can explain the impact of bodies on the senses by appealing to the motion of the parts of bodies acting on the sense organs only leads again to the ques-tion: how can the "transfer" of motion from bodies to the sense organs be accounted for without real accidents or something akin to them?

Le Grand's final argument against real accidents is the following:

> Besides, if accidents be real, we shall never be able to know what accidents belong to a body, and what to a spirit. For if accidents have no affinity with their subjects, save this only, that they inhere in their subjects, and yet are really distinct from them, we shall not be able to gather from the percep-tion of an accident, whether the substance in which it is be material or spiritual; that is, from the colour, figure and magnitude we shall not be able to conclude that it is a body rather than a spirit; neither shall we from understanding and willing, which are the modes of a spirit, be able to con-clude that the subject once endued with these accidents is a spirit. (LG I, IV, 8, 105)

But surely such dire consequences need not follow. The inability of acci-dents to translocate from one individual subject to another and the classifica-tion of substances which have certain accidents seem to be quite distinct prob-lems. Even without transmigration, a decision must be made as to whether we are confronted with a body or a mind. And one could hold that bodies can only be modified by certain accidents and minds can only be modified by certain accidents, because of their essences, without denying that accidents may migrate from body to body or, from mind to mind. In short, accidents might have an affinity for a *kind* of substance without having an affinity for a *particular* substance of that kind.

Le Grand's arguments against transmigration of accidents only preclude a particular theory of causal interaction. It is certainly a theory that Le Grand believes is very much alive in the Scholastic and neo-Cartesian philosophers of his day, and it is a theory that some, as we have seen, attribute to Descartes. But Le Grand's arguments are consistent with Descartes's own attack on real accidents (CSM II, 176). However, Descartes, as we have seen, was an interactionist even if he, like Le Grand, rejects the transmigration-of-accidents view of causation. Thus, Le Grand's argument is at best only a rejection of a particular kind of interactionism. And he does not rest his case for occasionalism solely on his rejection of real accidents.

MOTION AS WILL OF GOD

The interaction of bodies is a paradigm case of causal interaction for Descartes. It is this interaction that in the *Principles* is identified as one which we can clearly understand. Le Grand continues to focus on this kind of interaction; in fact much of his argument for occasionalism hinges on his ability to argue that no body can be a real cause of motion in itself or in another. Mind-body and body-mind interaction is conceded from the outset as being a miracle carried out by God (LG Preface). There can be no conceivable connection between mind and body except that "he who hath joyn'd them together shall suffer the body to produce its motions, with a dependency upon the cognitions of the mind, and the mind to exercise its cognitions dependently upon the motions of the body" (LG I, IX, 3, 325). But the case for body-body interaction cannot be so readily dismissed. First, because Descartes himself seems to say that we can understand this kind of interaction, and, second, because of the enormous amount of work that had been done to explain bow one body influences another—a way of talking which Le Grand continues.

The problem of motion in matter, in Cartesian terms, is simple:

> Matter being of it self sluggish and idle, and substantial forms, and real accidents having been rejected by us . . . we [must] procure it some principles whereby it may be enabled to procure its effects. (LG I, IV, 9, 106)

Like Descartes, Le Grand is aware that there are two notions of motion: first there is motion as translation (movement from one neighborhood of bodies to another), and, second, there is the motive force—the "action that translates it, or the cause of its motion" (LG, I, IV, 14, 115). It is the translation of matter that is the effect to be explained.

Matter itself is limited to the properties of extension, and since a body may move or not move, just as it may be square or round, motion as translation can only be accidental to a body (LG I, IV, 14, 116). Furthermore, if motive force were essential to a body, then that body would always be in motion (LG I, IV, 16, 119). Since motive force is not essential to bodies, bodies cannot be said to move themselves (LG I, IV, 16, 119). If motive force is not essential to bodies, then it would seem to be accidental to bodies. But the motive force moves from body to body, an accident cannot so move, hence motion is not an accident of bodies either (although it is accidental in the weaker sense of not being essential) (LG I, IV, 16, 119). A body that cannot move itself cannot move another body; it fails the principle that a cause cannot give what it does not have (LG I, IV, 16, 119). Hence, the motion of a body is by something external to the body, which could only be a mind or spirit. But created spirits, by admission, can only move a body through divine will. Hence what moves a body must be the will of God (LG I, IV, 16, 119). In Le Grand's words from *The Institution of Philosophy* concerned with the general physics:

> To know whether the body moved hath its motion from itself, or whether it receives it from some out ward cause, we are to suppose two things in motion; the one residing in the thing moved; and the other in the mover: The former of these is the successive application of the body moved, to the different parts of the body that doth immediately touch it; and the second is the force that causeth this application. Motion in the thing moved is nothing else but a mode, as hath been said in the foregoing chapter; and consequently cannot pass from this body into another, because every mode is inseparably tyed to its subject. But motion considered with respect to the mover, is not a mode of the body moved, because we find by experience that it passeth from that body into another; so that motion in the first sense is only modally distinct from the body, whereas the efficient mover is really distinct from it.

> It is evident therefore that a body hath not its motion from itself, in the first of these senses, because this motion consists in an application which is accidental to the body; and that every change which happens to any subject, proceeds from an external cause. Neither can it give itself the efficient motion; because this motion likewise is accidental to the body: wherefore it follows that the body must receive its motion from something that is without it. . . .

> If a body of itself had the power to move itself, this power would be essential to it, and consequently the body would move always, and with the same force,

which is contrary to experience, which teaches us that a body sometimes moves more, and sometimes less, and sometimes not at all: wherefore it receives its force to move from something without it. Now there is nothing without or external to matter but spirit; it is spirit therefore that moves body, that is to say, God, who makes the parts of matter apply themselves successively, as to their outsides, to other parts that immediately touch them. Wherefore, since God cannot produce motion without acting, nor act otherwise than by his will; we must own that the moving power is nothing else, but the will God hath to move the matter. (LG I, IV, 16, 119)

An oversimplification of Le Grand's argument is simply that Cartesianism is too impoverished to account for motion by anything except a "divine shove." Only a divine shove that is neither essence nor mode of created substances could be the kind of entity which passes from substance to substance. It is this entity that stands outside of the Cartesian ontology and that is communicated in interactions involving bodies. Le Grand's occasionalism is completed by his denial that bodies can act on bodies and his assumption that minds and bodies cannot interact. Still, he offers a further argument that supports both of these conclusions.

Divine Concursus Argument

The divine *concursus* argument is stated several times by Le Grand. The gist of this argument in Malebranche is that since God's will is both necessary and sufficient for every state of the universe at each moment of time, there cannot be other causes which are either necessary, since then God's will would not be sufficient, or sufficient, since then God's will would not be necessary. Hence there can be no other causes than God. Some of Le Grand's versions of this argument are stated as follows:

All things are continually procreated by him, as not being able to continue one moment without his concourse. (LG I, II, 12, 70)

God's omnipotence does not only appear in the production of things, but also in their conservation: for God is not only the principle of created beings when they are making, but also when they are made. Hence it is that he preserves them by a continual influence; and should he cease from his concourse, whatsoever he had produc'd would fall to nothing; because before they were created and he afforded them his concourse they were nothing.

For surely there is no less power in the creating of a thing, than to the conserving of it; and since no created thing acts on any thing by its own power, so neither can it give itself existence by the same. It remains therefore that all

> things must have their dependence on God, and that the things that are, be produced by venue only of the divine degree. (LG I, II, 14, 72)

> Besides the parts of time have no necessary dependence on each other; neither doth it follow that because a thing is now, it will be the next moment: Therefore to the end it may continue to exist, there must be some power, which may each moment reproduce it: But no such power is in the creature, and therefore there must be some being whose nature includes existence, and which is the cause why the thing that hath existed hitherto doth continue so to do. (LG I, II, 15, 73)

His claim in the final passage seems to involve the complication that the parts of time have no necessary dependence on each other; but in fact the reason for that is that things lack the power to sustain themselves. If things were to sustain themselves, they would violate the causal principle that a thing cannot give what it has not.

> For whatsoever is besides God, either hath the principle of its existence from it self, or from another: For natural light evinceth that things can not be made of nothing. If any thing was of it self, it would want nothing; yea, it would give it self all those perfections it hath any idea of, but nothing hath the power of bestowing those perfections on it self, for otherwise it would actually be possest of them. (LG I, II, 15, 73)

To make Le Grand's divine *concursus* argument into an argument for occasionalism, it must be assumed that in recreating a substance at each moment, God also recreates the entire state of that substance, that is, all of its properties, at that moment. With this assumption, then, it is plausible to argue that any causal efficacy by created substances has been completely preempted. As we noted, Descartes does *not* clearly make this assumption in his version of the divine *concursus* argument in the "Third Meditation" (CSM II, 33–34). And unless the argument is understood as preempting the causal efficacy of created things, it is compatible with a view in which God preserves substances but substances act on one another to produce changes in the properties of other substances, a view that would undermine occasionalism. Thus, Le Grand's argument requires that he bolster it with the assumption that God is not only the efficient cause of substances but also the efficient cause of each state of a substance at each moment of time. This assumption follows from a further argument in which Le Grand uses the Cartesian theological claim that in God will and knowledge are one and the same.

The Identity of Divine Will and Knowledge Argument

If God's knowledge and God's will are one and the same and if God knows everything that exists, then God wills everything that exists, and conversely. In short,

God's will is both a necessary and sufficient cause of everything which includes the existence and the state of each substance at each moment of time. Hence, there is no need for causally efficacious created substances. Le Grand's argument can be formulated:

> For in God to will, to understand and create are one and the same thing: Wherefore because he knows a thing, therefore it is true. (LG I, II, 6, 63)

> It belongs also to the idea of a most perfect being, that he be all powerful and all knowing. (LG I, 11, 7, 65)

> I say that God knoweth all things whereof he is the efficient cause, because as was said in the chapters on God's immensity all things are continually pro-created by him, as not being able to continue one moment without his concourse. (LG, I, II, 12, 70)

Elsewhere Le Grand embraces Descartes's doctrine that "all eternal truths are from God as from their efficient and total cause; for he is the cause of all creatures, not only as to their existence, but also with regard to their essence" (LG I, 11, 6, 63). A few lines latter Le Grand maintains the idea that "all truths" depend on God for their existence. The step to God as the cause of all truths is made by Le Grand because in God (all-powerful and all-knowing) will and understanding are one; and if to know something is to will it and to will it is to cause it, then God is the efficient cause of everything (LG I, II, 6, 63; LG I, II, 7, 65; (LG I, 11, 12, 70).

Le Grand sometimes talks as if *only* the existence and essence of things depend directly upon God as efficient cause; such a view would leave room for secondary causes to produce the modes of substances. But in other places, however, Le Grand is clear that modes of mind and body also depend upon God as their efficient cause (LG I, II, 14, 72). Le Grand readily admits that if God is the cause of modes including our volitions of will, then God must also be the efficient cause of our acts of volition. When, confronted with Descartes's doctrine of a free or undetermined will, Le Grand admits that the reconciliation of these two claims is "more than I do clearly perceive" (LG I, II, 14, 72). Thus, even at the price of denying that human volition is free, Le Grand stands by his occasionalist solution.

Two further concerns need clarification. The first concern is more easily clarified. One might concede that God is the total efficient cause of all things and their states at each moment and still argue that God acts through created things; hence Le Grand's divine *concursus* argument even with the identity-of-will-and-knowledge argument does not yield an occasionalist conclusion. Here Le Grand can invoke his earlier arguments to the effect that bodies cannot act on bodies and minds and bodies cannot interact. With these arguments in place, Le Grand can claim that all causal efficacy belongs only to God.

A second concern is less easily answered. If God's will and knowledge are one, then it is unclear how God can know a possible world without creating it. Le Grand suggests that God in fact creates possibles in much the same way that God creates actuals, by knowing (hence, willing) them, which suggests some ontological status for possible worlds.

> God therefore is the efficient cause of all things; not only of such as exist, but also of possibles. . . . (LG I, II, 6, 63)

Just what Le Grand means here is not clear. On the one hand, he stops short of Descartes's extreme voluntarism; God "can produce whatsoever doth not imply a contradiction" (LG I, II, 1, 55). On the other hand, he argues that "it is contrary to reason to think that any thing cannot be otherwise, because we cannot understand how it can be" (LG I, II, 6, 63). But however Le Grand conceives of possible things, he cannot argue with other moderns such as Leibniz that the difference between actual and possible worlds is that God wills the former but not the latter. In Le Grand's view, there must be some further characteristic of actual worlds that distinguishes them from the merely possible worlds and that suggests that God's will and knowledge are not sufficient to make a world actual.

The goal of philosophy, besides the discovery of first truths, is to provide deductions from these causes to their effects (LG Preface). Indeed most of the text in the second and third book is concerned with the explanation of effects from causes. Le Grand here means cause-as-premise, an ambiguity which he takes from Descartes, even though he is clear that there is no real cause-as-thing except God.

Like Descartes, Le Grand distinguishes between an analytical and a synthetical method. While both methods "proceed from that which is more known to that which is less known," synthesis proceeds from the general to the particular, whereas analysis proceeds from what is particular back to the general (LG I, I, 21, 44–45). Put another way, synthesis proceeds from causes to effects, whereas analysis proceeds from effects to causes. In Le Grand's example of analysis, he tries to show why the insensible parts of liquid are in motion (the better known fact) owing to more general causes which are hypothesized from that fact, whereas in the method of synthesis he tries to deduce that the soul of man is immovable from better-known maxims and definitions (LG I, I, 21, 46).

Le Grand's explanations, like those of Descartes, are often explanations of composition, that is, explanations of the states of a body in terms of its parts and their composition. Le Grand's metaphor of nature is to view "the world . . . [as]

a wonderful, and most artificially contriv'd *machine*, not the part of it taken severally, but as joined and orderly complicated together" (LG I, IV, 9, 107). And one understands such a machine when one understands what are its parts and how they are connected.

> Hence it is evident that the powers of bodies, or their faculties of action, are nothing else but the magnitude, figure, contexture, &c. of the *parts of bodies*; for by these all the effects we see in nature are produced. (LG I, IV, 9, 107)

Le Grand's quarrel with Gassendi, for example, is not that the world is a machine or that natural causes reduce to matter in motion—though motion is always produced by God—but in how the machine is constructed (LG II, I, 4, 7). Its parts are not atoms but divisible bodies that "can never be exhausted by any partition whatsoever" (LG II, I, 9, 8). But Le Grand's other explanations in terms of contact among particulars, where divisibility is set aside, would be familiar to Hobbes, Gassendi, or Descartes. Consider his account of the leavening of bread:

> The cause whereof is, because the stiff and sharp particles of sprouted wheat do infold themselves; and as the chymists express it are in their greatest exaltation: Wherefore, as soon as the dough begins to grow hot in the oven, the parts thereof become tumultuarily agitated, and driving the resisting bodies before them, do in a manner praecipitate them, and by this means the bread becomes spongy and light. (LG II, I, 5, 10)

And like his predecessors Le Grand is quite prepared to reduce heat, color, taste smell to the motion and collisions of particles (LG I, IV, 9, 107).

Le Grand sometimes hints at a demonstration of the basic laws of motion and the conservation of motion, but his position is less bold than Descartes's effort to infer these basic rules from the nature of God; instead, Le Grand claims that these rules can be demonstrated from "the immutability and simplicity of that operation whereby God conserves motion in the universe," which suggests that the justification for certain laws of nature is not so much the nature of the deity as their simplicity and elegance in comparison to other candidates (LG I, IV, 15, 118).

Finally, in an echo of Hobbes and what is clearly seen as an anti-Scholastic view of causation, Le Grand locates the causal "powers" of things in their possession of certain accidents.

> But it will be objected, that these modes cannot produce so many effects, forasmuch as all actions are attributed to the subjects themselves, and not to the accidents, which only operate by virtue of the substance.

> I answer that we acknowled no other subject, but matter furnished with mag-
> nitude, figure, &c. for matter being passive, cannot operate, but by their effi-
> cacy. And tho' indeed matter do not derive its essence from these modes, that
> is, tho' they do not fluke it to be a thing, yet do they cause it to be such a
> thing. Thus, that a pen is fit to write withal, and a key proper to open a lock,
> proceeds only from their disposition, figure, motion, &c. for when these are
> taken away, they are no longer useful. Wherefore, accidents do not operate,
> by vertue of their substance, as the schools wilt have it; but the substance
> rather works, by a vertue borrow'd from its accidents. (LG I, IV, 9, 107)

Le Grand takes all of Descartes's metaphysical theses and pushes them
toward his occasionalist answer to the metaphysical problem of causation. He
neglects doctrines that get in the way, for example, Descartes's claim that
because of God's immutability change must be explained by particular causes.
And Le Grand's single-mindedness leads him into direct conflict with some of
Descartes's claims, for example, that minds and bodies do interact and that
humans have free will. At the same time Le Grand promotes the idea that accidents are not true causes but explanatory "causes," although he seems obvious to the fact that he explains phenomena by "causes" that are not true causes. That explanations do not occur through the identification of true causes is
a doctrine that becomes especially evident in Malebranche, who is explicit
about his distinction between true causes (God's will) and explanatory "causes" (natural causes or occasions).

MALEBRANCHE

In a passage where he alludes to what others have to say about causation
Malebranche is clear that he believes that most philosophical talk about the
nature of causation is simply nonsense—people talking about things of which
they know nothing (LO, 242, 658–59). Malebranche lumps together "act,
potency, causes, effect, substantial forms, faculties, [and] occult qualities" as
entities about which philosophers speak unintelligibly (LO, 242). For the most
part he believes that either previous philosophers and scientists have no idea of
what they are talking about or, what may come to the same, causal powers are
simply reified entities whose only definition is that they are the causes of the
effects that led to their postulation in the first place. Thus, a ferment is that in
a thing which produces fermentation. The sentence "Fermentation is caused by
a ferment," then, is true but hardly informative (compare McCracken 1983,
96–97). Malebranche describes the reification process as follows:

> Here is what commonly happens to philosophers. They observe some new
> effect; immediately they fancy a new entity to produce it. Fire heats things—

therefore there is something in fire that produces this effect, something different from the matter of which fire is composed. And because fire is capable of several different effects . . . they liberally bestow on fire as many faculties or real qualities as effects it is capable of producing. (LO, 242)

Although the language of causation springs from "vague and indeterminate ideas" Malebranche, like Le Grand, is quite prepared to speak this language (LO, 243). But Malebranche is clear that when he speaks of the communication or transference of motion, the power to produce an effect, or a cause, such language is a sham (D, 161; LO, 425). It is necessary to use this language because talk about secondary causes has become philosophically and scientifically entrenched (LO, 661). The view that secondary causes are real causes is popular because, Malebranche believes, philosophers allow the evidence of their senses to defeat the evidence of reason. Even Malebranche worries that his senses may "seduce" him (LO, 659–60; LO, 673–74).

Malebranche began his mechanical philosophy as a strict Cartesian; bodies conserved their quantity of motion, moved in a plenuum, and changed directions only when involved in a collision (Hankins 1967, 198). Eventually, under the influence of Leibniz, whom Malebranche met in 1675 while Leibniz was in Paris, Malebranche came to revise Descartes's laws of motion (Hankins 1967, 198). By 1692 Malebranche was even prepared to abandon Descartes's belief that the quantity of motion is what is conserved (Woolhouse 1993, 124–26). At times, Malebranche seems more willing to criticize Descartes's science than his metaphysics, because he believes that Descartes has been successful in finding the clear and distinct first principles of philosophy (LO, 463). Thus, Malebranche prefers to read Descartes as an ally or, at least, as a proto-occasionalist whose clear and distinct principles entail the occasionalism that Malebranche defends.

Natural causes or *occasional* causes are unlike *true* or *real* causes (of which there is only one, namely, God) (LO, 448; D, 161–63). Malebranche's criterion of a true cause "is one such that the mind perceives a necessary connection between it and its "effect" and a natural cause is any cause where no necessary connection is perceived (LO, 450). But Malebranche realizes that even though God is the only real cause, it would be "ridiculous" to explain natural phenomena in this way; natural phenomena are best explained by natural causes (LO, 662).

Malebranche's God, unlike Descartes's God, is restricted by certain eternal, necessary truths, specifically the truths of logic and mathematics (LO, 615–18). Such truths are not the product of God's will, but they are truths according to which God "is constrained" to will (if there is to be a true science) (LO, 615). But while Malebranche's God "cannot do what is impossible or what contains a manifest contradiction," "God can freely will or create any law (decree) of nature that regulates associations of events" (D, 153, 173; compare Hankins 1995, 198).

Malebranche offers several arguments in favor of his total occasionalism. In this chapter I examine the three arguments which reveal the most about how Malebranche views the metaphysical problem of causation. I identify these arguments as "the argument from the Cartesian view of matter," "the argument from necessary connection," and "the divine concursus argument."

The Argument from the Cartesian View of Matter

Malebranche often focuses his defense of occasionalism on whether one body can move another. Philosophically, this is the most credible case of causal interaction, the one Descartes claims in the *Principles* to understand clearly. It is also the movement of one body by another that seduces the senses into thinking that natural causes are real causes.

> When I see one ball strike another, my eyes tell me, or seem to tell me, that the one is truly the cause of the motion it impresses on the other. . . . (LO 660)

Furthermore, as a mechanist Malebranche holds that "all the changes that occur in bodies have no other principle than the different communications of motion that take place in both visible and invisible bodies" (LO 660). For these reasons, Malebranche takes care to argue that material interaction, literally speaking, is impossible. He typically begins with the argument that a body is too ontologically impoverished to move another body or mind. Matter is nothing else than extension (it lacks a motive fore), which seems to suggest for Malebranche that matter is also impenetrable and divisible, and its modes are thereby limited to shape, size, and translocation (LO, 243–44). For Malebranche, everything is either a substance or a mode of a substance (LO, 513). Hence, if there is a power (motive force) in matter to move other parts of matter or to move a mind, it would have to be either a substance or a mode of substance. But a body's nature is exhausted by extension, hence it cannot have a power to move itself.

> It is clear that no body, large or small, has the power to move itself. A mountain, a house, a rock, a grain of sand, in short, the tiniest or largest body conceivable does not have the power to move itself. (LO, 448)

Since all physical change takes place through the action of one moving body on another, no body can move another body or act on a mind; bodies, by definition, simply lack the power to move (D, 151).

> What would that power be? Would it be a substance or a modality? If a substance, then it is not bodies that act but that substance which is in bodies. if the power is a modality, then there will be a modality in bodies which is neither motion [translocation] nor shape. (D, 147)

In short, Malebranche takes lack of a motive force in bodies as evidence that only God could be the source of their translocations.

The obvious rejoinder to this argument is to fall back on some version of the transfer model of causation and argue that there is a motive force that belongs at one time to this body and at a latter time to another body. In the *Dialogues* Malebranche considers such a theory of causation. He rejects such a move because he holds, with Descartes, Le Grand, and Leibniz, that "nothing belongs to it [a body] other than its modalities, inseparable from substances" (D, 159; LO, 273). Hence, the idea of a modality that transfers its dependency from one substance to another is as impossible for Malebranche as it was for Le Grand. Such "efficacious qualities" are "pretentions of human pride, chimerical productions of the ignorance of Philosophers" (D, 163).

Malebranche's argument goes some way toward establishing his occasionalism; however, it does not rule out the possibility of mind-body interaction. Toward that end, Malebranche offers more sweeping arguments.

The Argument from Necessary Connection

> A true cause as I understand it is one such that the mind perceives a necessary connection between it and its effect. Now the mind perceives a necessary connection only between the will of an infinitely perfect being and its effects. Therefore, it is only God who is the true cause and who truly has the power to move bodies. (LO, 450)

Malebranche's argument this passage is his most frequently used argument and his simplest. In a special case of this argument Malebranche also argues that bodies cannot act on bodies because there is no necessary connection between the motion of one body and that of the body with which it comes in contact (D, 161). Ultimately, this argument depends upon a necessary condition for causation that only God can satisfy.

Some scholars take Malebranche to mean quite literally that only God's will is *logically* necessary to the effects which it produces (Rome 1963, 179). Such a reading commits Malebranche to a necessitarian thesis, namely, the sentence C causes E is true, then it is necessarily true that C causes E. At the same time it seems to preserve divine free will, since God's acts of will are not themselves governed by the necessitarian thesis. But it is unclear what it means for one state of a substance to *logically* necessitate another. Logical necessity holds between propositions, not states of substances. Hence, Sleigh argues that Malebranche's arguments depend upon metaphysical rather than logical necessity (1990b, 171).

A third possibility that is not explored in the literature is that Malebranche means both logical and metaphysical necessity. Certainly, there is no incompatibility in holding both that true causation is metaphysically necessitated and that true causal statements are necessarily true. Descartes certainly treats causes both as premises and things. For Malebranche, God is a true cause, as an entity, but it is through knowing God (propositions about God) that we know (infer) truths about other things (LO, 236–37; see McCracken 1983, 54–87). What gives Malebranche confidence that God's will is necessarily connected to its effects is that God possesses an omnipotent and efficacious power, and that is surely, in part, a metaphysical claim (LO, 237; Loeb 1981, 200–202). Thus, Sleigh is surely right to insist that Malebranche's necessity between cause and effect is at least metaphysical. But given this metaphysical claim, it is also a contradiction then to argue that God willed that x occur, and x did not occur, which makes Malebranche's claim a logical one as well (D, 153; LO, 448). Indeed, it is a claim that we can perceive clearly and distinctly only for God's will (LO, 232–33, 448; D, 171–95).

Strictly speaking, Malebranche could stop the argument here, with the conclusion that only God *can* be a true cause (compare Loeb 1981, 202). But Malebranche also wants to show that God *is* the only true cause, which requires a few more steps, namely:

1. Every change must have a cause (D, 173).
2. There are effects (change) (LO, 448 ff.).
3. Hence, there are causes.
4. Hence, God is a true cause.

In other places, Malebranche offers a second argument to the conclusion that only God *can* be a true cause. It is an indirect proof. Suppose that God did make secondary causes into real causes. If there were real secondary causes, that would require that God communicate some of his power to these causes; in which case, they would be necessarily connected to their effects. Hence, to the extent that a secondary cause was a real cause, it would be independent of God (in that action). But it is a contradiction that God make a creature "independent of His volitions" (D, 155). Hence the supposition that secondary causes are true causes leads to a contradiction and is, thereby, false. Sometimes Malebranche puts this argument in the form that should there be a real cause other than God, God as creator would have to renounce his own attributes, and that is a "contradiction" (D, 157; compare D, 167). Hence, it is a logical constraint upon God that He "cannot even communicate His power to creatures. . . . He cannot make true causes of them, He cannot make them gods" (LO, 451).

This second argument seems to equivocate on the notion of *dependence*. Malebranche argues that if God gave power to a creature, then it would be independent of His volitions. But what does that mean? Aristes suggests that created things are dependent upon God because "God can annihilate them when He pleases" (D, 455). But how does that kind of dependence preclude God's giving a causal power to a creature? Malebranche seems to have some stronger notion of dependence in mind. That notion is that each thing depends upon God not only for its existence but for each state that it has throughout its existence. This notion of dependence lies behind Malebranche's next argument, the divine *concursus* argument.

The Divine Concursus Argument

We have seen other versions of the divine *concursus* argument in Descartes and in Le Grand. For all his other arguments, the divine *concursus* argument seems to bear the weight of Malebranche's occasionalism. This argument is repeated over and over in both the *Dialogues* and the *Search after Truth* (LO, 516 ff., 551–52; D, 153, 157). Perhaps the best-known version of this argument occurs in the *Dialogues*:

> Creation does not pass: the conservation of creatures is on the part of God simply a continued creation, simply the same volition which subsists and operates unceasingly. Now, God cannot conceive, nor consequently will, that a body be nowhere or that it not have certain relations of distance with other bodies. Hence God cannot will that this chair exist and, by this volition, create or conserve it without His placing it here or there or elsewhere. Hence, it is a contradiction that one body be able to move another. I say further; it is a contradiction that you should be able to move your chair. Even that is not enough. It is a contradiction that all the Angels and Demons joined together should be able to move a wisp of straw. The demonstration of this is clear. No power, however great we imagine it, can surpass or even equal the power of God. Now, it is a contradiction that God could will the existence of the chair yet not will that it exist somewhere and, by the efficacy of His volition, not put it there, not conserve it there, not create it there. Hence, no power can transport it where God does not transport it, nor fix or stop it where God does not stop it, unless it is because God accommodates the efficacy of His action to the inefficacious action of his creatures. . . . God communicates His power to creatures and unites them among themselves solely by virtue of the fact that He makes their modalities occasional causes of effects which He produces Himself . . . (D, 157).

Simply stated, God can create no substance without creating its complete complement of modalities (properties) and since God recreates each substance at each moment, God is the real cause of its modalities at each moment. Obviously, such an argument can readily be extended to all created substances, and Malebranche is prepared to defend his conclusion for minds as well as bodies (LO, 678–79). ". . . All creatures depend immediately on God, not only for their being, but for their operation as well" (LO, 679).

This argument from God's continuous creation does not of itself rule out any role for created substances. Descartes, as we have seen, accepted the idea that God preserves each substance at each moment, but, at the same time, Descartes seems to bold that God causes substances to be in particular states at certain times *by means of* other created substances. Thus, Descartes is a concurrentist. As an occasionalist, Malebranche must rule out what Descartes seems to allow, namely, that God through concurrence uses created substances as causes (compare Sleigh 1990b, 182). Malebranche holds that concurrentism is "not even conceivable to me" (LO, 658). One reason for concurrentism's inconceivability is the one we have already noted, namely, if God were to give causal efficacy to created substances, God would make his creations independent of him, which is a logical impossibility. But in presenting his divine *concursus* argument Malebranche hints at another ground for denying that God acts by means of created things or natural causes. For God to utilize any created thing would mean that God's will is neither sufficient nor efficacious in the production of change.

> God needs no instruments to act; it suffices that He wills in order that a thing be, because it is a contradiction that He should will and that what He wills should not happen. Therefore, His power is His will, and to communicate His power is to communicate the efficacy of His will. But to communicate this efficacy to a man or an angel signifies nothing other than to will that when a man or an angel shall will this or that body to be moved it will actually be moved. (LO, 450)

> Since God's volitions are efficacious by themselves, it is enough that He should will in order to produce, and it is useless to multiply beings without necessity. In addition, everything real in the natural determinations of our impulses also comes solely from God's action in us. . . . (LO, 679)

Always in Malebranche's version of the argument is the emphasis that to suppose that God uses instruments is to somehow demean God's divinity. McCracken notes that for Malebranche "occasionalism . . . was not merely a hypothesis embraced . . . to solve the perplexities of mind-body dualism; rather, it was the theoretical expression of what he took to be the very essence of the biblical concept of nature" (McCracken 1983, 104).

The difference, then, between Descartes and Malebranche regarding God's continuous creation of the world is twofold. First, whenever Descartes actually states the doctrine of continuous creation, he insists only that God is the continuous cause of *the preservation of substances.* Malebranche makes God continuously create substances *and* their qualitative states at each moment. Second, Malebranche insists against Descartes that God *needs* no instruments, so that God's will is the direct and single cause of everything (LO, 451). Of course, Descartes's God is all-powerful, and Descartes could agree that God needs no instruments without agreeing that God does not *use* instruments. In fact, the concurrentist theory defended by Descartes is precisely the theory that God does use instruments with which he acts concurrently as cause, although he need not use them.

What is Malebranche's alternative to interactionism? How does he articulate his positive view? Watson believes that as confused as the various earlier modern accounts of causation may be, Malebranche simply replaces one unknown with another. "God's power of will is an occult force of the highest degree, and it is this power we must understand to understand Malebranche's 'explanation'" (Watson 1993, 83). Malebranche does not "explicate the two substantive framework principles of his metaphysics—God and creation" (Watson 1993, 91). Watson is correct in arguing that there is very little that can be said to elucidate God's power except that God acts through willing or volition. But around that issue there have emerged three distinct philosophical interpretations of how Malebranche understands the operation of God's will. The first I call "the common view," the second "the general volition view," and the third "the omniscient volition view."

The common view is also the crudest form of occasionalism. The idea is that "God, by a vast number of distinct acts of will, meddles at every moment, and in innumerable ways, in the workings of nature" (McCracken 1983, 89). When I have a will to move my arm, God contracts my muscles and my arm moves; when my mouth bites an apple, God causes the appropriate sensations in me; when a car slides into another, God crumples both fenders. Nadler formulates it thus: "At the very moment when one billiard ball strikes another, God wills efficaciously *then and there* to move the second ball" [italics mine] (Nadler 1993a, 42). Nadler adds "to be sure, God's activity as cause is not *ad hoc*, but is governed by general laws instituted by God at creation" (Nadler 1993a, 32). Malebranche himself expresses something like the common view in passages such as:

> But this action, this moving force, does not belong to bodies at all. It is the efficacy of the will of the One who creates them and conserves them successively in different places. Matter is essentially movable. By its nature, it has a

> passive capacity of motion. But it does not have an active capacity, and it is in fact moved only by the continual action of the Creator. . . . And, because God is bound to act in a simple and uniform way, He had to set Himself laws which are general, and the simplest possible, so that, when change was necessary, He changed as little as was possible . . . (D, 161).

What I call the common interpretation reduces to the following three theses about God's will.

> (T1) God wills a set of general (natural) laws; the content of these volitions does not mention particular things. For example, God wills that any body in motion will continue in a straight line unless acted upon.
> (T2) God also has an infinite set of willings whose content is specific to individuals in particular situations. Thus, God wills that Joan raise her hand in philosophy class on such and such a day.
> (T3) God wills the general laws at the time of creation, but his specific acts of will are simultaneous with the particular actions or states produced.

Malebranche himself says much that undermines the common interpretation. In the first place he suggests that God does not act throughout time. His willings are never successive: thus, "in God, there is no succession of thoughts and volitions" (D, 473). In the *Treatise on Nature and Grace*, Malebranche writes: "If God causes a fruit to fall before it is ripe, it is not that he wills and no longer wills: for God acts not at all by particular wills, like particular causes" (R, 118–19). Thus, Malebranche seems to reject (T3) as incompatible with God's immutability and (T2) as incompatible with God's efficiency.

Malebranche's remarks in these passages suggest a second interpretation, which I have identified as the general volition view, namely, that Malebranche treats God's volitions as exclusively general and nonspecific (Nadler 1993a, 41). Antoine Arnauld (1612–1694), one of Malebranche's sharpest critics, also read Malebranche as saying that God's volitions were only for general laws (see Nadler 1993a, 33–34). Arnauld accuses Malebranche of confusing "acting in accordance with general laws" with "acting by general volitions" (Nadler 1993a, 37). And there are certainly passages wherein Malebranche seems to treat particular effects as the effects of general laws, for example, "natural effects are those that are the consequences of the general laws" (LO, 668). And Malebranche's *Treatise on Nature and Grace* is particularly suggestive of the general volition interpretation.

> . . . for God acts not at all by particular wills, like particular causes. He has not established the laws of the communication of motion with the design of producing monsters, or of making fruits fall before their maturity; he willed these laws because of their fruitfulness, and not of their sterility. (R, 118–19)

> If then it is true that the general cause ought not to produce his work by particular wills, and that God had to establish certain laws of the communication of motion which are constant and invariable, through whose efficacy he foresaw that the world could subsist such as we see it. (R, 119)

> Those who claim that God has particular plans and particular wills for all the particular effects which are produced in consequence of general laws ordinarily rely on the authority of scripture to shore up their feeling. (R, 136)

Under this interpretation God, at the time of creation, selects general laws which in turn serve as the causes of the particular events that follow the creation. God does not even intervene to perform miracles, that is, exercise acts of will whose content is a specific state of an individual thing, contrary to the general laws.

> He invariably follows that law which He has established thereby maintaining a perfect uniformity in His conduct. God never performs miracles, He never acts by special volitions contrary to His own laws. (D, 89)

> When a house crushes an honest man to death, there occurs a greater evil than when one beast devours another, or when a body is required to rebound by the impact of the body it strikes; but he does not multiply His volitions in order to remedy the true or apparent disorders that are the necessary consequences of natural laws. God must not correct or change these laws, although they sometimes produce monsters. He must not upset the uniformity of His conduct and the simplicity of His ways. He must ignore insignificant things, i.e., He must not have particular volitions to produce effects that do not merit them. . . . (LO, 665–66)

For God to will only general laws and never to have acts of will with specific content is most appropriate to his nature. As Clarke argues:

> The concept of God from which Malebranche works is that of an eternal, immutable, omniscient, and omnipotent creator. . . . Thus "everything which is outside of God must be produced by an action which is, in truth, eternal and immutable" ([R, 163]); in the interests of simplicity and the wisdom of his ways, "He ought not to multiply his wills . . . any further than necessity obliges" (R, 127; Clarke 1995, 502).

There is no easy resolution of the question of whether God's volitions are all general in content or whether God also wills that particular concrete things have particular states. The argument from divine *concursus* as well as many passages suggest that God wills in both ways. In other places Malebranche seems to deny that God acts by way of willing particular states of individual things. There is a third view which I have called "the omniscient volition view." Perhaps one way to introduce this view is to look at the debate between Leibniz and Malebranche on the issue of miracles. As we have just seen, Malebranche denies that there are miracles (D, 89). But Leibniz in his criticisms of Malebranche charges that Malebranche's occasionalism uses God's will as a *deus ex machina* and makes each cause a "miracle" (LL, 457).

For Leibniz, a miracle is anything that violates what Sleigh describes as his principle of spontaneity, namely, every noninitial state of every substance has a real cause in some preceding state of that substance (Sleigh 1990, 162). Or if, as Leibniz prefers, a miracle properly so called is a state that surpasses the powers of creatures, it need not be an unusual event (LL, 695). Thus, if Malebranche holds the common view, as Leibniz believes he does, then even when God wills in accordance with his general laws, it is a miracle because the change does not arise out of the agency of the individual substance. Malebranche, on the other hand, means that a miracle is some state of a substance which does not conform to the laws of nature, and even here, Malebranche hedges and suggests that there are no miracles, only events that occur which *seem* to violate the laws of which we are aware.

> Once for all, Aristes, when I say that God always follows the general laws which He has prescribed, I speak only of His ordinary and general providence. I do not exclude miracles or effects which do not follow His general laws. But besides . . . when God performs a miracle and does not act in accordance with the general laws that are known to us, I claim that either He acts in accordance with other general laws which are unknown to us, or what He does then is determined by the time of certain circumstances which He had in view from all eternity when He enacts that simple, eternal, invariable act which contains both the general laws of His ordinary providence and also exceptions to these very laws. (D, 175)

Thus, our discussion reveals another way to understand Malebranche's view of how God wills—the omniscient volition view. Malebranche, when he offers more detailed examples of God's volitions, seems to hold that the contents of God's will include both the general laws, the exceptions to these laws, if any, and the specific states of all substances throughout eternity. God's omniscience allows this kind of foresight. Hence God can will at once, in the time of creation, all that will ever happen and the order in which it happens *including any exceptions to the law.* Thus, there can be exceptions to laws and God can and does will particular states of particular things throughout all time without violating God's immutability. Malebranche articulates this idea as follows:

> . . . in God, there is no succession of thoughts and volitions—that, by an eternal and immutable act, He knows everything and wills everything that He wills. God wills, with a perfect freedom and a total indifference, to create the world. He wills to make decrees and establish simple and general laws in

order to govern it in a way that bears the character of His attributes. But, then decrees posited, they cannot be changed—not that they are necessary absolutely but are so ex hypothesis. . . . . When God made them, He knew so well what He was doing that they cannot be revoked. For, though some of them He made [only] for a time, it is not that He changed His mind and will when the time comes; but rather one and the same act of His will refers to differences in time which are contained in His eternity. So God does not change, and cannot change His thoughts, His designs, His volitions. He is immutable. (D, 173)

For His decrees, though perfectly free, are themselves eternal and immutable, as I have already told you. God made these decrees, or rather he fashions them unceasingly on eternal Wisdom which is the inviolable role of His volitions. And, although the effects of these decrees are infinite and produce thousands upon thousands of changes in the universe, the decrees are at all times the same. . . .

Thus, on the omniscient volition view, Malebranche holds:

(T1') At the creation God wills once and for all the general laws and any future exceptions.

(T2') At the creation God wills once and for all the specific states of all created substances through eternity, the order of those states being consistent with his general laws and their exceptions.

(T3') God wills everything at the time of creation and has no will that is successive to that.

I have termed this interpretation of Malebranche the omniscient volition interpretation because unlike the general volition view, some of God's volitions have specific events as contents; God also, however, wills general laws of nature. This view is compatible with an immutable divine nature (compare Nadler 1995). And as in the common view, God does will particular states of particular things, for example, when God conserves a particular thing God wills that it be in a particular place at a particular time. God may even will exceptions to general laws. But unlike the common interpretation, God's volitions are made once and for all time at the time of creation. What makes such a stupendous act of willing possible is God's omniscience, that is, God's complete knowledge of all things general and specific.

There is an obvious concern with any occasionalist causal explanation, no matter how it is understood that God wills. Watson states the problem:

The real problem, as we all know, is that God explains too much. God can do anything. And when God does everything, there is nothing to explain. Or, rather, the explanation of everything is this; God created the heavens and the earth. Nothing more is required. This, then, is what is bad about introducing God into philosophy. . . . There is no point in trying to explain things philosophically if God just does them by creative fiat. (Watson 1993, 83)

Malebranche addresses this issue:

I grant that recourse to God or the universal cause should not be had when the explanation of particular effects is sought. For we would be ridiculous were we to say, for example, that it is God who dries the roads or who freezes the water of rivers. We should say that the air dries the earth because it stirs and raises with it the water that soaks the earth, and that the air or subtle matter freezes the river because in this season it ceases to communicate enough motion to the parts of which the water is composed to make it fluid. In a word, we must give, if we can, the natural and particular cause of the effects in question. But since the action of those causes consists only in . . . the will of God, they must not be said to have in themselves any force or power to produce any effects. (LO, 662)

Malebranche's scientific explanations, then, look like the usual Cartesian "geometrical" explanations with the usual checks on experience and experimentation (compare LO, 12-13, 209–10). However, an occasionalist like Malebranche is aware that these "explanations," formulated in the same mechanical terms used by other scientists, really offer only evidence *that* something occurred, evidence *when* something occurred, but never why something occurred. Thus, they are not properly causal explanations.

Malebranche, like Descartes and Hobbes, is aware that the order of geometrical proof is not the order of scientific discovery. We may well go wrong in our reasoning and need to check our assumptions by experience. Nothing proves this more than Malebranche's revisions of the laws of motion (Hankins 1967). More to the point, we may actually embrace false assumptions, which simplify our reasoning and increase our powers of prediction even though they depend on literally false premises in our proofs. Malebranche is sophisticated enough in his discussions of the relationship between geometrical demonstration, the goal of science, and the nature of reality to realize that causal explanations that allow predictions need not be true. In places, Malebranche seems almost to embrace Gassendi's view that we only gain a neighbor of truth in our science.

Nature is not abstract; the lever and balls of mechanics are not the lines and circles of mathematics. . . . As far as astronomy is concerned, there is no perfect regularity to be found in planetary motion. . . . Thus, the errors we fall into in astronomy, mechanics, music, and all the other sciences to which geometry is applied, come not from geometry itself, which is an incontrovertible science, but from our faulty application of it.

We assume, for example, that planetary motion describes perfectly regular circles and ellipses, which is not true. We do well to make this assumption in order to reason, and also because it is not far from the truth; but we should always remember that the premise on which we are reasoning is an assumption. Likewise in mechanics, we assume that the balls and levers are perfectly hard. . . . If experience fails to agree with it, we see that our assumed premises are false. But without geometry and arithmetic, nothing that is somewhat difficult in the exact sciences can be learned. . . .

Geometry, then, should be regarded as a kind of universal science that opens the mind, makes it attentive, and gives it the skill to control the imagination and to draw from it all the help it can give. . . . (LO, 428–29)

Throughout his writings Malebranche embraces the criteria of clarity and distinctness as marks of truth. Thus, he argues that "one should attribute to a thing what one clearly conceives to be included in the idea that represents it" (LO, 317; compare LO, 437–38). And, like Descartes, Malebranche's rationalism and apparent distrust of the senses seem to conflict at times with his actual treatment of science that requires constant correction from the senses and experimentation.

It must be remembered that the strong inclination we have for diversions, pleasures, and generally for everything that affects our senses, throws us into a great many errors because, the capacity of our minds being limited, this inclination constantly distracts us from the clear and distinct ideas of the pure understanding needed for the discovery of truth, and causes us to apply ourselves to the false, obscure, and misleading ideas of our senses (LO, 324–25).

Malebranche's place in the causation debate can be viewed in two very different lights. In one light, Malebranche muddies the waters by introducing the ultimate occult force, God's will, abolishing causal explanations in terms of true causes, and thereby gains no advantage for the emerging mechanical philosophy. In another light, Malebranche greatly advances the cause of the mechanical philosophy. Malebranche saw more clearly than anyone that the debates of philosophers about the metaphysics of causation were nonproductive and confused:

In addition, when I think about the different opinions of philosophers on this subject, I cannot doubt what I am proposing. . . .

> There are some philosophers who assert that secondary causes act through their matter, figure, and motion . . . others assert that they do so through a substantial form; others through accidents or qualities, and some through matter and form; of these some through form and accidents, others through certain virtues or faculties different from the above. . . . Philosophers do not even agree about the action by which secondary causes produce their effects. Some of them claim that causation must not be produced, for it is what produces. Others would have them truly act through their action; but they find such great difficulty in explaining precisely what this action is, and there are so many different views on the matter that I cannot bring myself to relate them. (LO, 659)

Thus, Malebranche redirects the debate by creating a world totally without forces, a world in which events are ordered by before and after and where some kinds of events regularly follow other kinds of events. The only problem faced by philosophers should be the problem of the correct identification of *occasional* causes; the metaphysical problem of causation is buried in the mystery of God's will. And in denying that natural causes were true causes Malebranche forces those who would give God a major role in causal explanation to choose between denying that any account in terms of natural causes is a proper explanation or denying that proper explanations are in terms of real causes. Thus, Malebranche set the stage for Hume's assertion that there is "no foundation for that distinction . . . betwixt *cause* and *occasion*" (T, 171; compare McCracken 1983, 254–89).

CENTRAL THEMES

Both Le Grand and Malebranche work within the tradition of the mechanical philosophy; they conceive of the physical world as machinelike and change as occurring through the contact of its parts. But underlying their mechanism is the metaphysical thesis that because mechanistic reduction has not answered the metaphysical problem of causation, a further step must be taken. That step is to deny true efficacy to particular things (created things) and to boldly defend the thesis that only God is a true cause. Their thesis is bold because while occasionalism may make some sense for mind-body connections, it flies in the face of mechanism and its basic assumption that bodies can and do act on other bodies. Immediately, this view leads to a denial that proper scientific explanations make use of true causes. Instead, proper scientific explanations are in terms of merely apparent or occasional causes. Among occasional causes, Le Grand identifies accidents as the occasional causes of change. Le Grand and Malebranche both identify the occasional causes as those that best explain the changes in question. It is occasional, not real causes that occur in scientific explanations. In this way, occasionalism abandons any hope of settling the metaphysical problem of causation in terms that are either rationally or empirically understood. The power of God is even harder to comprehend than causal power, and neither Le Grand nor Malebranche count on a previous theological tradition to give meaning to such talk. But in the end, occasionalism leads to the challenge: Why not count occasional causes as true causes and thereby restore the principle that proper explanations are in terms of proper causes? Thus, occasionalism is not a dead end in the causation debate as much as it is a sharp turn toward a different conception of cause and causal explanation.

6.
Causes and Sufficient Reason: Spinoza and Leibniz

At roughly the same time as Le Grand was publishing expositions of Cartesianism in England, Benedict Baruch Spinoza (1632–1677) was doing the same in Amsterdam; in 1663 he published *Renati Descartes Principiorum Philosophie* (*Descartes's Principles*). The *Ethics*, which is Spinoza's major philosophical essay, builds on Descartes's *Principles* but fills in the many places where Spinoza disagrees with Descartes. The *Ethics* was not published until just after Spinoza's death in 1677.

Although Lodewijk Meyer, who wrote the preface to *Descartes's Principles*, claims that Spinoza "considered himself obliged not to depart a hair's breadth from Descartes's opinion," there are obvious differences in doctrine and proof that are noted by Meyer (EMC, 229; EMC, 229–30). Spinoza clearly expresses reservations about distinctions that are basic to Descartes, for example, that the mind and body are distinct substances (EMC, 244). Spinoza also seems to have consistently rejected Descartes's idea that matter was exhausted by extension or that one body could not in some sense be the cause of motion in another body (Woolhouse 1993, 92–94). *Descartes's Principles* and the *Ethics* are both efforts to produce the kind of geometrically deductive system (synthesis) that Descartes begins in his reply to the second set of objections. Spinoza, however, is much more thorough and persistent in formulating his philosophy in a deductive fashion.

Like Descartes, Spinoza was a serious scientist; his work in optics was both theoretical and practical. Spinoza was widely respected by his contemporaries for the microscopes and telescopes that he constructed (Savan 1986; Klever 1996, 33). Meyer, a prominent scientist in his own right, was attracted to Spinoza in part because of his scientific accomplishments. Spinoza went beyond the construction of scientific instruments and employed them to observe astronomical bodies as well as small bodies in the human blood (Klever 1996, 34).

Even more than Descartes, Spinoza encountered theological criticisms, especially from the Dutch Reform Church. At one place, he complains to his friend Oldenburg that certain Cartesians condemn his work (Klever 1996, 48). Spinoza was viewed by his contemporaries as an atheist who denied of free will and divine retribution, and their hostility led him to fear for his personal safety. Spinoza's views were well known in Europe by 1665. But the publication of his *Theological-Political Treatise* (in 1670) was so vilified that he began a serious retreat from public life, and although he had finished the five parts of the *Ethics* by 1670, publication was withheld at his request until after his death.

Unlike Descartes and other moderns whose goal was knowledge, Spinoza's ultimate goal is happiness or well-being. This state can only be achieved, however, by understanding the world (gaining knowledge), by which Spinoza means grasping the true deductive causal explanations of things. Knowledge produces freedom from the emotions and passions that are caused by ignorance. Thus, for Spinoza, the metaphysical and epistemological problems of causation serve as a means to the moral end of happiness or freedom.

In his later years, when Spinoza had withdrawn from public life, one of his supporters, Baron von Tschirnhaus reestablished Spinoza's contact with Leibniz, who had originally written to Spinoza on a matter of optics in 1671. Tschirnhaus, who was living in Paris, offered to transmit to Leibniz parts of the *Ethics*. Spinoza declined this invitation, fearing further condemnation, but despite Spinoza's reluctance, Tschirnhaus passed on many of Spinoza's ideas to Leibniz anyway. Thus, Leibniz began his study of Spinoza's philosophy, a study which resulted in a correspondence between them until the time of Spinoza's death. And Leibniz continued to comment on Spinozism throughout the remainder of his own life.

No philosopher entered into the causation debate with greater enthusiasm and energy than Gottfried Wilhem von Leibniz (1646–1715). In his mature philosophy Leibniz creates a new view of causation, a view that offers answers to the metaphysical and epistemological problems as well as the central questions. Leibniz, with great pride, distinguishes his own theory of the preestablished harmony from the occasionalists, the Cartesians, and the Scholastics. According to his theory of preestablished harmony, the states of each substance arise spontaneously from the active force of that substance, and the states of each substance are regularly parallel to one another. As Kulstad notes, the theory of preestablished harmony is the "doctrine that God created finite substances in such a way that they do not causally interact but nonetheless exhibit parallelism in virtue of their own spontaneity" (Kulstad 1993, 97; compare Clatterbaugh 1973, 58)

When Leibniz visited Paris in 1672–76, he met Malebranche and became acquainted with Cartesianism. Malebranche did not make much of an initial impression on him, and Leibniz at that time may not have distinguished sharply between Descartes and Malebranche as well as other Cartesians and occasionalists (Kulstad 1993a, 105). During his stay in Paris it is likely that Leibniz would have been made aware of other occasionalists, particularly, La Forge, Cordemoy, and Geulincx (Kulstad 1993a, 100). It was on his return to Germany that he visited Spinoza in Holland, just a year before Spinoza's death. Leibniz may well have been inspired in his rejection of the interaction of mind and body by Spinoza's rejection of any causal connection between the two (Kulstad 1993a, 114–16). Approximately ten years after his contemplations of occasionalism and Cartesianism and his flirtation with Spinozism, Leibniz wrote the *Discourse on Metaphysics*, which is generally agreed to be his first articulation of his mature views on causation.

Leibniz's scientific writing makes clear his belief that Descartes's laws of motion are wrong—quantity of motion is not preserved under a change of direction—and he believes that the Cartesians should have made force (active and passive forces) essential properties of matter (AG, 148; AG, 106; AG, 250–56). But Leibniz seems to have a deeper dissatisfaction with Descartes's theory of causation. Leibniz probably places Descartes among the influx philosophers (O'Neill 1993). If there is an influx from one body to another, then Leibniz believes that there must be a transmission of a metaphysical entity like an accident, quality, or species. Certainly, we have seen that Descartes sometimes talks as if the quantity of motion is passed from one bit of matter to another. This kind of transmission is metaphysically impossible in Leibniz's view (AG, 145; Clatterbaugh 1973).) Leibniz's rejection of the way of influx (causation) became a critical basis for his defense of his theory of preestablished harmony.

Spinoza and Leibniz share certain general commitments. Both philosophers embrace what Bennett calls "explanatory rationalism." They hold that "there is a satisfying answer to every 'Why?' question" (1996, 61). Another way to put it is to say that both are fundamentally committed to the principle of sufficient reason: There is a reason why everything is the way it is and not some other way (AG, 217; EMC, 446; EMC, 91). Bennett denies that Descartes was com mitted to explanatory rationalism, but we have offered reasons to think that Descartes, too, held that there was in principle reason at least for every particular event (1996, 61). Both Spinoza and Leibniz deny that there is any causal interaction between mind and body or between bodies and minds. Spinoza explains the correlation between mind and body by means of a dual aspect theory, wherein a mental state and a physical state are simply two aspects of one and the same reality. For Leibniz, mind and body are related by the preestablished harmony. And finally, both Spinoza and Leibniz are necessitarians, that is, they both hold that if a proposition P is true, it is necessarily true, a view which applies to causal truths just as much as to any other kind of truth.

SPINOZA

It is often noted that the moderns, with a few notable exceptions such as Leibniz, displace final causation in favor of efficient causation. For example, Burtt makes this claim in *The Metaphysical Foundation of Modern Physical Science* (1925, 89). But as Osler argues, "rather than rejecting final causes, many important seventeenth-century natural philosophers reinterpreted the notion of final cause, retaining the concept as part of their insistence on providential Christianity as a framework for natural philosophy" (1996, 389). For these moderns, final causes were God's purposes or manifestations of Divine Nature, and they were external to the creation instead of being immanent (intrinsic) in creatures as were Aristotelian/Scholastic final causes. Descartes argues for example, that the laws of motion must conserve the quantity of motion in matter because God is immutable (CSM I, 240; compare Osler 1996, 391). As we have seen, Gassendi offers similar arguments.

One of the most striking aspects of Spinoza's discussion of causation is the harshness of his attack on final causes—immanent or extrinsic. He goes much further than any predecessor in holding that "All final causes are nothing but human fictions" (EMC, 422). And, he explicitly rejects Descartes's attempt to relegate final causes to the abyss of God's wisdom, since for Spinoza God has no purpose, hidden or otherwise. "All the prejudices I here undertake to expose depend on this one: that men commonly suppose that all natural things act, as men do, on account of an end; indeed, they maintain as certain that God himself directs all things to some certain end. . . ." (EMC, 439). Let us now turn to some of the arguments by which Spinoza would utterly overthrow this doctrine.

First, Spinoza suggests that to hold that there are final causes is to reverse cause and effect (EMC, 442). At one level he may simply be claiming that causes are prior to their effects; to pretend that a later (end) state is the cause of some prior state is to place the cause after the effect, to reverse them. Of course, to a defender of final causes, this argument simply begs the question, and it is not clear from his writing that Spinoza embraces the view that causes are always prior to their effects, Delahunty suggests a further reading of Spinoza's remark (1985, 168). Those who believed in final causes, philosophers such as Gassendi, argue that God's creations reveal God to us. In the "Fifth Set of Objections" Gassendi remarks that through consideration of final causes we find "the principal argument for establishing by the natural light the wisdom, providence and power of God, and indeed his existence" (CSM II, 215). But Spinoza clearly rejects the epistemic possibility that we can conceive of things in nature prior, even in the order of discovery, to our knowledge of God (EMC, 454). Instead, we must begin with the adequate idea of God (Nature or Substance) and through that come to understand what are really God's attributes or modes.

In a second argument Spinoza suggests that "mathematics, which is concerned not with ends, but only with the essences and properties of figures . . . [has] shown men another standard of truth" (EMC, 441). And Spinoza's goal in the *Ethics* is to achieve truth modeled on mathematics. Thus he writes in the *Preface* to Part III:

> It will be doubtless seem strange that I should undertake to treat men's vices and absurdities in the Geometric style. . . . But my reason is this: nothing happens in nature which can be attributed to any defect in it, for nature is always the same, and its virtue and power of acting are everywhere one and the same, i.e., the laws and rule of nature according to which all things happen, and change from one form to another, are always and everywhere the same. (EMC, 492)

This argument does not so much demonstrate that final causes are useless as it demonstrates that truth can be found without using them. At the same time, Spinoza clearly believes that the arguments in favor of final causes, especially conceived as God's purposes, are irrational attempts to place all events into an anthropocentric framework. Although the evidence is that "conveniences and inconveniences happen indiscriminately to the pious and the impious alike," they (those who believe in final causes) still hold onto their prejudice that there is a purpose to these things—it is just unknown (ECM, 441).

What is implicit in Spinoza's discussion of final causes is that where causal explanation is appropriate it should be in terms of some other kind of causation. More specifically, Spinoza recognizes only efficient causation, which is the cause of both the existence and essence of things (EMC, 431). Spinoza is clear in his exposition of Descartes's *Principles*: "The act of creation admits of no cause except the efficient . . . which is God" (EMC, 334). But what does it mean for God to be the efficient cause of all things, and does Spinoza leave room for other things to be causes besides God?

Individual minds and bodies are what Spinoza calls "finite modes"; since Spinoza reserves the term "substance" for God or Nature, and God is the only substance, one might suppose then if causes are substances, God is the only cause or only true cause, to use Malebranche's language. As we shall see, however, Spinoza does not restrict the notion of cause to substances; he also allows that finite modes and even attributes may be causes.

Throughout his writing, Spinoza's concept of cause has both epistemological and metaphysical content. In Part I of the *Ethics* he offers the following causal principles:

> A3: From a given determinate cause the effect follows necessarily; and conversely, if there is no determinate cause, it is impossible for an effect to follow.
>
> A4: The knowledge of an effect depends on, and involves the knowledge of its cause.
>
> P3: If things have nothing in common with one another, one of them cannot be the cause of the other. (EMC, 410)

In a further elaboration on causation in Part I, Proposition 17, Spinoza adds that "from God's supreme power, or infinite nature, infinitely many things in infinitely many modes, i.e., all things, have necessarily flowed, or always follow, by the same necessity and in the same way as from the nature of a triangle it follows, from eternity and to eternity; that its three angles are equal to two right angles" (EMC, 426).

To many scholars, Spinoza's elaboration in Proposition 17 together with the other claims he makes about causation suggest a view of causation in which God's nature is like the nature or definition of a triangle and everything follows in a logical sense from that nature; or the relationship of cause (God) to effect is little more than the relation between ground and consequent (Parkinson 1954, 64; Curley 1969, 45; Allison 1975, 71; Bennett 1984; 30). Thus Bennett argues:

> Associated with this [explanatory rationalism] is a view about, or attitude toward, causation. Spinoza did not distinguish what is absolutely or logically necessary from what is merely causally necessary. In his way of thinking, there is a single relation of necessary connection, which links causes with effects in real causal chains and premises with conclusions in valid arguments. (Bennett 1996, 61)

Curley also states that Spinoza held "causal rationalism," that is, a view in which "a cause relates to its effect as a premise does to a conclusion which follows from it" (Curley 1969, 45). Since the ground consequent relationship holds between or among propositions, Curley goes so far as to identify the power of God (God's omnipotence) with propositions—specifically, "the scientific laws that govern phenomena" (Curley 1969, 49). Curley bolsters this identification by noting that Spinoza uses "logical language" in talking about God's omnipotence as being "actual from eternity and will remain in the same actuality to eternity" (EMC, 426; Curley 1969, 46, 49). This view of Spinoza on causation, which I shall call the "inferential view," holds that causes are premises and their effects are conclusions from those premises and that Spinoza's view of causation is exhausted by the relationship of premise to conclusion. Furthermore, God is the total efficient cause of everything in the sense that God is the grand proposition from which all truths follow.

Spinoza's other remarks on causation in Axiom 3 and Axiom 4 as well as Proposition 3 above are seen as harmonious with the inferential view. Axiom 3 simply states that one version of the principle of sufficient reason, the inferential view, makes clear that a sufficient reason for some truth is a set of premises from which it follows. Axiom 4 simply reveals that to know a truth is to be able to justify it, that is, provide a sufficient reason. And Proposition 3 of Part I is a claim very like Descartes's causal principle: it means that one cannot infer (supply the cause) for a truth from premises that do not contain at least that truth within them. Or as Spinoza prefers to say, "if they have nothing in common with one another, then (by A5) they cannot be understood through one another, so (by A4) one cannot be the cause of the other, q.e.d." (EMC, 411).

There are at least two obvious reasons for rejecting the inferential view of causation suggested by the triangle analogy. First, it is implausible that Spinoza thinks that God or God's creatures are simply propositions, although he may think that there are propositions that mirror every fact. Second, and more significantly, the inferential view seems to conflict with other passages wherein Spinoza offers a much richer conception of causation and wherein Spinoza draws a distinction between God as immanent cause and finite modes as transitive causes. In these passages Spinoza is clear that God is not the only cause of everything, specifically, "particular things," which Spinoza defines as "affections of God's attributes, or modes by which God's attributes are expressed in a certain and determinate way"; particular things or finite modes can only be produced with the help of other particular things or finite modes (EMC, 431, 432). Spinoza, like his predecessors, struggles with the boundary between God's causation in the world and the causation of particular things (finite modes). On the one hand, he makes it clear in Part I, Proposition 25, that God is the efficient cause of both the existence and the essences of all things (EMC, 431). On the other hand, Spinoza argues in Part I, Proposition 28, that only through the action of one finite mode on another can a change take place in a particular thing (EMC, 432).

Let us pursue some suggestions as to how Spinoza can draw the boundary between God's causal efficacy and that of finite modes. Commentators, such as Watt, argue that the inferential view is only one of *two* different versions of what it means for God to be the cause of all things (1972). Thus, Watt argues that the inferential model in which God is the only premise and things follow directly from God is appropriate only for the timeless essences of things. Everything has an essence for Spinoza: "I say that to the essence of any thing belongs . . . that without which the thing can neither be nor be conceived. . . ." (EMC, 447).

> The ideas of singular things, or of modes, that do not exist must be comprehended in God's infinite idea in the same way as the formal essences of the singular things, or modes, are contained in God's attributes. (EMC, 452)

In other places, Watt notes, Spinoza seems to suggest that God is not the *sole* cause of everything. In the *Ethics*, Part II, Proposition 9, Spinoza says:

> The idea of a singular thing which actually exists has God for a cause not insofar as he is infinite, but insofar as he is considered to be affected by idea of a singular thing which actually exists; and of this [idea] God is also the cause, insofar as he is affected by another third . . . [idea] and so on, to infinity. (EMC 453)

In Part I, Proposition 28, Spinoza proves that a finite mode "can neither exist nor be determined to produce an effect unless it is determined to exist and produce an effect by another cause, which is also finite and has a determinate existence" (CSM, 432). Thus, in the realm of particular things there is an infinite series of causes over and above God reaching out into the past and future of each particular thing (Watt 1972, 175–76). As Savan puts it: "Each finite mode is an intersection of the two causal axes [God and other finite modes]" (Savan 1986, 105). If one can make sense of this "intersection," Spinoza's view of God's relationship to creation bears a strong resemblance to Descartes's concurrentism.

Leibniz finds fault with Spinoza's construction of the causation of finite modes:

> How will they [finite modes] finally then spring from God? For they cannot come from him mediately; in this case, since we could never reach in this way things which are not similarly produced by another finite thing. It cannot,

therefore, be said that God acts by mediating secondary causes, unless he produces secondary causes. (Wiener 1959, 497)

Leibniz argues in this passage that finite modes cannot come from God immediately, which Spinoza admits, or mediately, which Spinoza does not admit, since mediately they come from other finite modes and so on *ad infinitum*. They must come from God either mediately or immediately. Therefore, they cannot come from God. There is a version of this dilemma that faces the inferential view as well. Either everything follows from the nature of God alone, or it does not. if everything follows, then the inferential view seems plausible. But in the case of finite modes Spinoza suggests that other premises are necessary, namely, premises about other finite modes. Thus, it would seem that the inferential view is wrong to treat the Divine Nature like the nature of a triangle from which everything follows.

Spinoza throws some light on the causal duality of God and finite modes in Part I, Proposition 18, where he asserts: "God is the immanent, not the transitive, cause of all things" (EMC, 428). God is the *immanent* cause of all things because everything must be conceived through God and because there is no substance outside of God. In saying that God is the immanent cause, then, Spinoza is asserting the epistemological priority of God in the order of conception.[1] To conceive a thing is to conceive its essence, and it is from God that all essences come—"a man is the cause of the existence of another man, but not of his essence, for the latter is an eternal truth" (EMC, 427). The second aspect of God's immanent causation is that God does not stand apart from the world but is in some sense identical with the world (Delahunty 1935, 127). Transitive causes—the mother is a transitive cause of the son—are apart from that which they cause, and though they must have something in common with their effect, the effect need not be conceived through the cause (EMC, 427). Without transitive causes, Spinoza would have no scientific explanations of finite modes; he would face the same uninformative account of everything— it follows from God—that Malebranche faced.

Curley, who defends the inferential view of causation in Spinoza, allows that God is the sole efficient cause only in the sense that God is *required* for the inference to a particular existing thing and that God is ultimately the source of the particular things as well (1969, 66–67). At the same time, Curley admits that God is only a "partial cause" of finite modes (1969 73).[2] Curley cites the dilemma, noted by Leibniz. But Curley tries to find a way out of the dilemma without abandoning the inferential view of causation. The way out for the defenders of the inferential interpretation is to fall back on Spinoza's radical monism (Woolhouse 1993, 35–36). Since God is in some sense identical with the laws of physics *and* the bodies that bump other bodies at particular places at particular times, God is the cause of everything. "God is their adequate cause, not insofar as he is infinite, but only insofar as he is modified both by finite and by infinite modifications" (Curley 1969, 74). Unfortunately, while radical monism provides a kind of answer, it is hardly satisfactory. In the first place there seem to be two questions that are being conflated: Can Spinoza maintain that God is the sole cause of both the essence and existence of all things infinite and finite and can Spinoza make God the sole cause as premise from which everything follows? Clearly, Spinoza can answer the first in the affirmative, along the lines suggested by Curley and in Proposition 25 of Part I. God is the sole cause precisely because everything is a modification of God, so even particular things that cause other particular things are in some sense God. At the same time there is reason to doubt that God is the cause only in the sense of a first and sufficient premise from which all (true) conclusions follow. Second, however, the appeal to Spinoza's radical monism leaves unexplained what it means to say that God is identical with and at the same time distinct from the particular things that cause other particular things to exist. Here we come up against the pervasive and yet unanswered problem in Spinoza's metaphysics, namely, what it means to say that God both is and is not the same as the many "parts" of nature (MacIntyre 1967; Bennett 1996; Donagan 1996).

In Part III Spinoza introduces his own distinction between adequate and inadequate causation, a distinction that raises further questions for the inferential view. In Definition I of Part III Spinoza writes: "I call that cause adequate whose effect can be clearly and distinctly perceived through it. But I call it partial, or inadequate, if its effect cannot be understood through it alone" (EMC, 492). This definition suggests that while God may be an adequate cause of all general truths, God is not an adequate cause of particular things since there are no clear and distinct (adequate) ideas of finite modes from the idea of God (EMC, 467 ff.). Thus, God is in this sense only a partial cause of finite modes. The inferential view's notion of cause is closer to adequate cause than to partial cause; this is another way of saying that for the existence of particular things, including their changes to particular states, the inferential view fails to capture Spinoza's conception of causation.

Thus, we must look for a richer concept of causation in order to do justice to Spinoza's views on causation. Causes may be either immanent or transitive and adequate or inadequate. God is an immanent and inadequate cause of finite modes, although he is an immanent and adequate cause of infinite modes and essences. Finite modes are generally transitive and inadequate causes of other finite modes. In a few places Spinoza hints that there may be particular things—acts—of which we are the adequate cause when it follows from our nature, but since our nature cannot be conceived except through God, that does not resolve the question of whether everything in some sense depends upon God. Certainly, God is an immanent and adequate cause of the essences of all things finite and infinite; and it is only in this last case that one can plausibly argue that from God's nature one can infer all things (that is, all essences).[3]

With regard to the interaction of bodies Spinoza relies on transitive and inadequate causes exclusively; he agrees with Descartes, Hobbes, and Gassendi that material bodies interact in a single mechanical system without causation acting from without that system. While Spinoza disagrees in certain particulars about the motion and rest of bodies, his overall view is thoroughly mechanistic (Woolhouse (1993, 115–16). As Hampshire writes,

> Spinoza is in effect saying that the extended world is to be conceived as a self-contained, and all-inclusive, mechanical system in which the total amount of energy is constant; and, secondly, he is in effect saying that all the changing qualities and configurations of extended bodies can be adequately represented solely as transmissions or exchanges of energy within this single mechanical system. (1951, 71)

Spinoza's conception of bodies is thoroughly corpuscular and mechanistic. He sees each body as divided into smaller bodies and changes of states in the greater body are, after the manner of Hobbes or Gassendi, caused by changes in the states (motion or rest) of the smaller bodies (EMC, 459–62). Ultimately, Spinoza tells us in Lemma VII of Part II of the *Ethics*, the whole of nature can be conceived as a body composed of parts, which are other bodies (EMC, 462).

In contrast to his views of body-body interaction, Spinoza is equally clear that mind and body do not interact: "The Body cannot determine the Mind to thinking, and the Mind cannot determine the Body to motion, to rest or to anything else (if there is anything else) (EMC, 494; Loeb 1981, 157–89). At the same time, Spinoza is clearly aware we do correlate the activities of mind and body. "Nothing can happen in that Body which is not perceived by the Mind" (EMC, 457; EMC, 494). To some extent the very success of the *Ethics* in describing the road to happiness depends upon such correlations—when our minds have knowledge, our bodies are free of certain passions and emotions. When we will to move our arm, our arm moves; when our eyes scan the pages of the *Ethics*, we gain adequate ideas of substance. But Spinoza is clear that no philosopher has been able to explain the interaction of mind and body. He notes and rejects Descartes's suggestion that the pineal gland is the locus of connection (EMC, 595).

Mind and body cannot be causally connected for Spinoza for the simple reason that such a causal link would violate Proposition 3, Part I, which asserts that among things with nothing in common one cannot be the cause of the other. This proposition is interpreted by Spinoza as precluding the causal interaction of any two entities that are not conceived under the same attribute. Thus, ideas can cause ideas, bodies move bodies, but ideas cannot move bodies or bodies cause ideas (EMC, 410–11; 494 ff. compare Loeb 1981, 159 ff.). Spinoza's discussion in the arena of mind-body connections treats mind and body as dual aspects of one and the same reality—thereby making their interaction more intimate than that of causation and making that correlation simultaneous. In Part III, Proposition 2, Spinoza summarizes his view:

> The Mind and Body are one and the same thing, which is conceived now under the attribute of Thought, now under the attribute of Extension. The result is that the order, or connections, of things is one, whether nature is conceived under this attribute or that; hence the order of actions and passions of our Body is, by nature at one with the order of actions and passions of the Mind. (CSM, 494)

As we noted in discussing the sense in which God is and is not identical with finite modes, the greater debate within Spinoza scholarship is whether one can make sense of God as both identical and not identical with finite modes, infinite modes, and attributes (see, Delahunty 1985, 119–23; Donagan 1973). In some places, for example, Spinoza suggests that mind and body (also the attributes of thought and extension) are really distinct—each can be conceived without the other—but parallel to each other (EMC, 416). In other places he suggests that there is a kind of identity between them—a mode of thought and a mode of extension are one and the same thing (God) (EMC, 451). Delahunty summarizes this perplexity in Spinoza thus:

> If we stress the real distinctness between the attributes, we must incline to a "parallelist" interpretation of the mind-body problem; if, on the other hand, we emphasise the fact that the attributes are necessarily inherent, we should favour the "identity" interpretation. (Delahunty 1985, 121).

When Spinoza tries to shed light on his dual aspect theory in a letter to De Vries, he only seems to reassert what is in question (EMC, 195–96; compare Delahunty 1985, 122):

> Nevertheless, you want me to explain by an example how one and the same thing can be designated by two names (though this is not necessary at all). Not to seem niggardly, I offer two: (i) I say that by Israel I understand the third patriarch; I understand the same by Jacob, the name which was given him because he had seized his brother's heel; (ii) by flat I mean what reflects all rays of light without any change; I understand the same by white, except that it is called white in relation to a man looking at the flat surface.

We need not resolve this issue in order to recognize Spinoza's effort is to account for the correlations between mind and body without any reference to causal connections between the two. What Spinoza tries to substitute in place of the causal connections is a theory of multiple descriptions of one and the same thing. The problem for Spinoza is that he sometimes talks as if these descriptions are not descriptions of the same thing but different things (really distinct attributes). Similarly, when Spinoza tries to state the causes of a particular finite mode—say, a tropical storm—he appeals to other finite modes—other weather systems—that are both one and the same as God (nature) and yet distinct. Thus, the account of causation in Spinoza ends with a greater perplexity about his radically monistic philosophy, namely, how to have diversity within this radical unity.

Spinoza's God, unlike Descartes's, does not freely will the world (EMC, 435). Spinoza holds a version of *necessitarianism*, that for any state of the world if it is actual, it is necessary (Delahunty 1985, 160–65). This doctrine derives in part from his positive view about causation. Simply stated, necessitarianism is a form of determinism in which the causes both necessitate the effects and are themselves necessitated. Contingency for Spinoza is a matter of ignorance of an infinite sequence of causes (Delahunty 1985, 161).

We noted in Chapter 2 that Descartes raises the possibility that a perfect explanation would be a deductive sequence of premises or causes each of which followed from the first cause. That sequence would begin with clear and distinct ideas of God and proceed through the effect to be proved. Thus, a perfect explanation would also yield perfect understanding. A cause could be described as that through which a thing is understood or known—it is also a reason why something is the way it is. Spinoza makes these connections explicit. The principle of sufficient reason in modern philosophy is frequently stated as: "There is a reason why everything is the way it is and not some other way." Spinoza accepts a version of this principle in Proposition 11: "For the existence or non-existence of anything there must he a cause or reason" (EMC, 417). The principle of sufficient reason (cause) serves a dual purpose; it is an assurance that the world is comprehensively causal, that is, there exists a cause for everything, and it is an assurance that the world is comprehensively intelligible, that is, there exists an explanation (proof or demonstration) of everything. Spinoza seeks to produce in the *Ethics* the deductive sequence of explanations (synthesis) that Descartes only promises in his "Reply to the Second Objections." And he can do this only if he holds explicitly the principle of sufficient reason and if the first principles that begin the deduction are available to a mind that can carry out the deduction.

LEIBNIZ

Coming toward the end of the early modern period, Leibniz is sensitive to his place in the causation debate. He regularly alludes to his predecessors and frequently contrasts his own views on causation with those of his near contemporaries. Leibniz was frequently in contact with major figures in the debate—Spinoza and Malebranche, and in some cases representatives of various positions—Des Bosses (Scholastic), De Volder (Cartesian), and Clarke (Newtonian). But like all those in this debate, Leibniz began thinking about causation through the works of Descartes:

> After I established these things [true substances are monads]. I thought I was entering port; but when I began to meditate about the union of soul and body, I felt as if I were thrown again into the open sea. For I could not find any way of explaining how the body makes anything happen in the soul, or vice versa, or how one substance can communicate with another created substance. Descartes had given up the game at this point, as far as we can determine from his writings. But his disciples, seeing the common opinion is inconceivable, judged that we sense the qualities of bodies because God causes thoughts to arise in the soul on the occasion of motions of matter, and that when our soul, in turn wishes to move the body, it is God who moves the body for it. . . . That is what they call the system of occasional causes, which has been made very fashionable by the beautiful reflections of the author of the *Search after Truth*. (AG, 142)

Leibniz clearly identifies some of the tensions within Descartes's views on causation, and he accurately notes that many of Descartes's followers abandoned Cartesian interactionism in favor of occasionalism. Leibniz tends to see Descartes as holding some version of a transmission or influx theory. There is disagreement about whether Leibniz rejects the transmission model entirely or is willing to accept it as a way to explain body-on-body motion. O'Neill argues that "Leibniz thinks there is nothing wrong with a transmission model as long as it is used to account for purely bodily change at the macro level" (1993, 52). At the same time, O'Neill acknowledges that Leibniz finds this account unsatisfactory at the level of substances—substances are immaterial and simple, and therefore cannot add or subtract parts—between which there can be no such communication (1993, 52).

There are good reasons to think that Leibniz's talk of body-body interaction is nothing more than a heuristic device. Leibniz finds any transmission or influx model of causation unacceptable at the level of true substances *or* at the level of bodies. In his *Specimen Dynamicum* (1695) Leibniz argues that "every passion of a body is spontaneous or arises from an internal force, though upon an external occasion" (LL, 448). At the same time, like Malebranche, Leibniz is prepared to make concessions to ordinary language and of talking (LL, 312–13; compare Loeb 1981, 270). Strictly speaking, for Leibniz "one particular substance never acts upon another particular substance, nor is it acted upon by it . . . what happens to each is solely the result of its own complete idea or concept" (LL, 312).

Scholars such as Loeb often speculate as to why Leibniz held that nothing external can act on any other substance (God is the exception) (1981, 269 ff.). One answer lies in the fact that Leibniz, like Malebranche, finds previous efforts to answer the metaphysical problem about causation unintelligible. And part of the reason for this unintelligibility is that he tends to understand these theories of causation as involving some transmission or influx. Leibniz takes very seriously the view that dependent entities such as accidents or attributes are individual and uniquely attached to particular substances; this doctrine applies both to true substances (monads) and phenomenal substances (bodies) and makes any view of causation as transference or influx impossible (Clatterbaugh 1973). His argument is closely akin to the argument against real accidents offered by Descartes and Le Grand. In his letter to de Beauval in 1696, Leibniz argues:

> The way of influence is that of the common philosophy; but since we can conceive neither material nor nonmaterial qualities or species that can pass from one of these substances to the other, we must reject this opinion. (AG, 148; compare O'Neill 1993)

In the *Monadology* true substances are said to be windowless, and that metaphor is another way of denying the causal interaction of substances through a transfer of metaphysical entities:

> The monads have no windows through which something can enter or leave. Accidents cannot be detached, nor can they go about outside of substances, as the sensible species of the Scholastics once did. Thus, neither substance nor accident can enter a monad from without. (AG, 214)

Leibniz's commitment to the doctrine of individual properties is closely tied to another metaphysical doctrine, namely, the principle of spontaneity, which we will examine in a moment. Together Leibniz uses these doctrines to provide grounds for his rejection of the ways of influence (intractionism); furthermore, he argues that his own system of preestablished harmony will do everything that interactionist accounts will do without violating true metaphysical principles. He further suggests that his view of causation is somehow more worthy of God as a creator—unlike constant occasionalism, which requires constant miracles (AG, 143; AG, 159).

Spinoza's views on causation were attractive although ultimately unacceptable to Leibniz. They were attractive because Spinoza also denies an interaction between mind and body. Yet we have seen that Leibniz rejects Spinoza's view as unable to account for changes in particular things, a problem which he attributes to Spinoza's radical monism: Spinoza's error comes "entirely from his having pushed too far the consequences of the doctrine that denies force and action to creatures" (LL, 583). Furthermore, Leibniz is unhappy with Spinoza's necessitarianism and Spinoza's rejection of final causes (AG, 273).

> You know that I once strayed a little too far in another direction, and began to incline to the Spinozist view which allows God infinite power only, not granting him either perfection or wisdom, and which dismisses search for final causes and explains everything through brute necessity. (RB,73)

Leibniz consistently argues that final causes are useful—contrary to the views of Descartes and Spinoza. His argument on behalf of final causes is twofold. First, he argues that explanations by means of final causes may provide a shorter and easier route to certain conclusions about the world than explanations solely in terms of efficient causes (mechanical explanations) (AG, 54). His favorite example is Snell's law:

> For by seeking the easiest way to lead a ray from a given point to another point given by reflection on a given plane (assuming that this is nature's design), they discovered the equality of angles of incidence and angles of reflection. . . . Descartes's [attempt] to give of this same theorem by way of efficient causes is not nearly as good (AG 55).

His second argument is that although final causes are not necessary to explain particular phenomena, they are required to explain the laws which govern particular phenomena. In two passages with a very Gassendi-ist flavor, Leibniz writes:

> And it is surprising that, by a consideration of efficient causes alone, or by a consideration of matter, we cannot give the reason for the laws of motion discovered in our time, some of which I myself have discovered. For I have found that we must have recourse to final causes for this . . . and that these laws do not depend upon the principle of necessity, as do logical, arithmetical, and geometrical truths, but upon the principle of fitness, that is, upon the choice of wisdom. And this is one of the most effective and most evident proofs of the existence of God. . . . (AG, 211)

> For, all in all, whatever Descartes may have said, not only efficient causes, but also final causes are to be treated in physics, just as a house would be badly explained if we were to describe only the arrangement or its parts, but not its use. I already warned earlier that, although we say that everything in nature

is to be explained, mechanically, we must exempt the explanation of the laws of motion themselves, or the principles of mechanism should . . . be . . . derived from a metaphysical source, namely, from the equality and effect and from other laws of this kind. . . . (AG, 255)

The metaphysical sources that explain the laws of nature are conceived by Leibniz to be the designs of God, not only to create the world but to create the world according to certain guiding principles such as plenitude, perfection, equality of cause and effect—all of which presumably follow from his nature (AG, 52–55). Thus, Leibniz equates denial of final causes with denial of God's perfection and wisdom.

> . . . it is unreasonable to introduce a supreme intelligence as orderer of things and then, instead of using his wisdom, use only the properties of matter to explain the phenomena. This is as if, in order to account for the conquest of an important place by a great prince, a historian were to claim that it occurred because the small particles of gunpowder, set off by the contact of a spark, escaped with sufficient speed to push a hard and heavy body against the walls of the place, while the little particles that make up the brass of the cannon were so firmly interlaced that this speed did not separate them, instead of showing how the foresight of the conqueror enabled him to choose the suitable means and times and how his power overcame all obstacles. (AG, 53)

Leibniz, like Spinoza, holds to a principle of sufficient reason that he states in various ways. At one level it is equivalent to the vulgar claim that nothing happens without a cause. Another version is that every truth has an a priori proof that begins with its complete concept (LL, 646; LL, 337; compare Mates 154 ff.). Leibniz allows that if the individual concept of a particular were known, it would be possible to know everything that is true of it past, present, and future (AG, 33; AG, 47). The easy claim here is that Leibniz, like Descartes and Spinoza, seems to conflate causes with premises and reasons. For Leibniz, however, it is not a conflation so much as it is a self-conscious ambiguity in these terms.

> A reason is a known truth whose connection with some less well-known truth leads us to give our assent to the latter. But it is called a "reason" especially and *par excellence*, if it is the cause not only of our judgement but also the truth itself—which makes it what is known as an *"a priori reason."* A *cause* in the realm of things corresponds to a reason in the realm of truths, which is why causes themselves—and especially final ones—often called "reasons." (RB, 475)

Sufficient reasons, then, come out of individual concepts. Sufficient reasons are both causes and reasons for why things are the way they are. When God is the individual concept, final causes are revealed, that is why we have the particular *kinds* of series that we do—the particular laws of nature that we do. After all, God's purposes (final causes) are for Leibniz the sufficient reasons for the laws of nature that we have. "The reasons for the world lie hidden in something extra mundane, different from the chain of states, or from the series of things, the collection of which constitutes the world" (AG, 149–50).

> Since matter is in itself indifferent to motion and rest, and to one motion rather than another, we cannot find in matter the reason for motion, still less the reason for a particular motion. And although the present motion found in matter comes from the preceding motion, and it, in turn, comes from a preceding motion, we will not make any progress in this way, however far back we go, for the same question always remains. Thus, the sufficient reason, which needs no other reason, must be outside this series of contingent things, and must be found in a substance which is its cause, and which is a necessary being. . . . (AG, 210)

If final causes, God's designs, explain why mechanical causes follow the laws that they in fact follow, then Leibniz has a general argument that holds not only against Descartes and Spinoza but against the occasionalists as well. They all seem to lack an explanation of why things unfold in the regular patterns that they do:

> The same difficulty found in the hypothesis of a real influence of soul on body, and vice versa, is also found fit in the hypothesis of occasional causes, insofar as we can see no connection nor can we see a foundation for any rule. (AG, 83)

At the same time, we must not allow Leibniz to claim too much originality. Descartes could agree with Leibniz that there are reasons why we have the scientific laws that we do; the reasons are simply unavailable to us because they are designs or purposes. But, in fact, both Descartes and Spinoza hold that we can infer that we have the scientific laws that we do from an understanding of God's nature. Descartes derives certain laws of conservation in the *Principles* from God's immutability, and Spinoza is clear in the first part of the Ethics, Proposition 29," that "all things have been determined from the necessity of the divine nature, not only to exist, but to exist in a certain way, and to produce effect in a certain way" (EMC, 434). Leibniz slides between talking about God's nature and talking about God's Purposes, and since he seems to hold that God's purposes follow from God's nature, it would seem that his disagreement with either Descartes or Spinoza is minimal: both of them allow justifications for the laws of nature based upon God's nature, although neither of them recognize such inferences as grounded in final causes (compare Adams 1994; Sleigh 1990, 59–67).

Leibniz, although he sometimes links himself to the occasionalists, clearly views his theory of preestablished harmony as an advancement not only over Malebranche (AG, 100) but over the Cartesians and Scholastics as well (LL, 494). At bottom, Cartesian interactionism, Scholastic interactionism, and occasionalism all violate Leibniz's principle of nonspontaneity or autonomy of substance—namely, that each state of a substance is a consequence of the internal workings of that substance.[4]

Before we turn to the details of Leibniz's own theory of preestablished harmony, let us note some other concerns that lead Leibniz away from occasionalism, although he agrees with the occasionalists that substances do not, metaphysically speaking, interact. Of the necessary connection argument, Leibniz contends:

> Malebranche's strongest argument for why God alone acts reduces to this in the end—a true cause is that which the effect follows from necessarily, but an effect follows necessarily from the will of God alone [therefore, etc.]. However, it should be noted that if the state of any entity is known perfectly, then the state of any other entity can he inferred infallibly (although not, I grant, necessarily, i.e., not in such a way that it could ever be demonstrated that the contrary implies a contradiction, since analysis goes on ad infinitum). (as in Sleigh 1990b, 170)

The divine *concursus* argument, as we have noted, is only effective with the lemma that concurrence is an unintelligible alternative (Sleigh 1990b, 182). Leibniz, however, sides with the concurrentists against Malebranche. Indeed, Leibniz feels that if concurrence "physical co-operation" is unintelligible, then we might as well be Spinozists (FH, 139; FH, 234 ff. FH, 352).

> . . . the concurrence of God consists in giving us continually whatever there is of reality in us and our actions in so far as it contains some perfection; but what there is therein of limitation or imperfection is a consequence of preceding limitations, which are originally in creatures. (FH, 141)

Sleigh interprets Leibniz's concurrentism as follows:

> The basic idea is obvious enough: in an action with respect to which God and some creature concur, God's causal contribution pertains to the perfections exhibited in that action, whereas the creature's causal contribution pertains to the limitations exhibited in that action. (1990b, 185; see AG, 96–97)

The example of concurrent causation used by Leibniz in the *Theodicy* is that of two boats of similar construction moving downstream; the stream powers both boats, but the more heavily laden is held back in its motion (FH, 140; compare Sleigh 1990a, 185). Thus the motion of the more heavily laden boat is attributed to two causes. Although Leibniz is sometimes, by his own words, classified as an occasionalist, he is prepared to deny the central occasionalist tenet, namely, that God alone is causally efficacious.

There is some debate as to when Leibniz formulated his positive theory of causation, namely, the theory of preestablished harmony (Kulstad 1993a). In the 1670s he seems to have held a view that bodies can interact with minds and minds with bodies (Kulstad 1993a, 103). However, by the time of the *Discourse* in 1686, he had arrived at the central claims of his view, which were clearly amplified in his *New System of Nature* and his letters to de Beauval and Arnauld.

Leibniz's concern with his theory is not to change the way that interactionists or occasionalists talk, but to restructure their metaphysical understanding of that talk (Sleigh 1990b, 164).

> Yet I do not disapprove at all of the assertion that minds are in some way the occasional causes, and even the real causes, of the movements of bodies. For, with respect to divine resolutions, what God foresaw and pre-established with regard to minds was the occasion for his regulating bodies from the beginning so that they might fit together in accordance with the laws and forces he will give them. (AG, 85)

The metaphysical understanding that Leibniz would substitute is nicely summarized by Mark Kulstad:

> By *spontaneity* I mean the view that created substances can be real causes, or, more specifically, that each state of a created substance arises causally from its preceding state. (Thus, Leibniz can allow for causation—intrasubstantial—in creatures while denying them intersubstantial causation.) By parallelism I mean the thesis that the states of each creature correspond or agree perfectly with the sates of every other creature at any given moment. And by *concomitance* or *preestablished* harmony I mean the doctrine that God created finite substances in such a way that they do not causally interact but nonetheless exhibit parallelism in virtue of their own spontaneity. (Kulstad 1993a, 96–97)

Sleigh's summary is similar:

> According to the thesis of spontaneity every non-initial non-miraculous state of every created substance has as a real cause some preceding state of that very substance. According to the world-apart thesis no state of ally substance has as a real cause some state of some other created substance. . . . What we have is an affirmation of the ubiquity of real intra-substantial causality and the denial of inter-substantial causality. (Sleigh 1990b, 162)

Leibniz's view is that although there are no interactions among created substances, they do correspond with each other—this view he shares with occasionalists (Clatterbaugh 1973, 21–25). And that there are causes apart from God—this view he shares with the interactionists. In the preestablished harmony each substance is an "automaton" driven from internal forces and appetites to live out its own history, a history that happens to coincide with the histories of other automata—"the natural agreement of two very exact clocks" (LL, 494).

> But in my opinion it is in nature of created substance to change continually following a certain order which leads it spontaneously (if I may be allowed to use this word) through all the states which it encounters, in such a way that he who sees all things sees all its past and future states in its present. And this law of order, which constitutes the individuality of each particular substance, is in exact agreement with what occurs in every other substance and throughout the whole universe. I shall not claim too much if I say that I can demonstrate all this, but for the present the question is merely to maintain it as a possible hypothesis which is suitable for explaining phenomena. (LL, 493)

> For why should God be unable to give substance, from the beginning, a nature or an internal force that can produce in it, in an orderly way (as would happen in a spiritual or formal automaton, but free in the case where it has a share of reason), everything that will happen to it, that is, all the appearances or expressions "it" will have, without the help of any created being? This is especially so since the nature of substance necessarily requires and essentially involves progress or change, without which it would not have the force to act. (AG, 144)

There are two points which need clarification at this juncture. First, although Leibniz is committed to the view that nothing interacts with anything else, except God, he has no difficulty in accepting standard mechanistic explanations. Thus, Leibniz realizes that he departs from "ordinary usage" and that he must reconcile his metaphysics with this common usage (LL, 312–13).

> All bodily phenomena can be explained mechanically, or by corpuscular philosophy, following certain principles of mechanics granted without troubling whether souls exist or not; but in the final analysis of the principles of physics and of mechanics even, it is found that these principles are not explicable purely by the modifications of extension, the nature of force already requires something else. (as in Woolhouse 1993, 59)

The second point goes to the heart of Leibniz's theory of causation. There is general agreement among Leibniz scholars that in his mature philosophy, which began about the time of the *Discourse on Metaphysics* in 1686, Leibniz held that monads were the only substances and that bodies were somehow constructed out of the perceptions of these basic substances (Sleigh 1990; Adams

1994; Rutherford 1995). Thus, the mechanistic interactions among bodies, the correlations between body and soul all "reduce" in some way to changes in the monad. The question then is: what causes the changes in the monads? If we understand that these changes are lawful, according to the purposes of God (final causes) and that change of and other alterations in bodies are founded in the changes in the monads, the metaphysical problem of causation becomes the problem of understanding what produces monadic change. Here, there are at least three schools of thought (see Bobro and Clatterbaugh 1996).

The first view that is accepted by many is "the conceptual unfolding view," according to which the changes in monads are due to (caused by) the individual concept of that monad. Certainly Leibniz scholars such as Rescher and Woolhouse have been drawn in this direction (Rescher 1981; Woolhouse 1982). And Leibniz himself contributes to this view with passages such as:

> What happens to each [individual substance] is solely a consequence of its complete idea or notion alone, since this idea already contains all its predicates or events. . . . (AG, 47; compare AG 33)

There is, however, a compelling reason to deny that the cause of change in substances is the individual concept of that substance. Recall that Leibniz objects to Malebranche's occasionalism on the grounds that it requires constant miracles, that is, it requires that changes in substances are due not to normal causation but to God. Leibniz is prepared to allow that if there are miracles they come from outside of the normal causation that occurs in substances (AG, 82). If, however, the different states of a substance are caused by its concept, then since the concept of a substance contains everything that will ever be true of it, every state of a substance is caused by the same cause and there is no way to draw the distinction between miraculous and nonmiraculous states of a substance (AG, 41–47). Thus, we must reject the conceptual unfolding view of substantial change; the cause of change in substances cannot be the individual concept of that substance.

Once the cause of change is separated from the individual concept of the substance that changes, we can better understand why Leibniz holds a necessitarian view while, at the same time, denying that he should be in the company of necessitarians like Hobbes or Spinoza (FH, 234). In many writings, especially his correspondence with Arnauld, Leibniz makes the point that a true proposition is one in which the subject concept contains the predicate concept . . . the notion of the predicate is in some way included in that of the subject. *Praedicatum inest subiecto*; otherwise I do not know what truth is" (LL, 337; compare LL,334). Thus, individual concepts are reasons that entail (move us to the truth of) all claims about individual substances. Thus, for any proposition P, it is necessary that P. Causal propositions are as necessary as any other, for example, that I act in such a way as to go on a journey (LL, 334; compare Adams 1994, 57 ff.). In principle, one could begin with the individual concept and prove all the states of a substance past and future (AG, 45). This framework lies behind Leibniz's claim that there exists a proof a priori for every true proposition (AG, 101). At the same time, because the states of a substance are infinite, we cannot actually carry out such a proof, hence Leibniz claims that such indemonstrable propositions are contingent, not necessary (AG 28; AG 217). Adams, in his detailed analysis of Leibniz's determinism argues correctly that this notion of contingency does not enable Leibniz to escape necessitarianism (1994, 25 ff.). But since Leibniz seems to have held this theory of contingency throughout much of his life, he can argue that unlike Spinoza or Hobbes, all particular propositions are contingent.

The second interpretation of nomadic change is more tempting than the conceptual unfolding view. Loeb states the position and its defense:

> Leibniz holds that everything that exists or happens has a sufficient reason or cause. . . . The states of a substance at a given time must therefore have some sufficient reason or cause. Since nothing external acts upon a substance, the only candidate for causes of states of a substance at one time are states of that same substance at previous times. (1988, 270)

This view, which has been called "the efficacious perception view," is also espoused by Sleigh and Kulstad. Sleigh's version is: "Every non-initial, non-miraculous state of every created substance has as a real cause some preceding state of that very substance" (1990b, 162). Kulstad's version comes up in his articulation of Leibniz's theory of preestablished harmony: "I mean the view that created substances can be real causes, or, more specifically, that each state of a created substance arises causally from its preceding state" (1993a, 96).

Leibniz seems to suggest such a view in passages such as:

> The present state of each substance is a natural result of its preceding state. (LL, 495)

> Everything that happens in each substance is a consequence of the first state that God gave it in creating it, and extraordinary concourse aside, his ordinary concourse consists simply in the conservation of the substance itself, in conformity with preceding states and with the changes that it carries with it. (AG, 81–82)

In addition to these passages, there is an obvious argument that can be found in Loeb's discussion, namely, that every change must have a cause, the only candidates for a change in the state of a substance are in its previous states, therefore, the previous states of a substance are the cause of subsequent states. The efficacious perception view also fits with other aspects of Leibniz's philosophy. It allows, for example, a clear-cut way to distinguish miraculous states from nonmiraculous. Any state of a substance that arises from previous states is nonmiraculous, whereas any state that does not, which would include all initial states, is miraculous. Furthermore, this view acknowledges the distinction between cause and reason that is implicit in much of Leibniz's writing—the *cause* of a state is another state, whereas the *reason* for the state is to be found a priori in the individual concept.

Frankel and others have noted, however, that this view of causation makes Leibniz's view of causation into a Humean view in which regularly associated events become the cause of other events, and that view is at best anachronistic when applied to Leibniz's substance/accident metaphysics (1989, 57; Bobro and Clatterbaugh 1996). This view becomes even more doubtful when one notes that Leibniz is careful not to use causal language in talking about the movement from one state to another; instead he prefers terms such as "consequence," "leads," "follows," and "results" when talking about the passage from one state to another (AG, 33, 47).

Throughout his mature writing Leibniz holds what he calls "the principle of continuity" that no change takes place through a leap or discontinuity (AG, 131; AG, 297). For Leibniz, the principle of continuity applies to phenomenal states such as motion or change of color as well as changes in monadic states (AG, 297–298). It also provides a criterion by which Leibniz distinguishes natural from nonnatural (miraculous) states (AG, 298). Thus, there is good reason in Leibniz's philosophy to hold that each state of a substance follows from, results from, is a consequence of previous states, without those states being the cause of that state. if this understanding is right, then we are brought back to Loeb's question: if previous states are not causes of subsequent states, what is the cause or change in the monad?

Throughout his philosophical life Leibniz holds the view that ". . . activity is the essence of substance . . ." (RB, 65), and in his mature philosophy this idea is understood as a "created, active force inherent in things" (AG, 156). Leibniz contrasts his view with that of Spinoza, Descartes, and the occasionalists by noting that he is willing to allow these created things forces of their own that are the cause of spontaneous change arising from their own depths (RB, 65). The mistake of others, especially Spinoza, is to deny causal powers to created being (LL, 587). Thus, what may be called "the agency view" of change holds that in each substance there is an intrinsic force that is causally responsible for its changes (Bobro and Clatterbaugh 1996; compare Sleigh 1990a, 79). This "primitive active force" in Leibniz's mature philosophy drives the changes of perceptions in the monad, which in turn drives the changes in the states of phenomenal substances (AG, 119; compare Clatterbaugh 1973; Garber 1995).

The agency view conforms even better to the overall structure of Leibniz's philosophy than the efficacious perception view. Both views allow Leibniz's distinction between miraculous and nonmiraculous states of substances and both allow for Leibniz's distinction between causes and reasons. But the agency view better fits with Leibniz's substance/accident philosophy by making substances, not accidents, causes, and the agency view fits better with the fact that Leibniz avoids causal language when talking about how one state of a substance follows upon another. Finally, the agency view seems to tie together Leibniz's discussion of causation and the Aristotelianism implicit in much of Leibniz's treatment of causation (AG, 118).

Perhaps Leibniz's view of causation can best be understood as a way of talking about interlocking "causal" sequences at different ontological levels (compare, Garber 1995). At the phenomenal level, causation is mechanistic and explanations of one phenomenal state are in terms of another—"we have no means of explaining them except through magnitude, figure, and motion, that is, through mechanism" (LL, 173; AG, 42–43). At the same time, since phenomenal change reduces, metaphysically, to change in perception of monads, there is a further metaphysical level that explains phenomenal change (AG, 119). And at this level the explanation stops at the "primitive force" that is in each monad and which causally carries out the blueprint or formal cause that is the individual concept.[5] But even the blueprints, which constitute the plan for individual change, are explained at another level in terms of God's plan or the final causes (AG, 54–55; AG, 225). If one wanted to press the Aristotelianism of Leibniz's view, the states of substances or the accidents of substances could be viewed as the material causes that are manipulated by the agency of the substance in accord with the formal cause or plan (the individual concept). But any such Aristotelian reading should also make it clear that Leibniz's metaphysics are not Aristotle's; rather it is that one is able to find Aristotelian analogs within his metaphysics.

Ultimately, Leibniz's treatment of the substance as having an internal force that causes its changes is largely metaphorical, although metaphysically real. It does not serve to explain, in a scientific way, phenomenal change. "Indeed, primitive force corresponds . . . only to general causes, which are insufficient to explain the phenomena" (AG, 119). It does, however, give a response to the metaphysical problem of causation. Of all the early moderns, Leibniz is perhaps the clearest in his realization that solutions to the metaphysical problem of causation will not necessarily spill over into science or influence the scientific quest for particular causes, although Leibniz clearly believes that knowing God's nature can facilitate the discovery of scientific laws. The next moderns, the scientist-philosophers, are inclined to throw up their hands at the metaphysical problem of causation. If, as Leibniz observes, the metaphysical question of what happens in a causal sequence and the scientific question of what are the causes of a particular change can be answered independently of each other, the next group of moderns is inclined to simply abandon the metaphysical problem in favor of concrete explanations of particular events or particular binds of events.

CENTRAL THEMES

At this point in our discussion the debate has several notable features. Descartes, Hobbes, and Gassendi all assumed that causal interactions between bodies and between bodies and minds occur. Hobbes may have tempered his view by making minds material, and Descartes and Gassendi were somewhat mystified by the interaction of mind and body, but that such interactions occur was never seriously in question. Divine interaction with the created world was also never questioned, although it was never fully analyzed because of the enormous power of God. The metaphysical problem of causation, then, was taken to be a problem about how to account for what goes on metaphysically mainly between or among bodies. By the time of Le Grand and Malebranche there has been a general rejection of the assumption that causal interactions occur between bodies or between minds and bodies. Something happens, but it does not involve true causation; it is a kind of pseudocausation. The only true causation is between God and the creation, and that is as much a mystery for the occasionalists as it was for their interactionist predecessors. Leibniz, in the most general sense, keeps faith with the occasionalists. He talks about causal connections between and among created things, but what is happening is a kind of pseudocausation, not true causation. Leibniz denies all interaction in his theory of preestablished harmony; all connections are elaborately planned, yet lawful, coincidences. Spinoza talks about one finite mode conditioning another, but God remains the only true efficient cause in his system. Thus, mechanism, although it is embraced for scientific reasons in the philosophies of Le Grand, Malebranche, Spinoza, and Leibniz, is not an effort to provide scientific explanations in terms of true causes. This denial makes the metaphysical problem or causation moot, if that is understood to be a metaphysical account of what goes on in true causation. From the very beginning, the metaphysical problem of causation was never satisfactorily resolved; the attempted solutions to it end in vague metaphors, such as divine impulse (Descartes), primitive active force (Leibniz), divine will (the occasionalists) or divine necessity (Spinoza), or even in endeavors of intrinsic motive force in bits of matter (Hobbes and Gassendi). Thus, it is small wonder that the scientist-philosophers, whom we consider next, find no advancement of knowledge in exploring the metaphysical problem. Indeed, they think that such speculations have proved to be a positive detriment to the advancement of science.

7.
The Limits of Classical Mechanism: Boyle, Rohault, and Newton

Robert Boyle (1627–91) published *Origin of Forms and Qualities According to the Corpuscular Philosophy* in Oxford in 1666; Jacques Rohault (1620–72) published *A System of Natural Philosophy* in Paris in 1671; and Issac Newton (1642–1727) saw his *Philosophiae Naturalis Principia Mathematica* appear in print in 1687. All three men were among the finest and best-known scientists of their time. Their essays appear during the height of the causation debate in the late 1600s. While these scientist-philosophers are not unfamiliar with the philosophical debate about causation, their focus is elsewhere—they are far more interested in discovering causes than in understanding causation. Indeed, there is evidence that they focus on particular causes because they believe that the debate concerning the metaphysics of causation is fruitless, at least for the purposes of science. Accordingly, one cannot expect clear statements about the nature of causation or detailed arguments that favor one or more of the various conditions upon causation. Thus, how they view causation must be gleamed from the isolated remarks that they make when in their rare philosophical moods and from the kinds of entities they are willing to consider as candidates for causes in scientific explanation.

Boyle's *The Origin of Forms and Qualities* was conceived as an "introduction to the Mechanical philosophy"—the belief that changes in the physical realm are best understood in terms of matter (corpuscles) in motion and that the physical world is a well-ordered machine (S, 2). This essay remains one of the best theoretical statements of the corpuscularian or mechanical perspective (Alexander 1990, 35). Boyle conceives it as a statement and defense of corpuscularianism in its most general form—a position which includes himself, Cartesians such as Rohault, and atomists such as Gassendi—without a clear preference for any particular school of corpuscularianism (S, 7).

Rohault's *System* dominated physics for the fifty years after its publication. Anthony Le Grand brought out a Latin edition in 1692, two years before he published his own English writings. Samuel Clarke subverted the Cartesian system and gained entry into the universities for Newton's ideas by publishing four separate editions of Rohault's *System* between 1697 and 1713. By the 1713 edition, Clarke's footnotes constitute twenty percent of the edition. John Clarke, brother of Samuel, brought out an English edition in 1723. Of course, Newton, himself a Cartesian for twenty years, had published the *Principia* in part as a refutation of the Cartesians; but it was due to Clarke's ingenuity that that refutation was accomplished (RS, Laudan, Introduction).

The changes in the debate that Boyle, Rohault, and Newton introduce are themselves a matter of debate among scholars of the modern period, although there is general agreement that Boyle is a practical scientist who seeks to avoid unnecessary metaphysical debate. Marie Boas's classical paper "The Establishment of the Mechanical Philosophy" argues that Boyle is best understood as the *restorer* of the mechanical philosophy; he successfully uses it to understand physical phenomena and as a devout Christian, he tries to rescue it from Hobbesian atheism (1952). Joy argues that Boyle was able to extract the mechanical philosophy from a number of metaphysical disputes about the indivisibility of matter, the existence of the plenum, or the innateness of motion (1988). Sargent argues that Boyle sides with Bacon against Descartes in holding that it is the construction of elaborate metaphysical systems that impedes the advancement of science (1995, 35–36). Alexander sees Boyle's work as the final demolition of systems of the late Scholastics or Aristotelians. In this chapter, I concur with these themes; I argue that Boyle's restoration, which was taken up by Newton, does excuse itself from some of the muddiest and most contentious metaphysical problems, such as the metaphysical problem of causation, that perplexed earlier mechanists such as Descartes and Gassendi. At the same time, I argue that Boyle does not hesitate to engage in certain foundational questions, if they are perceived as germane to the defense of the mechanical philosophy. At the same time, by turning his back on the metaphysical debate and metaphysical constraints, Boyle is free to pursue causes that are not allowed in classical mechanism.

Rohault gets scant attention in the history of science and philosophy, although in many ways he best exemplifies the changes these scientist-philosophers make in thinking about causation. And since Rohault is a Cartesian, it is all the more significant that his views about metaphysical speculation tend to coincide with those of Boyle and Newton who oppose the Cartesians on many fronts. Basically, Rohault takes the stand that metaphysical speculations have borne no fruit in part because the level of metaphysical speculation is too abstract and general—such work is of no use in explaining particulars, and it is the explanation of particulars that is the test for the adequacy of any system (RS, Author's Preface). In one of the few treatments of Rohault, Garber notes:

> God appears nowhere. Furthermore the preface contains a diatribe against metaphysics and in the body of the work Rohault explicitly endorses a hypothetical mode of reasoning, collecting phenomena, making conjectures, and testing them against experience. The content is clearly Cartesian, but the dependence of physics on metaphysics Descartes himself took such pains to emphasize is all but ignored. (1992, 62)

Newton's place in this debate is also a matter of contention among scholars. Boas lumps him with Boyle, whereas Westfall argues that while Boyle's mechanism treats matter as "shorn of every active principle," Newton introduces attractive and repulsive forces as a way of perfecting mechanism (1971b, 41, 143). Certainly with Newton it becomes most obvious that the debate is no longer directly about the nature of causation but about the kinds of entities that are needed as causes to successfully articulate the causal laws and to explain the phenomena of interest. Newton, as Westfall notes, focuses his attention on the phenomena that are most difficult to explain by causation by contact—he looked at the phenomena of electrical attraction, gravity, and light (1971b, 159 ff.). In the end, Newton finds the earlier mechanisms wanting and is prepared, with some vacillation, to accept "hidden" forces of attraction and repulsion. In his own time and since, Newton's views have been examined to see if he in fact abandons or advocates"occult qualities." In his *Theodicy* of 1710, Leibniz charges Newton publicly with advocating an occult quality (FH, 85–86). Leibniz's controversy with Newton was already enflamed by the "calculus question" that had arisen in 1705. Newton, in turn, responded to Leibniz in the second edition of the *Principia*, and Roger Cotes, Newton's disciple, charges Leibniz—not by name—with Spinozistic necessitarianism in this same edition (TH, 116 ff.). Contemporary scholars such as Hall believe that Newton does abandon "occult" qualities (1952, 469 ff.). But other authors, such as Westfall, McGuire, Henry, and Hutchison, have argued that while there is an effort to get rid of Scholastic occult forms, other occult or hidden causes that were in some way "intelligible" were acceptable to Newton and others who were part of the scientific revolution in the seventeenth century (Westfall 1972, McGuire 1968, Henry 1986, 1971b, and Hutchinson 1982).

Newton, as a Cambridge student in the early 1660s, was familiar with many of the major figures of the causation debate, probably through the instruction of Henry More (Westfall, 1971b, 323 ff.). Newton, of course, knew the works of Rohault and Descartes; Rohault's work had received a favorable review in the *Philosophical Transactions of the Royal Society* immediately upon its publication in 1671. Newton was acquainted with Gassendi through Charleton's interpretations. Hobbes he studied directly, and Leibniz was familiar to him as an antagonist, although both Leibniz and Newton changed the classical mechanical philosophy forever by building it on a foundation of intrinsic force (Westfall 1971b, 323). Boyle, who was a scientific peer, he read throughout his life.

In this chapter, I argue that rather than being presented simply as opponents to late scholastic forms and virtues, these scientist-philosophers should be read as resisting questions about the value of metaphysical speculation itself. Not only are they not interested in the metaphysical question of causation but also they seem to believe that that question, among certain other metaphysical concerns, is harmful to the progress of science. Of course, such a questioning of metaphysics makes them hostile to powers, occult qualities, substantial forms, accidental forms, or real qualities—the postulation of any of which they believe derives from metaphysical concerns rather than scientific ones. At the same time, these thinkers are not rigidly antimetaphysical; like the twentieth-century logical positivists, they happily embrace metaphysical concerns when they see the issue as one of defending a principle that is required for their vision of a science. And they exhibit a pragmatic streak that allows them to postulate, accept, and defend causes that are yet unknown or little understood, if those causes are deemed justifiable based on their views about what counts as a good scientific explanation. The work of these thinkers marks an explicit reformulation of the terms of the debate. Whereas the earlier thinkers (Le Grand, Malebranche, Spinoza, and Leibniz) openly engaged in metaphysical speculation and were led by that to deny that what had been paradigm cases of causal interaction were in fact truly causal interactions. These scientist-philosophers go back to the tradition of Descartes, Hobbes, and Gassendi in reasserting that the paradigm cases of interaction are true interactions, and they consciously reject the metaphysics that led Le Grand and others to think otherwise.

BOYLE

Boyle is remarkably casual about causation. If one compares his summary of mechanism with Charleton's views on mechanistic causation, Boyle avoids claiming that everything has a cause or that causation occurs only through contact. Boyle presents a succinct summary of his version of the mechanical philosophy in *The Origin of Forms and Qualities* where he articulates its ten central tenets as follows:

1. That the matter of all natural bodies is the same, namely, a substance extended and impenetrable.

2. That all bodies thus agreeing in the same common matter, their distinction is to be taken from those accidents that do diversify it.

3. That motion, not belonging to the essence of matter . . . and not being originally producible by other accidents as they are from it, may be looked upon as the first and chief *mood* or affection of matter.

4. That motion, variously determined doth naturally divide the matter it belongs to into actual fragments or parts. . . .

5. Whence it must necessarily follow that each of these minute parts of *minima naturalia* . . . must have its determinate bigness or size, and its own shape. And these three, namely *bulk, figure,* and either *motion* or *rest* . . . are the three primary and most catholic moods or affections of the insensible parts of matter, considered each of them *apart.*

6. That when *diverse* of them are considered *together,* there will necessarily follow here below both a certain position or posture in reference to the horizon of each of them, and a certain order or placing before or behind or beside one another. . . . And indeed these several kinds of location . . . , attributed . . . to the minute particles of bodies, are so near of kin that they seem all of them referable to . . . situation or position.

7. That yet there being men in the world, whose organs or sense are contrived in such differing ways that one sensory is fitted to receive impressions from some, and another from other sorts of external objects or bodies without . . . the perceptions of these impressions are by men called by several names, as heat, colour, sound, odour...[that] are but the effects or consequents of the above-mentioned *primary affections* of matter. . . . (S,50–51)

8. That when a portion of matter, either by the accession or recession of corpuscles, or by the *transposition* of those . . . happens to obtain a *concurrence of all* those qualities which men commonly agree to be *necessary* and *sufficient* to

denominate the body which hath them . . . [then it ranks as] a determinate species of bodies. . . .

9. This convention of essential accidents . . . discriminates it from all other sorts of bodies.

10. Now a body being capable of many other qualities besides those whose convention is necessary to make up its form, the acquisition or loss of any such quality is by naturalists, in the more strict sense of that term, named *alteration*, as when oil comes to be frozen, or to change colour. . . . (S, 50–53)

Boyle's summary reveals a theory of the structure of matter that is as metaphysically neutral as possible; for the most part these tenets would have been acceptable to almost all of his predecessors. Boyle avoids calling the particles of matter "atoms," but he also avoids commitment to the Cartesian position that every bit of matter is further divisible. Among the various properties that are formed by arrangements of particles, those that are said to be essential are so designated by convention [theses (8), (9) and (10)] (S, 38–39, 45). And Boyle is eager to reject the position that every property that is *attributed* to a corporeal object is *inherent* in that object; he calls this the "grand mistake" (S, 28, 31–32). To use one of his examples: the echo in a cave is not a distinct property of the cave, but it is "nothing else but" the hollowness of the cave (S, 34). As stated in thesis (7), Boyle treats the "secondary properties" of corporeal objects as "nothing else but" the effects of the primary properties on the senses; writers like O'Toole and Alexander among others are able to identify the considerable influence of Boyle upon Locke's distinction between primary and secondary properties (1974; 1935). It is interesting to note here that while Boyle disagrees with Hobbes on such metaphysical issues as whether there are spirits distinct from corporeal substances, he is willing to go further than Hobbes in denying the reality of secondary properties such as taste, smell, and color.

The first six theses simply assert a kind of naturalistic corpuscularianism which posits small impenetrable bodies that all have shape and size and are either in motion or at rest. Motion is not essential to a body—otherwise, it could not be at rest. At the same time, motion is singled out as the chief mood of matter, which seems to mean that it has special status among the properties of matter. Boyle is content, like Descartes, to speak of one body communicating its motion or some degree of it to other corporeal bodies (S, 43). And, like Descartes, Boyle does not make a metaphysical commitment to a particular kind of causation in which, for example, an accident is transferred from one body to another. Indeed, Boyle endorses Descartes's abhorrence of "real accidents," that is, accidents that can exist without being in a particular subject (S, 22). Noticeably absent from Boyle's list is the classical mechanist principle articulated by Charleton that nothing can act on a distant object.

When Boyle cites examples of proper causation, he offers a variety of entities that qualify as causes. Whereas he seems to agree with Hobbes that we do not need to appeal to God in our discussions of the "nearest and most immediate causes," he does not agree that we can have a satisfactory account without acknowledging an intelligent Author or Disposer of things" (S, 156–57). Boyle dismisses "final causes" or divine design as explanations of particular physical changes (S, 19). Like Descartes, Boyle is prepared to allow that spirits do cause changes in matter, but he excludes spirits from mechanical explanations because, however it is that spirits or immaterial principles do operate on matter, it is more complicated than the mechanical philosophy and may even be unintelligible to us (S, 153). Boyle, unlike Descartes who believes that understanding God or God's design helps to establish the primary principles or laws of the physical world, is more interested in using our knowledge of the physical world to prove that there must be a supreme being who constructed this marvelous machine. Boyle frequently uses the metaphor of a watch:

> And thus in this great automaton, the world (as in a watch or clock), the materials it consists of being left to themselves could never at the first convene into so curious an engine and yet, when the skilful artist has once made and set it a-going, the phenomena it exhibits are to be accounted for by the number, bigness, proportion, shape, motion (or endeavour), rest, coaptation, and other mechanical affection, as the spring, wheels, pillars, and other parts it is made up of; and those effects of such a watch that cannot this way be explicated must, for aught I yet know, be confessed not to be sufficiently understood (S, 71).

Boyle is generally clear that he is a deist, that is, he believes that God gave matter its design and set it going, although we need not make these suppositions in order to explain particular phenomena (S, 19, 172; compare Westfall 1958). That Boyle is a deist in this sense has been challenged by McGuire, who argues that Boyle denies causal powers to any created things except moral agents (1972). While Boyle clearly allows that there are spirits that act on matter in some mysterious way, he is certain that "whatever is done among things inanimate . . . is really done but by particular bodies, acting on one another by local motion, modified by the other mechanical affections of the agent, of the patient, and those other bodies that necessarily concur to the effect or the phenomenon produced" (S, 91). In his preface to *The Origin of Forms and Qualities* Boyle clearly identifies qualities of bodies as causes:

> And as it is by their qualities that bodies act immediately upon our senses, so it
> is by virtue of those attributes likewise that they act upon other bodies, and by
> that action produce in them, and oftentimes in themselves, those changes that
> sometimes we call *alterations*, and sometimes *generation* or *corruption*. (S, 13)

Some scholars, notably McGuire, have argued that because Boyle conceived
of nature as a set of particulars (Boyle's nominalism) that were unrelated, he
actually embraced a form of occasionalism in which God's will is "the only
causally efficacious agency in nature" (1995, 525). If Boyle held the view
attributed to him by McGuire, he would never have made bodies and their
qualities the causes of change and he most certainly would never have entered
into a debate with More precisely on the question of whether matter was or
was not inert—Boyle taking the view that matter is not inert and that material change is not due solely to the action of spirits (Henry 1990).

However, Boyle's casual approach to causation can lead to confusions. He
speaks of both spirits and mechanical causes as agents and compares the regularities of inanimate bodies to those of rational agents (S, 81).[1] In some
places, Boyle even refers to the primitive, general, and fixed laws of nature (or
rules of action and passion among the parcels of the universal matter) as the
"catholic and primary causes of things"; he does this in the same paragraph
that he identifies as primary causes "the shape, size, motion, and other primary affections of the smallest parts of matter" (S,156–57).

While Boyle's language is casual about what counts as a cause—bodies,
qualities of bodies, laws of nature—his particular examples of causes are
almost always qualities of bodies (S, 82 ff.). And he consistently rules out a set
of entities that in his view have been inappropriately counted as causes of
physical change, specifically, powers, natures, real properties, and even spirits.
In his essay "About the Excellency and Grounds of the Mechanical
Hypothesis" Boyle argues rather straightforwardly that the mechanical philosophy that begins with matter and motion and allows matter only a limited set
of properties is the simplest and most comprehensive set of principles yet
devised (S, 141). Thus, further principles are unnecessary to explain physical
change, and because they are more complex or use entities like spirits that are
poorly understood, they are unintelligible or less intelligible than mechanical
principles.

Arguing specifically against powers, Boyle notes that explanations in terms
of powers, where powers are thought of as the ability to cause a property
change in another body, for example, the power of *aqua regia* to dissolve gold,
tend to multiply entities beyond necessity. Once we admit powers, over and
above the specific mechanical properties of a body, "we must admit that a body
may have an almost infinite number of new real entities accruing to it without

the intervention of any physical change in the body itself...."(S, 24). To admit indefinite powers would, for example, make the conventional notion of natural kind (essence) indefinitely complex. Thus, the inclusion of powers along with other properties threatens the simplicity of science, and it challenges its empirical basis (S, 25). The sun, in the ordinary way of speaking, has the power to harden clay, soften wax, melt butter, weather glass, evaporate water, catch eggs; these are not distinct properties of the sun over and above the fact that the sun has heat produced by the agitation of little particles (S,27).

Behind Boyle's confidence in his mechanical explanations lie two deeply held beliefs. The first, which is also Rohault's, is that a system should be judged by its ability to explain *particular* phenomena, and in that regard mechanism is far superior to competing types of explanation, which are too general in nature to explain particular phenomena.

> And accordingly, if you further ask them how white bodies in general do rather produce this effect of dazzling the eyes than green or blue ones, instead of being told that the former sort of bodies reflect outwards . . . you shall perchance be told that it is their respective natures so to act: by which way of dispatching difficulties they make it every easy to solve all the phenomena of nature in general, but make men think it impossible to explicate almost any of them in particular. (S, 16)

Boyle's second belief is that the cause of something is determined by the best explanation or, as he prefers to say, by a good or excellent hypothesis, that is, a hypothesis that explains better, more simply, is consistent with other accepted hypotheses, and allows for the successful prediction of future events (S, 19).

Having set what he believes to be rigorous standards for the acceptance of any hypothesis, Boyle applies them equally to qualities manifest or occult. That is to say, Boyle does nor rule out or rule in a quality as cause because it is not readily available to the senses or because it is readily available. For example, Boyle prefers explanations of color, taste, and other secondary properties in terms of nonmanifest properties of the insensible parts because he finds it a better explanation.

> Nor do I say that all qualities of bodies are directly sensible: But I observe that, when one body works upon another, the knowledge we have of their operation proceeds either from some sensible quality, or some more catholic affection of matter, as motion, rest, or texture, generated or destroyed in one of them. . . . (S 32)

As Sargent and other Boyle scholars argue, Boyle is not committed to an empiricist view of causation, that is, he does not believe that the cause of a phenomenon must be available for observation. What must be available is the effect and it must be available empirically (the cause is manifest in its effect) and, in principle, predictably (Sargent 1995, 105, 107; Henry 1994).

In his essay "Tracts about the Cosmical Qualities of Things," written in 1671, Boyle seems to explicitly abandon classical mechanism's commitment to push-pull causation (no action at a distance):

> ... there may be diverse unheeded agents, which by unperceived means, may have great operations upon the body we consider, and work such changes in it, and enable it to work such changes in other bodies, as are rather to be ascribed to some unheeded agents than to those other bodies with which the body proposed is taken notice of. (1772, iii, 306)

The causes, which Boyle seems to have in mind and which cannot be immediately deduced from the principles of corpuscles in motion, are "gravity," "fermentation," "springiness," and "magnetism" (Henry 1994, 123; S, 31; Boyle 1772, v, 26). As Henry notes in his discussion of "Cosmical Qualities," Boyle does not discount such causes as long as their effects are manifest. When Boyle talks of "occult" qualities as fictions, he clearly does not count such qualities as gravity; rather he is focusing on Scholastic forms and powers whose effects are not manifest (Henry 122; Boyle 1772 III, 307; S 79). And as Henry argues in another paper, Boyle's willingness to include insensible qualities as causes is quite consistent with the works of other practical scientists of his time. Robert Hooke, for example, accepts occult powers as long as their effects can be daily tested (Henry 1986, 361). Hutchinson has argued that the new mechanical philosophers took it as an advantage of their view that hidden or occult causes could be used to explain phenomena (1982).

Boyle emerges in the causation debate as a participant who found little value in the great systems of his predecessors—indeed he saw these systems as impediments to natural philosophy (Sargent 1995, 35–36; Boyle 1772, i, 26). They are an impediments in part because they identify causes that are too far removed from particular phenomena, which are always better explained by local causes and motions (S, 146). To the extent to which Boyle avoids these great systems, he avoids metaphysical debate. At the same time, when he needs an assumption to make his explanations in terms of local causation work, he does not hesitate to venture into metaphysics—as in his debate with More. And he certainly does not fall into a naive empiricism that requires that causes be observable; he does not even fall into the category of one who holds that the hidden causes, while they may be hidden, must be at least like the causes that are observable—small insensible atoms act much like visible sensible billiard balls. He allows that there may be causes that are unlike any cause that is experienced. The test of a cause is simply whether as a hypothesis it satisfies Boyle's conditions for a scientific explanation, that is, is it simple, better than its competitors, and does it allow for experiment and prediction?

In his manuscript notes on a good and excellent hypothesis, Boyle offers a radically new way of thinking about causation, and nowhere does he require a solution to the metaphysical problem of causation. What he does insist upon is that a good hypothesis is "intelligible," that "it contain nothing impossible or manifestly false," that it not presuppose anything impossible, "that it be consistent with it self," that it be sufficient to explain the effect, and that it be consistent with other phenomena and truths (S, 119). An *excellent* hypothesis is a good hypothesis that is supported by other evidence, that is the simplest of the good hypotheses, that is the best explanation, and that allows experiments and prediction ("a skilfull Naturalist to Foretell Future *Phenomena*") (S, 119). This epistemic turn is to one degree or another supported by the remainder of the participants in the debate; it is a critical turning point in which successful science prevails over philosophical and metaphysical concerns. And while elements of this approach to causation can be found in participants of the debate such as Gassendi, no one before Boyle presents this view as clearly and as unencumbered by tradition or metaphysics; and certainly no one is as capable as Boyle of putting this view of causation into practice.

Rohault

On the surface, Boyle and Rohault appear to be very different in their scientific outlook. Rohault is a Cartesian committed to basic Cartesian principles: the essence of matter is extension, there is a plenum but no void, and much of physical change (including gravitation) is explained through vortices of subtle matter. Rohault is adamantly opposed to attractive forces (occult forces) such as gravity. Rohault and Boyle are not, however, as directly antagonistic as they could be because Boyle does not possess the fervent anti-Cartesianism of Newton or Clarke, and both Rohault and Boyle are cautious about their metaphysical commitments. Thus, although Boyle seems to favor a vacuum and deny the existence of the *materia subtilis*—Rohault's preferred explanation— he avoids categorical denunciations of these metaphysical doctrines. Of *materia subtilis* he says, "if it be at all," and although he seems to be satisfied with experiments demonstrating the existence of a vacuum, he concedes that the vacuum might be a "thing impossible" (S, 103, 146). And in case there are no true vacuums but all empty space is filled with *materia subtilis*, Boyle postulates that that subtle matter will not affect the phenomenon in any way, so it can be disregarded for the sake of experiment (S, 403). Thus, Boyle, even when he prefers one metaphysical stance to another, hedges whenever possible, that is, when the position does not affect an experimental outcome or a best explanation.

Rohault's response to those who argue like Boyle is to agree with them that arguments about nature abhorring a vacuum are "ridiculous" (RS I, xii, 56). At the same time, Rohault argues that if there were no matter in a Torricelli tube, then light could not pass through it, as it does (RSI, xii, 64). Thus, Rohault rests his case, as does Boyle, ultimately on what are the outcomes of experiments with different presuppositions. Rohault's arguments on behalf of a plenum reflect his fundamental belief that philosophers have failed to discover much about nature because they adopt methods that are "wholly from reasoning" and "they judge it superfluous to make any experiments" (RS, Author's Preface). Rohault's preferred method is to use both reasoning and experiment as in the vacuum case; this approach fits well with Boyle's own style of argument.

In his "Author's Preface" Rohault identifies several things that have hindered the progress of natural philosophy; there has been too much respect for ancient authority, too little experiment, too little reasoning, not enough mathematics, and especially too much attention to general metaphysical questions:

> Another thing which hinders the progress of natural philosophy, is the treating thereof in a matter too metaphysical and the disputing about questions so abstract and general, that though all philosophers were agreed in their notions or them, yet they could not help to explain the least particular effect in nature; whereas every useful science ought to descend immediately to particulars. For instance, what good do those long and nice disputes do about the divisibility of matter? (RS, Author's Preface)

Boyle would agree wholeheartedly with the sentiment expressed here; Boyle, like Rohault, finds general principles only of interest when combined with local motions that can help explain particular effects (S, 153; compare S, 145, 165).

Rohault's critique of the metaphysical debates and abstract definitions that do not descend to particulars is at times openly sarcastic; consider his reference to the attempts to define motive force:

> It is very useful, without doubt, to find out the nature of motion in general. And it may not be very improper to examine a little whether it be well or ill defined thus, *The act of being a power, so far forth as it is in power.* But we should not spend too much time in determining this, and such like questions; I should rather think, that after having considered a little the true

nature of motion in general, we should particularly and distinctly examine all the properties of it, so that what we affirm concerning it, may be applied to some use; in a word, I think we should carefully enquire into the cause why matter produces such a particular effect rather than any other. (RS, Author's Preface)

The need to descend to particulars encourages the scientist-philosophers to identify specific states or properties of things as causes of specific states or properties in other. Both Boyle and Rohault make it abundantly clear that qualities or properties—not substances—are the appropriate causes of change or alteration of other qualities or properties. As Boyle puts it in the preface to *The Origin of Forms and Qualities*, we "scarce know anything else in bodies, upon whose account they can work upon our senses, save their qualities" (S, 13). The movement away from substances as causes, which was aggressively promoted by Hobbes, was also championed in the debate by Le Grand (LG I, IV, 9, 107).

But not just any quality is to be acknowledged as suitable for a scientific explanation. For Boyle and Rohault it is the principal properties of size, shape, and motion or rest that are the causes of changes not only in principal properties but in the secondary properties as well (S, 153; RS I, vii, 22 ff.). And occult properties are to be dismissed because they too fail to provide any particular explanation of particular phenomena—Rohault says that there is no difference in quality between the answer of a plowman who claims not to know why a loadstone attracts iron and that of a natural philosopher who claims that the attraction is due to a power to attract iron (RS, Author's Preface). Rohault seems to believe that all attractive qualities are of such a nature, whereas Boyle, as we have seen, allows for attractive causes that produce particular effects. Thus, the metaphysical debate about causation is increasingly reduced to a debate about *which* qualities provide the best causal explanations of particular phenomena where "best explanation" includes a set of epistemological principles such as simplicity, comprehensiveness, availability, and usefulness.

A comparison of Boyle's essay "Of the Imperfection of the Chemists' Doctrine of Qualities," published in 1675, and Rohault's Chapter 20 of Part I, entitled "Of the Elements of the Chemists," nicely illustrates the criteria that both scientist-philosophers use in identifying proper causes.

The Chemists were a school of scientists who sought the composition of things by heating them; ultimately they identify sulfur, salt, and mercury as the building blocks of other substances—building blocks that they discover through their analysis. Both Rohault and Boyle reject what they take to be the foundational principles of the Chemists. Both note that the Chemists' doctrine is far from comprehensive—they leave a great many phenomena unexplained (RS I, xx, 110; S, 123). Boyle and Rohault also note that the terms salt, mercury, and sulfur are ambiguous; there are multiple kinds of salt, mercury, and sulfur, which gives the Chemists' explanations a vagueness and imprecision. Rohault writes: "Thus, there are a great many sorts of mercury, sulfur, salt and company" (RS I, xx, 110). Boyle observes: ". . . those substances themselves that chemists call their principles are each of them endowed with several qualities. Thus salt is a consistent, not a fluid body, it has its weight; it is dissoluble in water, is either daiphanous or opacous, fixed or volatile, sapid or insipid . . ." (S, 126). Both Boyle and Rohault reject the Chemists' doctrine as not providing a deep enough explanation. Boyle says it is not "deep and radical enough" (S, 127). And Rohault notes that they stop their analysis with a few sensible qualifies, never reaching the depth of the mechanical philosophy (RS I, xx, 110). Finally, what seems to be the decisive argument is that the analysis of the Chemists is "contradicted" by many experiments (RS I, xx, 111). Or as Boyle puts it, "I observe in the chemical doctrine of qualities . . . that in many cases it *agrees not well* with the phenomena of nature" (S, 130). Rohault also mentions that the method of heating a substance to determine its composition actually transforms the substance and its components, so it is an unreliable method; Boyle prefers to note that the method of analysis by heat is unnecessary (RS I, xx, 110; S, 123). In all these discussions the focus is on what qualities count as causes, not what goes on metaphysically when these qualities are causes. Natural philosophy, Rohault states, and Boyle would agree, is concerned with finding the "reasons and causes" of "every effect which nature produces" (RS I, i, 1). Indeed, Rohault comes close to holding that to know a thing is to know what effects it can produce by way of its properties (RS I, i, 13).

Perhaps because he is a committed Cartesian, Rohault is prepared to make more general metaphysical remarks than Boyle, who tries to stay free of such debates. For example, Rohault embraces the Cartesian claims that nothing can have no properties, that substance is that which can "subsist of itself," and "that a mode, or an accident, cannot be transferred from that substance which is that subject of it, to any other substance; for if it could it would not then have depended entirely upon the first substance" (RS I, iv, 15–16). He accepts a plenum filled with subtle matter, and he accepts the infinite divisibility of matter. But even in accepting these traditional Cartesian principles, there is a Boylean attitude of avoiding unnecessary metaphysical debate. For example, in discussing the infinite divisibility of matter Rohault says that he is concerned with things in the natural state and he does not intend to trouble himself with questions about the ultimate constituents (RS I, xxi, 141–15). Thus, the kinds of divisions that he is interested in are not the mathematical reductions but divisions into parts that are causally connected such as the parts of a mite (RS I, xxi, 114). Unlike Boyle, who adopts a conventionalist view of essence for natural kinds, Rohault seems to hold to a realist view. Yet neither is concerned to debate the issue; rather they are content to simply use the natural kinds for scientific purposes regardless of how they were determined (RS I, iv, 16; S, 52, 62, 72). Both Boyle and Rohault hold that matter itself has some "essential" properties. For Boyle, it is size, shape, and motion or rest (S, 20). For Rohault, the essence of matter is extension, size, and shape, although motion plays as central a role in Rohault's explanations as in those of Boyle (RS I, ii, 3; I, vi, 21 ff.).

When he turns to causation, Rohault diverges from Descartes in some interesting respects. He allows that "every effect presupposes some cause" (RS I, v, 19). And "if we ourselves are not the cause of any effect, it must necessarily depend upon some other cause" (RS I, v, 19). Applying Descartes's principles of inertia to all change, he also holds that any state will endure unless it is acted upon by an external cause (RS I, v, 19–20). When he turns to Descartes's causal principle, he formulates it without the Scholastic language of "formal and eminent reality." For Rohault, Descartes causal principle reduces to the simple truism that when something is produced, it has ingredients; something does not come out of nothing:

> It is impossible that something should be made of absolute nothing; or that mere nothing can become any thing. . . . When I said that it is impossible for something to be made of nothing, I expressly added the word absolute, because I do not at all doubt, any more than any other person, that a thing may be made out of what has nothing of that thing in it, or to speak more clearly, may be made out of that which is not that thing. Thus for example: No one can doubt, but that bread may be made of water and meal, which are not yet bread. (RS I v, 19)

Thus there is no hint in his work that Rohault is struggling with the metaphysical problem of causation in the same way as Descartes when he formulates his causal principle. Rohault does acknowledge a general principle to the effect that "every alteration is always proportional to the force of the agent which causes it" (RS I, vi, 20). Just what Rohault means by this is unclear for the simple reason that he avoids discussion of the force that moves things and concentrates on motion as translocation of a body from one neighborhood to another (RS I, x, 45). Motion, for Rohault, is not an essential property of bodies but it is something attributable to bodies, something initiated by the creator (RS I, x, 45). Rohault leaves motive force a mystery; indeed he leaves it unexplained how motion is communicated or transferred or how one body moves another. Rohault, however, is clear that created things have causal efficacy, and, like Leibniz, he explicitly denounces occasionalism as requiring constant miracles (RS I, xi, 46, 50 ff.). But throughout his discussion, it is the regularities of how one body of a particular kind moves another body of a particular kind or how to explain a certain kind of phenomena that occupies his attention.

In many ways Rohault's mechanism is closer to the classical mechanism of Hobbes and Gassendi than the new mechanism of Boyle or Newton. He literally tries to explain all phenomena—for example, the circulation of blood, comets, wind, sensation, magnets—in terms of matter in motion pushing and pulling by contact. In his chapter on the continuation and cessation of motion Rohault disallows all attractive forces:

> For as to *attraction, sympathy,* and *antipathy,* they ought not to be allowed at all, by reason of their obscurity. That they are obscure is very evident; for if we take a loadstone; for example, it is manifest to all the world that to say it has an attractive virtue or a sympathy with the iron, does not at all explain the nature or the properties of it. (RS I, xi, 54–55)

When Rohault turns to three theories of gravity in Part II, chapter 28, he denounces all of them as unsatisfactory. The first theory is that there are two inclinations in matter, one to descend toward the center of the earth and the other to ascend away from that center. Then Rohault considers two further simple theories, one of which posits *only* the inclination to descend. In this view ascension is only the failure to descend by bodies that lack as much inclination. And the other is the view that there is only the inclination to ascend and descending is having less of the inclination to ascend. All three views are "unsatisfactory":

> For if by the word, inclination, we understand any inward sensation, or any particular sort of thought; I can't think that it can without absurdity be ascribed to mere material beings, such as stones are. And if by this word be meant only in general, a cause whatever it be, which produces these motions by which bodies are carried upwards and downwards, then it is only a mere sophism; because it is saying nothing, but only purely giving the name inclination to something we know not what. (RS II, xxviii, 93)

Rohault's three theories of gravity are clearly founded upon an Aristotelian conception of bodies having natural places toward which they gravitate. Thus, these theories bear little similarity to Newton's theory of gravity.

But Rohault also speculates about the nature of gravity. One view is that gravitational forces are an inward sensation in matter; such a theory clearly comes into direct conflict with his Cartesian theory of matter as an inert, extended thing. But his second notion of gravity as a general cause does capture some of Newton's way of thinking about this force. Rohault regards gravity as a general or universal force as a mere sophism, a "something we know not what." He rejects it on two grounds. The first is that we do not know what properties (principles or laws) belong to such a cause (RS II, xxviii, 92–93). The second is that Rohault believes in a theory that accounts for the phenomena of gravity without positing such a force or attraction, namely, the theory of vortices. His own theory requires subtle or fluid matter that penetrates all things and all space. This matter, depending on its quantity of motion, will carry something out and others in from the center of the many vortices that fill space (RS II, xxviii, 9 ff.). Rohault is consistent with his method and cites an experiment where water was rotated in a vessel and bits of wax that were on the bottom moved to the center of the vessel (RS I, xxviii, 94). He concludes:

> By this experiment we see clearly that gravity is, properly speaking, nothing else but less levity; and though it follows from hence, that the bodies which descend have no disposition in themselves to descend; yet this motion ought however to be called natural, because it is the result of the established order of nature. (RS I, xxviii, 94)

Clarke's (and Newton's) response to Rohault is properly directed toward this second notion of gravity. For Clarke, gravity is an essential and universal property of matter, although as we shall see for Newton, gravity is a nonessential but universal property of matter (RS II, xxvi–ii, 96, n. 1). Newton and Clarke argue, contrary to Rohault, that the properties of gravity, the laws, are well known and that subtle matter and the vortices neither explain what they were intended to explain nor make sense (TH, 49; compare RS II, xxviii, 99, n. 1). Clarke also points out that many phenomena cannot be explained by classical mechanisms contact or the impulse of one body acting upon another (RS I, xi, 54, n. 1). While Clarke in his footnotes in *A System* identifies gravity as a general cause, he concedes that this force or cause of the phenomena for which there are laws is itself occult and unknown. Thus, Clarke writes:

> It seems to me farther, that these particles (of matter) have not only a vis inertia, accompanied with such passive laws of motion, as naturally result from that force, but also that they are moved by certain active principles, such as is that (Attraction which we call the attraction of gravity), and that which causes fermentation, and the cohesion of bodies. These principles I consider not as occult qualities presupposed to result from the specifick forms of things, but as general laws of nature, by which the things themselves are formed: Their truth appearing to us by phenomena though their causes be not yet discovered. (RS I, xi 54–55, n. 1)

> And the Aristotelians gave the name of occult qualities not to manifest qualities, but to such qualities only as they supposed to lie in bodies, and to be the unknown causes of manifest effects: such as would be the cases of gravity, and

of magnetick, and electrick attractions . . . if we should suppose that these forces or actions arose from qualities unknown to us, and uncapable of being discovered and made manifest. Such occult qualities put a stop to the improvement of natural philosophy, and therefore of late years have been rejected. To tell us that every species of things is endowed with an occult specific quality by which it acts and produces manifest effects, is to tell us nothing. But to derive two or three general principles of motion from phenomena and afterwards to tell us how the properties and actions of all corporeal things follow from those manifest principles, would be a very great step in philosophy, though the causes of those principles were not yet discovered: And therefore I scruple not to propose the principles of motion above-mentioned, they being of a very general extent, arid leave their causes to be found out. (RSI, xi, 54–55, n. 1)

Gravity usually appears as just one attractive force among others such as magnetism and electricity.

Clarke's argument is a bit disingenuous; he really does not have a way to know the force of gravity, but he trades on our knowledge of the laws of gravity and presumed manifestness of such phenomena. But the manifestness of the phenomena is true of Rohault's theory as well. The real question is, then, which theory provides the better explanation and allows more accurate predictions of these manifest phenomena. As to whether such causes are discoverable, Clarke's view fares no better than that of Rohault, who can at least point to some experimental support for how a vortex might work. Newton is perhaps more honest than Clarke about the occult nature of gravity. He seems to admit that in some innocuous sense gravity is an occult force, but argues that the success of the theory in dealing with appearances or phenomena justifies its acceptance:

> All sound and true philosophy is founded on the appearances of things; and if these phenomena inevitably draw us, against our wills, to such principles as most clearly manifest to us the most excellent counsel and supreme domination of the All-wise and Almighty Being, they are not therefore to be laid aside because some men may perhaps dislike them. These men may call them miracles or occult qualities, but names maliciously given ought not to be a disadvantage to the things themselves. (TH, 133)

Newton

Within Newton's philosophical and methodological observations we find an explicit abandonment of the classical model of mechanism. Noticing this change is not to deny that Newton, like Boyle, still believes that the universe is an intelligible and in some sense a mechanical system. Like Boyle, he dwells on the virtues of the simplest explanation; ". . . for Nature is pleased with simplicity and affects not the pomp of superfluous causes" (TH, 3). Newton often prefers the term "rational mechanics" as contrasted with the "geometrical mechanics" of his predecessors, notably, Gassendi, Hobbes, Descartes, and Rohault. And it is rational mechanics that is presented in the *Principia*.

> Rational mechanics will be the science of motions resulting from any forces whatsoever accurately proposed and demonstrated. (TH, 10)

The forces that Newton mentions by name are those of gravity, levity, elastic force, and the resistance of fluids—these are forces "attractive or impulsive" (TH,10). The model of science which Newton proposes is to investigate "from the phenomena of motions . . . the forces of nature, and then from these forces to demonstrate the other phenomena" (TH, 10). The last step is crucial because it provides the justification for the postulation of forces unknown and not manifest. Newton draws on the success of his own physics; speaking of the *Principia*, he writes:

> I wish we could derive the rest of the phenomena of Nature by the same kind of reasoning from mechanical principles, for I am induced by many reasons to suspect that they may all depend upon certain forces by which the particles of bodies, by some causes hitherto unknown, are either mutually impelled toward one another and cohere in regular figures, or are repelled and recede from one another. These forces being unknown philosophers have hitherto attempted the search of Nature in vain; but I hope the principle here laid down will afford some light either to this or some truer method of philosophy. (TH, 10–11)

This passage captures Newton's answer to what McGuire calls his central problem, "How can we obtain experimental knowledge of hidden forces in the invisible realm of nature?" (McGuire 1968, 164).

When Newton is confronted with the objection that his forces, such as gravity, are just as occult as those of the Scholastics, his response in the 1713 *Principia* is to appeal once again to the success of his suppositions:

> Some I know disapprove this conclusion [gravity belongs among the primary qualities of bodies alone with extention, mobility, and impenetrability] and mutter something about occult qualities. They continually are cavilling with us that gravity is an occult property, and occult causes are to be quite banished from philosophy. But to this the answer is easy: that those are indeed occult causes whose existence is occult, and imagined but not proved, but not those whose real existence is clearly demonstrated by observations.

> Therefore gravity can by no means be called an occult cause of the celestial
> motions, because it is plain from the phenomena that such a power does real-
> ly exist. Those rather have recourse to occult causes who set imaginary vor-
> tices of a matter entirely fictitious and imperceptible by our senses to direct
> those motions. But shall gravity be therefore called an occult cause and
> thrown out of philosophy because the cause of gravity is occult and not yet
> discovered? (TH,125–26)

A similar justification appears in the "Queries," which were first appended
to the *Optics* in 1704:

> It seems to me further that these particles have not only a *vis inertiae*, accom-
> panied with such passive laws of motion as naturally result from that force,
> but also that they are moved by certain active principles, such is that of grav-
> ity....These principles I consider, not as occult qualities supposed to result
> from the specific forms of things, but as general laws of nature by which the
> things themselves are formed, their truth appearing to us by phenomena,
> though their causes be not yet discovered. For these are manifest qualities,
> and their causes only are occult. And the Aristotelians gave the name of
> "occult qualities," not to manifest qualities, but to such qualities only as they
> supposed to lie hid in bodies and to be the unknown causes of manifest
> effects, such as would be the causes of gravity, . . . if we should suppose that
> these forces or actions arose from qualities unknown to us and incapable of
> being discovered and made manifest. Such occult qualities put a stop to the
> improvement of natural philosophy and therefore of late years have been
> rejected. (TH, 176)

In this and other passages Newton identifies forces like gravity as "occult,"
"active principles," "general laws of nature," and "unknown to us." But he
distinguishes them from the occult properties of the Scholastics which he
takes to be "incapable of being discovered and made manifest." Thus, the difference with the Aristotelian/Scholastics is twofold. On the one hand, they
cannot point to scientific success in explaining and predicting phenomena;
and their hidden forces are in principle unknowable, whereas Newton's are in
principle knowable. These passages are, however, confusing. If gravity is a
law of nature that Newton has presumably already formulated, then it can
hardly be unknown to us or hidden. At the same time, if gravity is an active
principle that lies behind the phenomena described by the laws of nature,
then it is not a manifest property, it is unknown to us, and can only be identified with the laws of nature by conflating cause (force) with effect (regularity of phenomena).

Newton does little to help sort out these confusions. In the "General
Scholium" to the *Principia* he takes the stance that he has not yet developed
any theory of gravity that lies behind the phenomena except that it does not

"operate . . . according to the quantity of the surfaces of the particles upon which it acts (as mechanical causes used to do)." At the same time, unable to discover the cause of these phenomena, he denies that he has framed any hypotheses whatsoever because "hypotheses, whether metaphysical or physical, whether of occult qualities or mechanical, have no place in experimental philosophy" (TH, 45). Elsewhere, in a 1692 letter to Bentley, he suggests the opposite when he argues that the idea of gravity as a force acting at a distance is absurd:

> That gravity should be innate, inherent, and essential to matter, so that one body may act upon another at a distance through a vacuum, without the mediation of anything else, by and through which their action and force may be conveyed from one to another, is to me so great an absurdity that I believe no man who has in philosophical matters a competent faculty of thinking can ever fall into it. Gravity must be caused by an agent acting constantly according to certain laws, but whether this agent be material or immaterial I have left to the consideration of my readers. (TH, 54)

Newton's remarks in this passage are strikingly at odds with those made by Clarke, who, presumably with Newton's approval, describes gravity as a universal force, that is, not accidental, and one that can cross a vacuum (RS II, xxviii, 96–97; compare TH, 125 ff.). The difference between Newton and Clarke may be this: Clarke seems to think of gravity as essential in the sense that it belongs to every body by virtue of being a body; in denying that gravity is essential, Newton seems to mean that it is not invariant—"immutable" is his word—in a body—gravitational attraction, for example, varies with the distance between bodies (TH, 5).

Such passages introduce a number of questions. If gravity is not a mechanical cause and if it might even be immaterial, then why is it governed by the principles of mechanism that deny action at a distance or across a vacuum? Is not such a supposition about how gravity operates a hypothesis about the nature of the force behind the phenomena? Newton scholars such as McGuire explain some textual inconsistencies by arguing that Newton changed his mind about gravity. In the earliest period of Newton's thought he seriously considers an aether as the cause of gravitational phenomena, as in his letter to Boyle (TH, 115-16). But by the time of the *Principia* 1687 to 1707, he was content to leave it an open question whether gravity was mechanical or not and seems to set the aether hypothesis aside (McGuire 1968, 155). In part this shift was motivated by the suggestion that large parts of space were a vacuum and that seemed incompatible with the aether hypothesis. However, around 1706 Newton began, again, to offer speculations about gravity's being the result of a subtle aether in a quasi-mechanical manner (McGuire 1968, 157 ff.). In what looks almost like a return to the subtle matter of the Cartesians, Newton notes that a thermometer in a vacuum will grow warm as the room grows warm. He explains this by the following hypothesis:

> Is not the heat of the warm room conveyed through the vacuum by the vibrations of a much subtler medium than air, which, after the air was drawn out, remained in the vacuum? And is not this medium the same with that medium by which light is refracted and reflected, and by those vibrations light communicates heat to bodies and is put into fits of easy reflection and easy transmission? And do not the vibrations of this medium in hot bodies contribute to the intenseness and duration of their heat? And do not hot bodies communicate their heat to contiguous cold ones by the vibrations of this medium propagated from them into the cold ones? And is not this medium exceedingly more rare and subtle than the air, and exceedingly more elastic and active. And does it not readily pervade all bodies? And is it not (by its elastic force) expanded through all the heavens. (TH, 141–42)

> And though this increase of density may at great distances be exceedingly slow, yet if the elastic force of this medium be exceedingly great it may suffice to impel bodies from the denser parts of the medium toward the rarer with all that power which we call gravity. (TH, 143)

Newton's struggles with the nature of gravity constantly skirt the issue of causation. When Newton dismisses a hypothesis such as action at a distance, is his view guided by any systematic understanding of causation? Or is his greatest concern always to successfully explain the phenomena by way of the best explanation, understood along the lines outlined by Boyle? The texts make it difficult to determine to what extent, if any, Newton is guided by a theory of causation. He certainly seems to embrace certain restrictions on causation. Newton clearly embraces some version of the "same cause, same effect" principle; the second rule of natural philosophy is:

> Therefore to the same natural effects we must, as far as possible, assign the same causes. (TH, 3)

The Cotes preface to the second edition (1713) makes the point as follows:

> The foregoing conclusions [such as there is universal gravitational attraction among the heavenly bodies and that gravitational attraction varies inversely with the squares of the distances of the bodies] are grounded on this axiom which is received by all philosophers, namely, that effects of the same kind, whose known properties are the same, take their rise from the same causes and have the same unknown properties also. For if gravity be the cause of the descent of a stone in Europe, who doubts that it is also the cause of the same descent in America? . . . All philosophy is founded on this rule; for if that be taken away, we can affirm nothing as a general truth. The constitutions of

particular things is known by observations and experiments; and when that is done, no general conclusion of the nature of things can thence be drawn except by this rule. (TH, 124–125)

At one level the above passage simply indicates that the laws of nature are universal, applying in all times and all places. And Newton certainly embraces the universality of the laws of gravity; they apply at both the macro and the micro levels of matter. Newton frequently notes that all bodies, observable and unobservable, have the properties of gravity, mobility, impenetrability, and extension (TH, 3, 125, 159). This form of the principle of universality is especially important because it contributes to his belief that there are no new forces that enter the picture at the corpuscular level, unlike the atomists whose atoms introduce properties such as indivisibility and substantial sameness. In this sense, for Newton, nothing is hidden. Yet as Newton's many statements about gravity make clear, he is quite prepared to live with its unknown features and properties as long as the laws of gravity are satisfactory in predicting the movements of planets, the tides, and the pendulum. In notes for the projected fourth book of the *Optics*, Newton writes at length about the explanatory power of the hypothesis of gravity:

> Hypoth. 2. As all the great motions in the world depend upon a certain kind of force (wch in this earth we call gravity) whereby great bodies attract one another at great distances: so all the little motions in ye world depend upon certain kinds of forces whereby minute bodies attract or dispell one another at little distances. . . . This principle of nature being very remote from the conceptions of Philosophers I forbore to describe it in that Book (*Principia*) least I should be accounted an extravagant freake & so prejudice my Readers against all those things wch were ye main desgne of the Book: but & yet I hinted at it both in the Preface & in ye book it self. . . . The truth of this Hypothesis I assert not, because I cannot prove it, but I think it very probable because a great part of the phaenomena of nature do easily flow from it wch seem otherways inexplicable: such as are chymical solutions, precipation, unions, separations, fermentations, the cohesion, texture, fluidity and porosity of bodies, the rarity & elasticity of air, the reflexions & refraction of lights, . . . (as in McGuire 1968, 165–66)

Thus, Newton thinks of causes as nested in such a way that although A may be observed to behave in a certain manner in the presence of certain behaviors in B, and thereby the qualities of B are the cause of the states of A, there may well be a hidden common cause of these behaviors. Thus, even though *aqua fortis* dissolves silver and not gold and *aqua regia* dissolves gold and not silver, these properties are ultimately explained by more hidden and presumably more "basic" causes such as gravity (TH, 164). Science will always come up against certain forces or qualities that have yet to be understood, but the fact that they are not understood does not mean that they are not proven or that they may not become "manifest" as Newton states elsewhere (TH, 176). In the *Optics* Newton returns to this method of causal analysis which is obviously inspired by Descartes's two methods. But, for Newton, analysis is a way of going beyond particular causes—the moon stays in orbit because of the gravitational attraction of earth—to more general causes that lie behind an apparent diversity of such causes:

> By this way of analysis we may proceed from compounds to ingredients and from motions to the forces producing them, and in general from effects to their causes and from particular causes to more general ones, fill the argument end in the most general. This is the method of analysis; and the synthesis consists in assuming the causes discovered and established as principles, and by them explaining the phenomena proceeding from them, and proving the explanation. (TH, 179)

Both Newton and Boyle leave some confusion about what it means to make a cause manifest. In places it seems that having successfully explained and predicted particular phenomena from a supposition of a cause that offers a better explanation than any other is sufficient to make that cause manifest. Here, Newton's and Boyle's new mechanism abandons the principles of the classical mechanists. In one of the better discussions of what it means to make a quality manifest (in classical mechanism), Charleton suggests that in common usage a quality is manifest if and only if (i) it is a quality, (ii) it belongs to the "jurisdiction" of the senses, and (iii) it is dependent upon known causes and known faculties. (Hence we should note that Charleton's skepticism asserts itself in this discussion and he speculates that all qualities in nature are "immanifest" and "abstruse" to some extent (1654, 341–42). Charleton concedes that this notion is too strict since there are qualities that are intelligible but unsensed that may be causes (1654, 342). Charleton's account of how some use the term "manifest quality" is certainly a view that is too strict to capture what Boyle and Newton mean by "manifest" since they deny that all causes must be sensible in order to be intelligible. The Cotes preface to the second edition, done under Newton's supervision, makes the point in more detail.

> But shall gravity be therefore called an occult cause and thrown out of philosophy because the cause of gravity is occult and not yet discovered? Those who affirm this should be careful not to fall into an absurdity that may overturn the foundations of all philosophy. For causes usually proceed in a continued chain from those that are more compounded to those that are more simple; when we are arrived at the most simple cause, we can go no farther. Therefore no mechanical account or explanation of the most simple cause is to be expected or given; for if it could be given, the cause were not the most

simple. These most simple causes will you then call occult and reject them? Then you must reject those that immediately depend upon them and those which depend upon these last, till philosophy is quite cleared and disencumbered of all causes. (TH, 126)

These passages shed some light on Newton's views on causation; but they also reveal the limits or vagueness of that view. In some places Newton speaks of gravity itself as the unknown cause; in other places he speaks of the cause of gravity as the unknown cause (TH, 176). In part this may depend upon how he thinks of gravity. If gravity is identified with the laws of nature, then gravity is manifest in the sense of being understood in Newton's rational mechanism and what is unknown is the cause of gravity (TH,126). When gravity is the cause of the phenomena described in the laws, then gravity itself is the unknown cause (TH, 176). But what is consistent in both accounts is that causes of a kind, known or unknown, are linked to the same kinds of effects. And the simpler causal explanation is to be preferred to the more complex. Finally, Newton always seems to find the justifications of causal explanations to be contingent upon fitting the phenomena. In the third edition of the *Principia* Newton articulates a rule, similar to Boyle's rules for an excellent hypothesis.

> In experimental philosophy we are to look upon propositions inferred by general induction from phenomena as accurately or very nearly true, notwithstanding any contrary hypothesis that may be imagined, till such time as other phenomena occur by which they may either be made more accurate or liable to exceptions. (TH, 5)

In this way, Newton finalizes the turn toward cause as that which serves in the best explanation. What Newton brings to the debate is a resounding set of explanations that are regarded as the best, as successful science. And the prevailing view of the later philosophers, specifically Locke and Hume, begins with the presumption of Newton's success in finding causal explanations.

CENTRAL THEMES

In the writings of Boyle, Rohault, and Newton two notions of causation are employed. On the one hand, there are those qualities and qualitative changes that are immediately present to a physical change: the sugar added before fermentation, the acid into which gold is emersed, the creation of a vacuum in a tube. These are causes and they are phenomena; they are what all these scientist-philosophers call sensible (sometimes manifest) causes. That one set of qualities is the cause of another set of qualities (or, that one phenomenon is the cause of another) is determined by experiment and observation. But there is a second notion of causation that is deeper and seemingly more satisfying. These deeper causes are accepted as explanations of the relationships among the sensible causes; entities such as gravity and electricity are much more like a set of theoretical entities (intelligible causes) that explain why the phenomenal laws are as they are. Vortices and subtle matter play a similar role in the physics of Rohault. These causes are universal in scope in the sense that they lie behind the phenomena and in their different concatenations are causally responsible for all more sensible causal chains. Boyle, Clarke, Newton, and Rohault all extol the universality of the applicability of causes of the latter kind.

These causes are the real, true, deeper causes of phenomena and even when they are not observed, their effects are observable and predictable. It is tempting to say that these causes are to sensible causes what God's will, in Malebranche, is to natural or occasional causes. But this observation takes one in the wrong direction. God's will, unlike gravity, can never be understood even in principle by an appeal to mechanical interactions among bits of subtle matter or aether. But it does make causation, in the case of deeper causes, a matter of inference rather than direct observation. In a letter to Roger Cotes in 1713 Newton notes that "These principles [laws of gravity] are deduced from phenomena and made general by induction, which is the highest evidence that a proposition can have in this philosophy" (TH, 6). Glanville, the skeptic and member of the Royal Society, warns that such inferences are fraught with danger: "All knowledge of causes is deductive: for we know none by simple intuitions but through the mediation of its effects. Now we cannot conclude, any thing to be the cause of another; but from its continual accompanying it; for the causality itself is insensibly. . . . But now to argue from a concomitancy to a causality, is not infallible conclusive: Yea in this way lies notorious delusion" (1661, 189–90). At the same time, Glanville does not suggest that we can do any better.

We have often spoken of the metaphysical problem of causation's being ignored; perhaps it would be better to speak of its being displaced. Leibniz felt that one needed to address the metaphysics of causation to explain why the world has the particular natural laws that it does. The metaphysical account of causation in some way served to explain the phenomenal laws which science discovered. Newton, Boyle, and Rohault assign the same role to entities such as gravity, electricity, and subtle matter. One way to read this is to argue that these scientist-philosophers abandoned the traditional metaphysics of causation for a new metaphysics of causation of deep causal structures that can be tested empirically in that the assumptions about them allow for successful prediction. The impact of this way of thinking has altered, once and for all, the terms of the debate.

8.
The Attempted Alignment of Philosophy and Physics: Locke, Berkeley, and Hume

PLACES IN THE DEBATE

Although he was himself scientifically trained as a physician, John Locke (1632–1704) lived in the shadow of the great scientists of the late seventeenth century. He was familiar with the writings of Descartes, Gassendi, Hobbes, Boyle, and Le Grand. His "medical Common-Place Book" reads like a who's who of the seventeenth century, although reference to the "incomparable" Newton is missing (Romanell 1984, 65). *The Essays concerning Human Understanding*, first published in 1689, was strongly influenced by Gassendi and Boyle, and was openly hostile to Descartes.

It is standard among Locke scholars to take Boyle as Locke's inspiration for his view of matter and his distinction between primary and secondary qualities (Alexander 1974; Ayers 1991; Keating 1993). Yet, as Romanell has argued, Locke took much of his "historical plain method" from Sydenham, a physician with whom he had a close association from 1667 to 1672 (Sanchez-Gonzalez 1990; 676-77; N, 44). This method, which Locke employs in his *Essays*, is "observational, descriptive, intersubjective, and not interpretive" (Sanchez-Gonzalez 1990, 677). In Boyle's language, it avoids hypotheses that are speculative or ungrounded. In his "Introduction" Locke makes it abundantly clear that he does not intend to engage in speculations about how the changes in spirits or bodies occur: thus his method alone rules out interest in the metaphysics of causation (N, 43 ff.).

Locke does not see himself as a scientist-philosopher. In his "Epistle to the Reader" he consciously distinguishes himself from the great scientists of his time (Boyle, Sydenham, Newton). Instead he sees his work as philosophical, by which he means that he is an "Under-Labourer" whose job it is to remove "some of the Rubbish, that lies in the way to Knowledge" (N, 9–10). Leibniz, who considers Locke a mechanist of the Gassendi school, first saw an outline of Locke's Essays and then read them in 1690. He submitted criticism to Locke through Thomas Burnet and Lady Masham (AG, 291). His own page-by-page rejoinder to Locke, *The New Essays concerning Human Understanding*, was written by 1704. But Leibniz abandoned publishing his *New Essays* because the whole purpose of the project was to enter into a dialogue with Locke, who died in 1704 (RB, xiii). Leibniz's *New Essays* were not published until 1765. By 1710 Leibniz lumps Locke with Newton as a mechanist who used to be faithful to a classically mechanistic account of change but succumbed to the temptation of attractive forces (FH, 86).

George Berkeley (1685–1753) recorded his first philosophical thoughts in his *Philosophical Commentaries*, written between 1707 and 1708. His *An Essay towards a New Theory of Vision* and *A Treatise Concerning the Principles of Human Knowledge*, Part I, were published in 1709 and 1710, respectively. The *Commentaries* contain the prototypes of these two major philosophical works. While in London in 1713 Berkeley published *Three Dialogues between Hylas and Philonous*, which repeated his views from the *Essay* and contained passages that try to distinguish his views from those of Malebranche. In 1721 he published *De Motu*, an attack on the notions of force in Leibniz and attraction and repulsion in Newton, both of which Berkeley viewed as empty abstractions (Acton 1967, 295; DJ, 3 ff.). Berkeley's philosophy remained remarkably constant from his first conceptions in *Philosophical Commentaries* to his critiques of Newton. And although he is familiar with many participants in the causation debate, his focus is relentlessly on Locke. Locke's willingness to talk about material substance that causes ideas in us and exists independently of our mind is, to Berkeley's mind, the great metaphysical error of the seventeenth century. He takes Locke to be representative of the corpuscular philosophy. He also rejects Spinoza's views as atheistic materialism and Malebranche's occasionalism because Malebranche's total occasionalism violates Berkeley's view that spirits are true causes and because Malebranche's physical realism violates Berkeley's idealism (LJ, II, 219–20). At the same time, Berkeley's doctrine of causation is that natural causes are simply signs indicating their effects, whereas spirits (finite or infinite) are true causes of their different states (LJ I, 280).

David Hume (1711–76) is the modern philosopher who first comes to mind when discussing causation in this period. Hume's most detailed views on causation were published in *A Treatise of Human Nature* in 1739. Hume's disappointment with the reception of his work led to his publication of *Philosophical Essays concerning the Human Understanding* and *An Enquiry Concerning the Principles the Principles of Morals* in 1748 and 1751, respectively. Hume hoped that these writings would provide a better vehicle for his philosophy. The *Treatise* was modeled on Newton's *Principia*; its subtitle is "An attempt to Introduce the Experimental Method of Reasoning into Moral Subjects" (compare Woolhouse 1988, 135) Hume attempts to collect data and formulate and test hypotheses in what he takes to be a Newtonian fashion.

Hume's idea of a cause in the *Treatise* is a regularly prior event that is contiguous to its effect. In the *Enquiries* Hume seems to drop the longstanding mechanistic condition on causation that causes must occur through contiguous events. In any case, the relation of cause to effect is so freed of metaphysical restrictions that Hume is able to declare in the *Treatise* that "anything may produce anything" (T, 173).

Although Hume's thoughts on causation did not ignite a great debate among his immediate contemporaries, they were to become "the most celebrated and influential part of his philosophy" (Penelhum 1992, 98). In the twentieth century, for example, an elaborate philosophical debate developed over a forty-year period; much of this debate centered around Hume's concept of causation (Salmon 1990). But to get caught up in these responses to Hume is to treat Hume as the beginning of the contemporary debate about causation, which he is. But Hume is also the end of the modern debate about causation. With respect to the modern debate, Hume actively attacks the metaphysical problem of causation on epistemological grounds and then attempts to rebuild a positive concept of causation that is compatible with the new experimental science.

Hume is a student of the modern debate itself. He has read Malebranche carefully. He even footnotes with approval Malebranche's scathing remarks about the inability of philosophers to agree, on anything about causation (T, 159; compare McCracken 1983, 254 ff.). Loeb argues: ". . . it must have been Malebranche's position which provided the principal stimulus for Hume's examination of causation and shaped the strategy behind his discussion" (1981, 355). But Hume also knows and comments on the rationalist tradition or the Cartesians and the scientific and philosophical opponents of Cartesianism, namely, Locke and Newton, although there is some question as to how carefully he read Berkeley (Popkin 1964; Loeb 1981, 360; McCracken 1983, 254).

The standard interpretation of Hume is that his skepticism kept him from believing that any good could come out of philosophical speculations about the nature of causation. Certainly, his skepticism reinforced his views on causation, but had Hume never entertained a skeptical thought he could as easily have come to the view of causation that he defends. By the early eighteenth century, the metaphysical problem of causation is in disrepute; over and over again the focus on the metaphysical conditions leads to an untenable conclusion, namely, that the causes used in scientific explanations are not true causes. The impact of the successful science of the seventeenth century induces philosophers to assume, along with scientists, that there are causal interactions and that the philosophical task is to conceptually clarify the notion of causation so that it picks out those things that science identifies as causes and excludes those that are scientifically suspect. Berkeley is an exception, although he struggles mightily to make his views palatable to modern science. Thus, the debate under Hume's (and, to some extent, Locke's) guidance becomes a search for the criteria that identify true causes—the causes as they are discovered in the experimental tradition that Hume embraces (EHU, 36).

LOCKE

Occasionalism was in vogue in the late 1660s, and Locke made a study of Malebranche and other occasionalists. He wrote *An Examination of Père Malebranche's Opinion of Seeing All Things in God*, probably around 1665–70. This work was published among the posthumous works in 1706 (McCracken 1983, 120ff). McCracken notes that while Locke focuses his attack on Malebranche's theory of innate ideas, he does raise some standard objections occasionalism. Locke argues that if God is the only case, then why "has he wrought the elaborate contrivance in things that we find"? (McCracken 1983, 146). Locke also repeats the arguments that God's inability to give true causal efficacy to created things diminishes the power of God, the fact that God must act on the occasion of a created thing makes his power determined by the mundane, and, finally, Malebranche's denial that human minds cause their own ideas creates a system every bit as necessary as that of Hobbes and Spinoza (McCracken 1983, 147).

In his positive views, Locke seems to have agreed with Glanville, that true causation is hidden but we can glean, with considerable risk, cause and effect from concomitancy (Glanville 1661, 189–90). In his "First Draft" Locke states:

> I can have noe other certain undoubted knowledge of the constant connection of assigned causes and effects than what I have by my senses. Which too is but a grosse kind of knowledge is noe more than this, that I see when I apply fire to gold it melts it. . . . Because these alterations being made by particles soe small and minute that lthey come not within the observation of my sensses I cannot get any knowledge how they operate. . . . (as in Mccracken 1983, 150)

Locke's deep conviction that the nature of true causation lies beyond the power of the senses to detect immediately makes the metaphysical problem of causation moot. And his discussions of causation betray this belief. His positive account of causation in the *Essays* (third edition) is as openly epistemological and circular as that in the "First Draft."

> In the notice, that our Senses take of the constant Vicissitude of Things, we cannot but observe, that several particular, both Qualities, and Substances begin to exist; and they they receive this their Existence, from the due Application and Operation of some other Being. From this Observation, we get our *Ideas* of *Cause* and *Effect*. That which produces any simple or complex Idea, we denote by the general Name *Cause*; and that which is produced, *Effect*. (N, 324)

Locke is clear that causes may be either qualities or substances. He seems to agree with Malebranche and the occcsionalists that observation does not provide a clear idea of causal efficacy. Another occasionalist theme in Locke is his belief that the idea of power, which Locke does not distinguish sharply from the idea of cause, is best acquired by examining our ability to move our bodies (N, 131; compare McCracken 1983, 153). Locke spends little time in trying to explicate, define, or clarify the notion of causation. Having basically conceived of a cause as that which operates on another and effect as that on which there is operation, Locke uses the concept of cause or power readily throughout the essays. It becomes a mantra in Locke that ideas are caused by qualities in things, where quality is the power of a thing to produce ideas in us by way of its primary qualities (bulk, figure, texture, and motion) (N, 135). Although primary qualities are like or resemble the ideas which they produce, there is no evidence in Locke that he is committed to the view that causes are always like their effects; indeed, in the case of secondary qualities, he denies that there is a resemblance between cause and effect (N, 137).

The powers to produce certain effects are central to our idea of substances, that is, the nominal essence of substances that we make up in order to do science and assign a meaning to our words (N, 299; N, 453 ff.). As to the real essenccs of substances, these too have powers, but we are not epistemically situated to know these real essences (N, 418). Thus, for Locke, what causal properties a substance or quality has may be crucial to the identification of that substance or quality; the relation of causation is for Locke a central property that helps us to establish categories. But our knowledge of cause and effect, besides the general idea of power we get from the will, is limited to observing vicissitudes (changes or experiments?) in things. Thus, we observe the melting of wax when brought to the flame (M, 324).

On a first reading, Locke appears to be faithful to Boyle (compare Alexander 1985, 150 ff.). Locke is a corpuscularian, who holds that there is a distinction between primary and secondary qualities. Primary qualities are inseparable from matter. Essences, at least nominal essences, are conventions adopted for the purposes of scientific inquiry. Yet there are some differences that reflect other lines of influence in Locke's thought. Keating has argued that "Locke's theory of primary and secondary qualities is not Boyle's theory of primary and secondary qualities" (1993, 300). Her point is that Locke, who is interested in knowledge, looks for a feature in bodies that corresponds to each idea whether it is an idea of a primary or a secondary quality. Boyle has no such interest; he simply seeks the causes of qualities that we call white, square, etc., and he is only interested in showing that they depend on the mechanical qualities of things, not in finding some feature of a thing that that corresponds to an idea (Keating 1993, 319). To identify a quality for each idea is simply another version of the "great mistake"; and Boyle goes out of his way to deny that there is anything in a body that necessarily corresponds to many particular ideas (S,21).

We have already noted that for Boyle there is interaction between body and mind, but Boyle rejects any hope of understanding change based on the actions of an immaterial soul; they are too alien to mechanism. It is by mechanical principles that phenomena are best understood; where there are no mechanical causes or alien causes, science has nothing to say (S, 150 ff.). And when Boyle tries to explicate the notion of power, it is in terms of the shape, motion, and solidity of parts (S, 23). Thus, in his famous example of a key that can open a lock, Boyle writes:

> It was looked upon as a peculiar faculty and power in the key that it was fitted to open and shut the lock: and yet by these new attributes there was not added any real or physical entity either to the lock or to the key, each of them remaining indeed nothing but the same piece of iron, just so shaped as it was before. (S 23)

Locke, on the other hand, asserts in his long chapter on power in Book II of the *Essays*, that we can get our best idea of power from observing the power of the will to move our bodies and that the idea of power may be a simple idea.

Since power is a simple idea, it does not, by definition, contain within it other discernible ideas. Locke's view runs contrary to Boyle's message that power is ineffable and how minds move bodies does not shed any light on mechanistic causation. Furthermore, Boyle takes it to be a fundamental mistake to locate powers in things over and above the shapes and motions of the particles. For Boyle, the idea of power is not simple; it is complex, reducible to (the ideas of) the properties of corpuscles. Furthermore, the relation of power to quality for Locke is uninformative and circular. Locke defines qualities as the power to produce ideas in us by their primary qualities (N, 135). But this definition amounts to saying that qualities are powers to produce ideas in us by means of qualities. But defining "quality" in terms of "power" goes in the opposite direction from that of Boyle, who accepts the notion of quality as primitive and attempts to define power in terms of it (S, 24).

Leibniz, for one, believes that Locke retreats from the sensible mechanism of Boyle. In his essay "Against Barbaric Physics" Leibniz writes:

> John Locke, in the first edition of his *Essay Concerning Human Understanding*, judged that it is appropriate that no body is moved except through the impulse of a body touching it, as did Hobbes and Boyle, distinguished countrymen of his, and following them, many other who strengthened mechanistic physics. But afterwards, having followed the authority of his friends, I think, more than his judgement, he retracted his opinion and believed that I know not what wonderful things can lie hidden in the essence of matter. It is just as if someone believed that there are occult qualities hidden in number, in time, in space, in motion considered in and of themselves. . . . Robert Boyle once refuted such views quite nicely. . . . (AG 317)

In this passage, Leibniz is referring to Locke's treatment of the attractive force, gravity. Leibniz quotes Locke's 1699 letter to Stillingfleet:

> It is true, I say, "that bodies operate by impulse, and nothing else" [II. vii. 11]. And so I thought when I write it, and can yet conceive no other way of their operation. But I am since convinced by the judicious Mr. Newton's incomparable book, that it is too bold a presumption to limit God's power, in this point, by my narrow conceptions. The gravitation of matter towards matter, by ways inconceivable to me, is not only a demonstration that God can, if he pleases, put into bodies powers and ways of operation above what can be derived from our idea of body, or can be explained by what we know of matter, but also an unquestionable and every where visible instance, that he has done so. And therefore in the next edition of my book I shall take care to have that passage rectified. (RB, Preface)

As Jolley has pointed out, however, Locke's retreat is "deceptively modest" (1984, 59). In the second and third editions Section 11 in Book II, chapter viii reads: "The next thing to be consider'd is how Bodies operate one upon another, and that is manifestly by impulse, and nothing else" In the fourth edition, wherein he makes the change, he writes: "The next thing to be consider'd, is how Bodies produce Ideas in us, and that is manifestly by impulse, the only way which we can conceive Bodies operate in" (N, 135–36). What Locke actually means by this claim is not clear. He may not be abandoning classical mechanism at all; he may think that gravity can be explained by the insensible parts, as Gassendi argued. Or he may think that gravity is an "essential" power of matter, contrary to Newton's own view. Finally, Locke may think gravity is "a standing miracle"—in Jolley's words (1984, 61).

Locke's positive view of the nature of causation is complicated by his claim that there is a real essence of things as existing over and above the nominal essence that may be causally responsible for the other properties of things. The real essence is "that real constitution, on which the properties depend, it necessarily supposes a sort of things, properties belonging only to species, and not to individuals" (N, 442). In the same section, Locke allows that there may be causes entirely beyond our view on which what we observe depends (N, 445). Elsewhere he refers to the "real constitution of things" (N, 417). Thus Locke seems willing to venture into a metaphysical question that Boyle clearly seeks to avoid; Boyle acknowledges only nominal essences and these are necessary and sufficient to determine kinds (S, 52).

Locke's ulterior motive for talking about real essences is, as Jolley argues, that he seeks to hold onto a rationalistic model of explanation, that is, he takes the properties of a body to arise out of its real essence much as the properties of triangles arise out of the essence of triangle (1984, 61; compare Woolhouse 1988, 92–93; Wilson 1979). Of course, this model, were it to be taken seriously would undermine much if not all of Locke's discussion about causation. If we take Locke's frequent suggestions literally that real essences are the "foundation and cause" of nominal essences and all the properties of substances through a necessary connection akin to that between the essence of triangle and the properties of triangles, then we make nonsense of most of his discussion of causation (N, 439: N, 442). Furthermore, this account does not explain the role of other substances and qualities in the production of the properties of a substance. And it makes all of our attributions of causes false; the powers in the nominal essence are presumably or possibly only pseudo-causes. The real causes are inaccessible to us. If Locke were to hold this view, then he would be committed to a view reminiscent of Malebranche in which the true cause is unavailable to us and not part of scientific explanations. What we settle for are the apparent regularities and vicissitudes of substances. The rational scientific explanations to which we aspire are unattainable. But for all the conclusion it produces, such a view is consistent with the rather skeptical (Glanville-ian) view of causation with which we began our discussion of Locke's positive views on causation.

BERKELEY

Loeb's assessment of Berkeley's contribution to the causation debate is that it was a meager one at best:

> Berkeley's position on causation is feeble indeed. In the *Philosophical Commentaries*, there is little more than the assertion, and possibly the stipulation, that volitions are the only causes. In the systematic works, there is little advance. (1981, 267)

In spite of Loeb's assessment, however, Berkeley makes some significant contributions to the causation debate. Indirectly, Berkeley's sustained attack upon material substance as that which is other than a bundle of sensible qualities, rules out one whole area of the debate, namely, what if any powers can be located in substances and, more generally, whether material causes are substances. It helped to undercut Locke's appeal to real essences. In his own lifetime Berkeley's positive views about causation were conflated with those of Malebranche; specifically, in 1710 John Percival reported to Berkeley that Samuel Clarke and William Whiston took him to be a disciple of Malebranche. Berkeley's response in the Second Dialogue was to stress that he is not a Malebranchean occasionalist:

> Few men think, yet all will have opinions. Hence men's opinions are superficial and confused . . . I shall not be surprised, if some men imagine that I run into the enthusiasm of Malebranche, though in truth I am very remote from it. (LJ II, 214)

Berkeley exaggerates, however, when he asserts that his views are "very remote" from those of Malebranche. In his *Philosophical Commentaries* he seems to come close to subscribing to Malebranche's occasionalism:

> One idea not the cause of another, one power not the cause of another. The cause of all natural things is only God. Hence Trifling to enquire after second Causes. This Doctrine gives a most suitable idea of the Divinity (LJ, 54)

And entry 107 of the *Commentaries* is:

> Strange impotence of men. Man without God. Wretcheder than a stone or true, he haveing only the power to be miserable by his unperformed wills, these having no power at all. (LJI,18)

When Berkeley does set out to distinguish his view from those of Malebranche their agreements tend to outweigh their differences (compare McCracken 1983, 205 ff.). Berkeley does object to Malebranche's doctrine of abstract ideas, his assertion that the external world exists independently of being perceived, and that we know the true forms of things through reason (LJ II, 214). He also rejects Malebranche's view that created spirits are not causally efficacious (LJII, 215). Yet Berkeley agrees with Malebranche that sensible objects do not causally interact, that God orders our ideas by his wisdom and power, and that any form of concurrentism is unnecessary since God needs no instruments (LJ II, 69, 214, 218, 220). Berkeley approves of Malebranche's dictum: "in God we live, and move, and have our being" (LJ II, 214; compare LJ I, 99). As Loeb has argued, one gets Berkeley's view out of that of Malebranche simply by allowing finite wills to be causally efficacious in producing some ideas, deleting the material world in favor of Berkeley's idealism, and denying that we share in God's ideas (1981, 229). To spend too much time, however, on Berkeley's identity crisis obscures the fact that he does offer a different view of causation from that of Malebranche; specifically, he abandons Malebranche's insistence that a true cause is necessarily connected to its effect.

Berkeley does not abandon the metaphysical problem of causation—his own foundational claim that only spirits can be causes is grounded metaphysically in the belief that causes are active. Furthermore, in the first and second editions of the *Dialogues*, he seems to embrace the metaphysical causal principle that "nothing can give to another that which it hath not itself." This principle allows him to formulate an argument against material substance. If one adds the premise that an inert material substance causes ideas in us, then it follows that inert material substances must have ideas. But it is a contradiction for a material substance which by definition is unperceiving to have an idea (LJ II, 236). This argument begins with Le Grand's version of the causal principle, namely, "a cause cannot give that which it hath not" (LGI, 22, 50), adds a premise from Locke's materialism, and generates a contradiction. Berkeley ultimately deletes this argument in the third edition.

We are left to speculate as to why Berkeley drops the argument based on Le Grand's causal principle. The first and most obvious reason is that Locke does not use such a principle, and any argument, therefore, based on the principle will fail. Second, Berkeley has a replacement argument that gets the same result, namely, nothing can be like an idea but another idea; if our ideas of primary qualities are like the primary quality that causes the idea, then inert material substances must have ideas (LJ II, 206; compare LJ II, 44). Locke does seem committed to the premises of this argument (compare Cummins

1966), since Locke holds that knowledge consists in the agreement and disagreement of ideas and we have knowledge only to the extent that we have ideas. Hence resemblance, one form of agreement and disagreement, is defined in Locke's system *only* for ideas (N, 538). In this way, Locke is vulnerable to the other argument that Berkeley offers to show that Locke's conception of material substance is incoherent.

Berkeley's positive view of causation is that true causes are always active agents or powers in active agents, thus only spirits are true causes. In the *Commentaries* 828 and 829 Berkeley's view emerges:

> The Will is purus actus or rather pure spirit
>
> Substance of a Spirit is that it acts, causes, wills, operates . . . (LJ I, 99)

In the *Dialogues* and the *Principles* Berkeley continues the theme that only spirit or will can be a cause, because only spirit or will is active (LJ II, 67, 217). "There is no other agent or efficient cause than *spirit*, it being evident that motion, as well as all other *ideas* is perfectly inert" (LJ II, 85). Berkeley's metaphysics is exhausted by spirits that perceive ideas. Ideas, however, are not active. Therefore, only spirits can be true causes. Berkeley does not shy away from the consequences of this doctrine. He rejects both Locke's view that properties grow out of an inner essence and the mechanical philosophy of Boyle:

> One great inducement to our pronouncing our selves ignorant of the nature of things, is the current opinion that every thing includes within it self the cause of its properties. . . . Some have pretended to account for appearances by occult qualities, but of late they are mostly resolved into mechanical causes, to wit, the figure, motion, weight, and such like qualifies of insensible particles: whereas in truth, there is no other agent or eficient cause than spirit. . . . Hence to endeavour to explain the production of colours, or sounds, by figure, motion, magnitude and the like, must needs be labour in vain. (LJ II, 85)

The amended mechanical philosophy of Newton is no better off:

> The great mechanical principle now in vogue is attraction. That a stone falls to the earth, or the sea swells towards the moon may to some appear sufficiently explained thereby. But how are we enlightened by being told this is done by attraction? . . . Again, the parts of steel we see cohere firmly together, and this also is accounted for by attraction; but in this, as in the other instances, I do not perceive that any thing is signified besides the effect it self. (LJ II, 86)

Berkeley finds mechanical causal explanations unsatisfactory and in the case of gravity he suggests that gravity is simply another name for a set of effects or phenomena—hence it is not and cannot be an explanatory concept. At the base of Berkeley's argument is that gravity is not a sensible quality or sensible thing, hence there can be no idea of it, hence it is "occult" and hence useless in physics (DJ,75 ff.). Leibniz's efforts to introduce forces into matter suffer from the same objections (DJ, 80 ff.). Both Newton and Leibniz are charged with adducing "things which are neither evident to the senses nor intelligible to reason" (DJ, 82).

Having made these claims, however, Berkeley faces the same issue that Malebranche, Spinoza, Leibniz, and Locke face, namely, how to talk about the qualities or substances that the mechanical science ordinarily takes to be the causes of change. Berkeley readily allows that nature is lawful and that there is "a certain order and connexion between them [ideas or sensible qualities], like that of cause and effect" (LJ II, 68). But rather than attribute causal efficacy to anything other than spirits, Berkeley tries to impose a new meaning on the connection among ideas:

> . . . the connection of ideas does not imply the relation of cause and effect, but only a mark or sign with the thing signified. The first which I see is not the cause of the pain I suffer upon my approaching it, but the mark that forewarns me of it. . . . By this means abundance of information is conveyed unto us, concerning what we are to expect from such and such actions, and what methods are proper to be taken, for the exciting such and such ideas: which in effect is all that I conceive to be distinctly meant, when it is said that by discerning the . . . mechanism of the inward parts of bodies, . . . we may attain to know the several uses and properties depending thereon, of the nature of the thing (LJ II, 69).

Thus, scientific explanations and scientific knowledge are not knowledge of efficient causes. In *De Motu* Berkeley explicitly extends his causal framework to science—science is not in the business of discovering true causes; it discovers regularities among sensible phenomena.

> Because these things [motive forces like gravity] are not sufficiently understood, some unjustly repudiate mathematical principles of physics, evidently on the pretext that they do not assign the true efficient causes of things. When in fact it is the concern of the physicist or mechanician to consider only the rules, not the efficient causes, of impulse or attraction, and, in a word, to set out the laws of motion: and from the established laws to assign the solution of a particular phenomenon, but not an efficient cause. (DJ, 89)

At this point Berkeley begins to look more like Malebranche in one important respect. Occasional causes in Malebranche serve pretty much the same purpose as stand-in in scientific explanation. True, Berkeley's idealism is not Malebranchean realism, but Berkeley's answer suffers from the same afflictions as the answers of everyone who was led by metaphysical concerns to distinguish true causation from pseudocausation and finds that true causes do not occur in scientific explanations or scientific laws. This dichotomy which appears over and over in the debate—Malebranche and Le Grand allow only God's will as a true cause, Spinoza allows only God as a true cause, Leibniz allows monadic agency as the true cause, Locke talks about real essences as true causes—now reappears in Berkeley. It remains for Hume to destroy the dichotomy and to assert boldly that occasional causes are true causes (T, 171). Hume does not abandon Berkeley's view of science; science still seeks the regularities among sensible qualities, but for Hume these regularities are genuinely causal.

HUME

There are two great concerns that have confounded Hume scholars. The first concerns Hume's place in the causation debate, particularly, what are his arguments against the views of his predecessors and with whom is he most engaged in the debate.[2] The second has to do with how to articulate Hume's own positive conception of causation. Although there is considerable controversy over each concern, the first is probably the more easily answered. Clearly, Hume is deeply immersed in the debate, and he believes that he knows what is at stake, what must be eliminated, and what must be kept to gain a notion of causation compatible with his contemporary empirical or experimentalist science.

Hume introduces his discussion of causation with the warning with which we began this essay.

> There is no question, which on account of its importance, as well as difficulty, has caus'd more disputes both among ancient and modern philosophers, then this concerning the efficacy of causes, or that quality which made them be followed by their effects. (T, 156)

The *Enquiry* is equally direct:

> There are no ideas, which occur in metaphysics, more obscure and uncertain, then those of *power, force, energy or necessary connexion*, of which it is every moment necessary for us to treat in all our disquisitions. (EHU 7.1, 66)

Hume looks back on the causation debate and sees little progress in philosophical efforts to clarify the notion of causation; he sees no theory of causation worthy of his support. And Hume does so with Malebranche's own pessimistic assessment of the views of others set out before him—even his wording is similar (compare Mccracken 1983, 257).

> In this research we meet with very little encouragement from that prodigious diversity, which is found in the opinions of those philosophers, who have pretended to explain the secret force and energy of causes [footnote to father Malebranche, Book vi. Part 2. chap. 3]. There are some who maintain, that bodies operate by their substantial form; other, by their accidents or qualities; several, by their matter and form; some, by their form and accidents; others by certain virtues and faculties distinct from all this. . . . Upon the whole, we may conclude, that 'tis impossible in any one instance to shew the principle, in which the force and agency of a cause is plac'd; and that the most refin'd and most vulgar understanding are equally at a loss in the particular. (T, 159)

Like Malebranche, Hume concludes that if previous philosophers had any clarity about notion of cause, they would never have resorted to such obscure principles (T, 160: compare LO, 567).

Hume's first step is to show that experience does not directly yield an idea of power, agency, or necessary connection as a separate idea. Locke, as we have seen, supposes that there is a separate and probably simple idea of power: "Power, I think, may well have a place amongst other simple Ideas, and be considered as one of them" (N, 234). Hume's strategy, much like Berkeley's, is to examine his ideas of the operations of bodies, for example, and discover that there is no separate idea of power or agency to be found among their sensible qualities.

> In reality, there is no part of matter, that does ever, by its sensible qualities, discover any power or energy, or give us ground to imagine, that it could produce any thing, or be followed by any other object, which we could denominate its effect. Solidity, extension, motion; these qualities are all complete in themselves, and never point out any other event which may result from them. (EHU, 63)

The same conclusion is reached with respect to mind and body: In the *Enquiry* he summarizes his argument very nicely as follows

> But to hasten to a conclusion of this argument, which is already drawn out to too great a length: We have sought in vain for an idea of power or necessary connexion in all the sources from which we could suppose it to be derived. It appears that, in single instances of the operation of bodies, we never can, by our utmost scrutiny, discover any thing but one event following another; without being able to comprehend any force or power by which the cause operates. . . . The same difficulty occurs in contemplating the operations of mind on body—where we observe the motion of the latter to follow upon the volition of the former. . . . The authority of the will over its own faculties and ideas

is not a whit more comprehensible: So that, upon the whole, there appears not throughout all nature, any one instance of connexion which is conceivable by us. (EHU, 73–74)

In another place in the *Treatise*, Hume is even more succinct: "We never have any impression, that contains any power or efficacy. We never therefore have any idea of power" (T, 161).

Nor is Hume open to the claim that even if we lack an impression of power, there might be ideas of other causal principles that come through the senses.

> I begin with observing that the terms of efficacy, agency, power, force, energy, necessity. connexion, and productive quality, are all nearly synonymous; and therefore 'tis an absurdity to employ any of them in defining the rest. (T 1.3, 157)

This passage makes clear that Hume, unlike most modern participants in the debate, sees his task as a *definitional* one, that is, defining causation in terms of a set of ideas that he can locate in experience and which are not simply synonyms for causation. We have already seen that some participants in the debate, such as Locke and Hobbes, were content to "define" as cause that which operated on another or produced something in another and to define as effect that which was produced. Hume resists the temptation to define one term on this list in terms of others.

Having agreed with Malebranche's condemnation of previous theories of causation, and having agreed again with Malebranche that that experience does not provide us with a concept of causation, Hume goes on to argue that Malebranche himself chooses an option which does nothing to clarify our concept of causation.

> As to what may be said, that the connection betwixt the idea of an infinitely powerful being is connected "with that of every effect, which he wills, we really do no more than assert, that a being, whose volition is connected with every effect, is connected with every effect; which is an identical proposition, and gives us no insight into the nature of this power or connection. (T, 248–49)

And while Malebranche is right to reject concurrentist views of causation, placing true causation in God alone is just as bad:

> The efficacy or energy of causes is neither placed in the causes themselves, nor in the deity, nor in the concurrence of these two principles. . . . (T, 166)

Malebranche's mistake lies in his insistence that a true cause is necessarily connected to its effect. It is this doctrine that leads Malebranche to reject causal efficacy in all created things. Here, we must be careful to note that Hume agrees with Malebranche that necessary connection is a crucial part of our idea of cause.

> Shall we then rest contented with these two relations of contiguity and succession, as affording a compleat idea of causation? By no means. An object may be contiguous and prior to another, without being considered as its cause. There is a necessary connexion to be taken into consideration; and that relation is of much greater importance, than any of the other two above-mention'd. (T, 77)

But for Hume the necessary connection between cause and effect is neither logical necessity nor metaphysical necessity but a psychological necessity derived from custom or habit (T, 166):

> This connexion, therefore, which we feel in the mind, this customary transition of the imagination from one object to its usual attendant, is the sentiment or impression from which we form the idea of power or necessary connexion. Nothing farther is in the case. (EHU, 75)

However, before Hume can present his own view of the necessary connection between cause and effect and thereby establish his own definition of cause, he must demolish the claims of his predecessors, including Malebranche, that there exists a complex logical/metaphysical connection between cause and effect. In essence, Hume argues that just as cause and effect are not connected by a separate impression of power, agency, or causation, so there are no *rationally* discoverable principles of causation. In other words, reason is just as unable to produce a separate idea of power or causation as experience.

The tradition of the debate in which Hume is working is nearly unanimous in holding that cause and effect are rationally connected. Descartes, Hobbes, Gassendi, and Rohault thought that one could reason from cause to effect and effect to cause. Spinoza can be read along with Descartes and Hobbes as holding that there exists an entailment relation between cause and effect. Malebranche and Le Grand also seem to hold that there is an entailment between the true cause and its effect. Locke in some passages suggests that in principle one could infer the effects from the real essence, if the real essence were made available. There are also rational principles such as the principle that the cause must contain at least as much reality as its effect that help to establish rational connections between cause and effect. If these rational principles are true, then a number of things follow. We could, in principle, from a complete enough set of propositions about the cause deductively infer a proposition that describes the effect. Furthermore, among possible (nondeductive) inferences from effect back to cause, one could eliminate those that cannot be reversed. Thus, one important test for a good inductive inference, besides the truth of the propositions involved, is that when we reverse the order we arrive at a deduction. And depending upon which version of the causal principle one holds, certain candidates for the cause-and-effect relationship can be eliminated through this a priori principle. Thus, if one holds that a substance cannot give to another substance that which it has not, then in a room with only one warm oven, one can infer from the baked bread that emerges from the room that that oven was the cause.

Hume is, in principle, opposed to rational principles that would allow one to infer from cause A to effect B or from effect B to cause A in the absence of a lawful (empirically learned) statement of the form A causes B (EHU, 27–29). There is no role for reason in the discovery of the cause-and-effect connection; ". . . reason alone can never give rise to any original idea and . . . that reason, as distinguish'd from experience, can never make us conclude, that a cause or productive quality is absolutely requisite to every beginning of existence" (T, 156). "Causes and effects are discoverable, not by reason but by experience" EHU, 28). Hume's strategy is to deny any such connection between cause and effect; thus, he embraces the principle that there is no likeness required between cause and effect and there is never a logical entailment between the two:

> The mind can never possibly find the effect in the supposed cause, by the most accurate scrutiny and examination. For the effect is totally different from the cause and consequently can never be discovered in it. (EHU, 29; compare T, 14, 161-62).

Finally, then, Hume can conclude: "Any thing may produce any thing. Creation, annihilation, motion, reason, volition; all these may arise from one another, or from any other object we can imagine" (T 173). In short, there are no metaphysical or logical constraints on causation that can preclude one thing from being the cause of another. Hume's positive account of causation then must avoid the pitfalls of his predecessors. To Hume this means that causation must be definable in terms of empirically available ideas and that the definition must be free of logical and/or metaphysical conditions.

The two definitions of "cause" which Hume offers after collecting "all the different parts of this reasoning" to "form an exact definition of the relation of cause and effect" are (T, 169):

> We may define a CAUSE to be "An object precedent and contiguous to another, and where all the objects resembling the former are plac'd in like relations of precedency to those objects, that resemble the latter." (T, 169)

> A CAUSE is an object precedent and contiguous to another, and so united with it that the idea of the one determines the mind to form the idea of the other, and the impression of the one to form a more lively idea of the other. (T, 170)

In the *Enquiry* the definitions blend as follows:

> But when one particular species of event has always, in all instances, been conjoined with another, we make no longer any scruple of foretelling one upon the appearance of the other. . . . We then call the one object, *Cause*; and other *Effect*. (EHU, 74–75)

Hume scholars have raised a host of interpretive issues about Hume's two definitions. All possible interpretive schemes have been defended, namely, that Hume holds both definitions, that Hume holds neither definition, and that Hume embraces one but not the other definition (Garrett 1993). But before exploring the various interpretive schemes, let us take Hume at his word that these are his "exact definitions" of cause and that these two definitions are "only different by their presenting a different view of the same object" (T, 169–70).

Causation is defined for Hume in terms of three (empirically available) relations and their subsequent ideas. These relations stand between ideas, impression, or ideas and impression; the first is that of temporal priority, the second is that of contiguity, and the third is that of resemblance. Thus, when we observe that a particular event is prior to another, and that they are contiguous in space and time, and, with the aid of memory, notice that things like the first are regularly so related to things like the second, then the first is the cause of the second (T, 173).

> We have no other notion of cause and effect, but that of certain objects, which have been always conjoin'd and which in all past instances have been found inseparable. (T, 93; compare EHU, 159)

As Garrett notes, definitions are for Hume "an attempt to convey the idea that a term signifies" (1993, 174; compare T, 277). The complex idea conveyed by the terms "cause" and "effect" a composite of the three ingredients, resemblance, temporal priority, and contiguity. (In the *Enquiry* Hume is less insistent on the condition of contiguity, perhaps under the influence of Newton's theory of gravity.) Even though Hume defines the idea of causation in terms of resemblance, contiguity, and temporal priority, he does believe that the relation of necessary connection is of greater importance even than the relations of contiguity and succession (T, 77). But necessary connection is not for Hume a fourth empirical relation, a rationally discovered principle, or a logical relation. It is either a sentiment or a custom depending upon the text.

> This therefore is the essence of necessity. Upon the whole, necessity is something, that exists in the mind, not in objects; nor is it possible for us ever to form the most distant idea of it, consider'd as a quality in bodies. Either we have no idea of necessity, or necessity is nothing but that determination of the thought to pass from causes to effects and from effects to causes, according to their experience'd union. (T, 165–66)

> This connexion, therefore, which we feel in the mind, this customary transition of the imagination from one object to its usual attendant, is the sentiment or impression from which we form the idea of power or necessary connexion. Nothing farther is in the case. (EHU, 75)

A proper scientific account or explanation of some event comes out of a required set of experiences. Scientists must have numerous instances formulated into laws—or in rare cases, single instances very like other causal determinations—of prior regularly associated events, without exceptions. Further, there must be the habit of association of the events. In such cases, once we have the causal law or regularity, we can infer from cause to effect or effect from cause (T, 83; EHU, 26). Such causal reasonings can extend indefinitely as long as we have the requisite regularities.

Hume does not discuss at length his requirement that the cause is temporally prior to the effect, although he does note that some philosophers allow for a cause to be "co-temporary" with its effect (T, 76). Hume offers a *reductio* of the view that cause and effect are contemporary:

> 'Tis an establish'd maxim both in natural and moral philosophy, that an object, which exists for any time in its full perfection without producing another, is not its sole cause; but is assisted by some other principle, which pushes it from its state of inactivity, and makes it exert that energy, of which it was secretly possest. Now if any cause may be perfectly co-temporary with its effect, 'tis certain, according to this maxim, that they must all of them be so; since any one of them, which retards its operation for a single moment, exerts not itself at that very individual time . . . and therefore is no proper cause. (T, 76)

Here Hume seems to use an intuition about causation, namely, any view that a cause may coexist for a time with its effect before acting violates our intuition that time or duration alone cannot by itself produce any change. If one does not accept this argument, Hume is prepared to simply stipulate that temporal priority is a condition of all causes (T, 76). Besides, the scientific works on which Hume relies as background are filled with examples of causation that fully meet his conditions.

As Richmond has noted, however, Hume's view of causation has significant differences from that of Newton, on whose views Hume is trying to build. For example, while both authors insist upon simplicity of scientific explanation and both authors are committed to a principle of same cause, same effect, Hume takes this principle to require qualitative resemblance among particular sequences of cause and effect, whereas Newton often looks at such similar correlations as indicative of a common underlying cause (Richmond 1994, 40–41). Stated more bluntly, correlations for Hume provide explanations, whereas for Newton correlations are indicators that an explanation is needed. This difference is why Newton is able to formulate an overreaching theory of gravitation that explains a host of diverse yet similar phenomena—the pendulum, the tides, and planetary orbits. To this extent, Hume succeeds only in partially aligning philosophical discussion of causation with scientific practice. Perhaps because, like Berkeley, he is a radical empiricist, he is unable to sanction inferences from best explanations where the supposed cause is hidden. In a very strange passage in the *Enquiry* Hume seems to both endorse hidden general causes and to deny their value:

> These ultimate springs and principles are totally shut up from human curiosity and enquiry. Elasticity, gravity, cohesion of parts, communication of motion by impulse; these are probably the ultimate causes and principles which we shall ever discover in nature. . . . (EHM, 30)

If Hume's point is that we can never reach the answer to the ultimate "why" question, then that is consistent with Newton's view that there will always be some unexplained or not fully understood set of causes. But it seems odd to say that ultimate springs are beyond enquiry and then in the next sentence identify some of these ultimate springs. As someone who admires experimental science and is an empiricist, Hume, it would seem, should say that only time will tell what "ultimate springs" are discovered. The stretch in this passage is probably due to Hume's wanting to embrace Newtonian science on the one hand and wanting to deny Newton's views on causation on the other.

We now turn to the question: was Hume committed to both definitions? The first definition considers causation in terms of contiguity and regular prior association; the second, in terms of one idea's producing another. We might argue simply from the text that Hume is committed to both definitions; after all, he says he is presenting the same object from two points of view (T, 169; compare Robinson 1966). Yet the two definitions do not seem to be coextensive. Two events might be psychologically associated without being in contiguous space time, and, conversely, events might have the proper contiguity but not the proper psychological association. We might prefer the first definition to the second because it is widely used in Hume's writings and the second definition violates Hume's own conditions of avoiding circular definitions by defining "cause" in terms of a cognate "produce." At the same time, there are passages that suggest Hume seems to prefer the second definition. In the *Enquiry* Hume says that when we say one object is causally connected to another, "we mean only that they have acquired a connexion in our thought" (EHU, 76).

Perhaps the most devastating interpretation of Hume, from the standpoint of the thesis of this book, is the claim, advanced by several authors, that Hume ultimately rejects both definitions (Wright 1983; Strawson 1989). These scholars argue that Hume is committed to a Locke or Glanville hidden-cause view according to which there are "ultimate springs" that connect cause and effect and that are in principle unavailable to us. Thus, the causes that occur in scientific explanations are pseudocauses and Hume does not advance over his predecessors in this respect. The following passages are frequently taken as evidence for this reading:

> It is confessed, that the utmost effort of human reason is to reduce the principles, productive of natural phenomena, to a greater simplicity, and to resolve the many particular effects into a few general causes, we should in vain attempt their discovery; nor shall we ever be able to satisfy ourselves, by any particular explication of them. These ultimate springs and principles are totally shut up from human curiosity and enquiry. Elasticity, gravity, cohesion of parts, communication of motion by impulse; these are probably the ultimate causes and principles which we ever discover in nature. . . . (EHU, 30)

> The small success which has been met with in all attempts to fix this power, has at last oblig'd philosophers to conclude, that the ultimate force and efficacy of nature is perfectly unknown to us, and that 'tis in vain we search for it in all the known qualities of matter. (T, 159)

> This is our aim in our studies and reflections: And how must we be disappointed, when we learn, that this connexion, tie, or energy lies merely in ourselves, and is nothing but that determination of the mind, which is acquir'd by custom. . . . Such a discovery not only cuts off all hope of ever attaining satisfaction . . . since it appears, that when we say we desire to know the ultimate and operating principle, as something, which resides in the external object, we either contradict ourselves, or talk without meaning. (T, 267)

> The scenes of the universe are continually shifting, and one object follows another in an uninterrupted succession; but the power or force which actuates the whole machine, is entirely concealed from us, and never discovers itself in any of the sensible qualities of a body. (EHU, 63–64)

In spite of such remarks by Hume, there are good reasons for accepting both definitions of "cause" as Hume's only notion of cause. Foremost among

these considerations is the fact that words refer to ideas and in Hume's epistemology there can be no other idea of cause. In Hume's own theory of knowledge, when we talk of ultimate principles, etc., we are literally speaking nonsense; we are using words without ideas associated with them. Such principles
"have no place" in Hume's philosophy (EHU, 58). Furthermore, "there is no
known connexion between the sensible qualities and the secret powers" that
would allow us to at least attach a meaning to terms like "secret powers"
(EHU, 34). And Hume is inclined to treat such terms as meaningless (T, 267).
Furthermore, notions like gravity and cohesion do have sensible qualities in
terms of which they can be understood, because for them we can "trace up the
particular phenomena to, or near to, these general principles" (EHU, 30–31).
In Rohault's language these principles allow us to descend to particulars. To
take Hume's talk about secret powers seriously, even to think that such sentences are meaningful, would mean that Hume would have to set aside the
entire epistemological framework of his philosophy in the *Treatise* and the
Enquiry.

Hume obviously does not regard "gravity" as a meaningless term. But at the
same time, he does not regard it as a secret power either. Hume's best understanding of gravity must remain true to his definition of cause; he reminds us
that ". . . when an effect is supposed to depend upon an intricate machinery or
secret structure of parts, we make no difficulty in attributing all our knowledge
of it to experience" (EHU, 28). How, then, are ideas like that of gravity linked to
sensible qualities? And why are such causal powers not "secret" powers? Hume
offers little in response to these questions. Pressed on this issue, Hume might
well refer to Newton's *Principia*. It is this work that makes these powers manifest and gives meaning to terms such as "gravity."

Garrett believes that in the end there is a set of compelling reasons—
including the above—to think Hume holds to both definitions:

> There is considerable textual support for the interpretation of Hume as
> endorsing both of his two definitions of "cause". This support lies in (i) their
> manner of presentation, (ii) his uses of them to derive further conclusions,
> (iii) his further remarks seeming to endorse each of them, and (iv) their con-
> formity to his limitations on what can meaningfully be said and thought
> about causal relations. (1993, 179)

If we accept Hume's definitions of "cause" as his positive view of causation,
then ". . . the real power of causes is . . . their connexion and necessity" (T,
166). From which it follows that all causation talk in the previous debate is
about regularly associated events that are accompanied by the necessity of
custom or habit. Hence, Malebranche's occasions, if they satisfy these criteria
as they seem to do, are true causes.

> We may learn from the foregoing doctrine, that all causes are the same kind, and that in particular there is no foundation for that distinction, which we sometimes make betwixt efficient causes, and causes sine qua non; or betwixt efficient causes, and formal, and material, and exemplary, and final causes. . . . For the same reason we must reject the distinction betwixt cause and occasion, when suppos'd to signify any thing essentially different from each other. If constant conjunction be imply'd in what we call occasion, 'tis a real cause. if not, 'tis no relation at all, and cannot give rise to any argument or reasoning (T, 171).

Even if we accept that Hume's conception of causation is captured by his two definitions, his account is hardly free of difficulty (Brand 1976, 65 ff.).[3] First Hume's definitions cast too wide a net. There are many pairs of events that are regularly associated, contiguous, and temporally ordered and which are associated by custom or habit and that are not causally connected or that we do not want to include among our set of causally connected events, for example, symptoms or developmental sequences. Second, as Locke and Boyle suggest, what an object can do and what causal relations it enters into determine our understanding of its nominal essence, for example, gold is soluble in *aqua regia*. But if we use a notion of causation to understand what a kind is, then Hume's account of causation, which uses an implicit notion of kind when it requires that events like the first are regularly so associated with events like the second, is blatantly circular. Third, and finally, there is the Newtonian point that regularly associated events, instead of being a causal sequence, may well require that we look for a common cause that explains both. But most of these debates are part of the twentieth-century debate, and they raise concerns that go beyond the causation debate in modern philosophy.

CENTRAL THEMES

Locke, Berkeley, and Hume inherited a working science, a modified corpuscularian view that was not adverse to the admission of attractive and repulsive forces as long as they were made manifest. They beheld the power of this science in works by Boyle and Newton. They also read the warnings against metaphysical speculation about the nature of causation. Each tried accordingly to accommodate this shift in the debate. Locke simply does not worry about causation; he accepts as causes those things which Newton and Boyle identified. He does create controversy and confusion with his notion of the real essence of things. Perhaps the kindest thing to say is that Locke should have abandoned that notion. It fits neither his epistemology—knowledge is the agreement and disagreement of ideas—nor his own prohibition against meta-physical speculations. Berkeley, although he cannot bring himself to be rid of the notion that substances (spirits) are active causes and that true causes are active agents, does demolish the concept of material substance and introduces a clear theme that causes among sensible qualities are those sensible events that are or could be observed and that serve as a basis for prediction of others. It remains for Hume to pull the pieces together and to insist that such sensible events are not only the basis of prediction but also the basis of scientific explanation. Thus, Hume rescues the causation debate from its foolish conclusion that the causes by which we explain change are not true or proper causes. He does this, first, by attacking metaphysical conditions that he believes have inserted a wedge between true causes and explanatory causes and, second, by adopting science as a guide to the identification of true causes. With Hume, it appears then, that science and philosophy are once again in alignment as they were at the outset of the causation debate in modern philosophy.

9.
Summation and Final Ironies

We began our discussion of the causation debate in modern philosophy with a set of central themes about causation that were part of the Scholastic/Aristotelian legacy. Throughout the course of the causation debate these themes have been altered, so that by 1739 the counterpart themes can be formulated as follows:

(1) There are four kinds of causation—material, efficient, formal, and final—has become: (1) There is only efficient causation.
(2) Forms preexist in efficient causes has become: (2) Anything may produce anything.
(3) Causation requires that something is "communicated" from the cause to the effect has become: (3) Causation is regular association.
(4) Proper explanations are deductively inferential has become: (4) There is no logical connection between a cause and its effect, although we can discover laws that say that the first is the cause of the second and, using such a law, make scientific inferences.
(5) Cause and effect are necessarily linked has become: (5) Cause and effect are linked by custom or habit.
(6) Causes and effects are substances has become: (6) There are no substances; causes and effects are sensible qualities.
(7) Some substances (spirits or souls) are active agents has become: (7) There are no active agents, meaning there is no distinct kind of causation found in minds.
(8) Causation may be instantaneous has become: (3) Causes are always temporally prior to their effects.
(9) Proper explanations are in terms of the true or proper causes of change is unchanged.

(10) God is the total efficient cause of everything has become: (10) Whatever God's powers may be, they are distinct from the nature of efficient causation as understood in science.

As we noted in Chapter 1, only thesis (9) survives. And (9) has a new meaning, namely, true or proper causes are those that serve in proper scientific explanations and scientific explanations are those that involve true and proper causes; science is the arbiter of what counts as true or proper.

Throughout the course of the causation debate in modern philosophy, a number of ironies emerge. We have alluded to these ironies in the introductory chapter and throughout the presentation of the debate. In the remainder of this chapter I shall highlight the specific ironies that have emerged.

First. The metaphysical problem about causation that appears early in the debate was an attempt to understand what went on in true or proper causal processes. Hume's understanding of the philosophical motivation for this problem is correct; philosophers wondered what "quality" in the cause makes itefficacious (T, 156). Or, to put it another way, philosophers were concerned to describe metaphysically the "how" of causation. Thus, metaphysics is logically prior to science because it helps us to understand what kinds of entities are involved in every true causal relationship and how those entities are connected. Of course, it is obvious that philosophers with different metaphysics will offer different accounts of the nature of causation. Descartes's causal principle is one of the outstanding efforts to articulate a metaphysical condition on causation.

The irony of these efforts to identify at least certain necessary conditions for the occurrence of proper or true causation is that many of philosophers engaged in this enterprise came to the conclusion that these very requirements preclude true causation from occurring in precisely those cases that earlier participants in the debate had identified as paradigms of true or proper causation. Thus, Malebranche argues that it is precisely because causes are necessary to their effects that ovens cannot bake bread or my will cannot cause my arm to rise. Le Grand, Foucher, Princess Elizabeth, and others doubt that there is enough similarity between mind and body to allow for a causal connection either in sensation or in volition. Thus, the first irony properly stated is that the very explications that early participants, especially Descartes, offer to show how proper causes bring about change or produce effects end up being used to show that proper causes are not, after all, proper causes but something else.

Second. Descartes's radical view about the inertness of matter compounds doubts about his theory of causation by denying that the force that moves bodies is either an attribute or a mode of bodies. Thus, the paradigm case of causal interaction, one body acting upon another, came to be a paradigm case of a noncausal connection. How can one body move itself or another if there is no motive force in bodies? What is the point of contact between physical causes and their effects if matter is merely extension? Some philosophers such as Hobbes, Gassendi, and Leibniz and scientists such as Boyle and Newton try to add properties to bodies such as force and impenetrability in order to make bodies the proper causes of motions in other bodies. But other philosophers take Descartes's point to be that only spirit or perhaps God can move bodies. The second irony, then, is that Descartes, who is the founder of classical mechanism, is also the founder of a kind of antimechanistic metaphysics that holds that in any proper sense of cause, one body cannot move another body and that causation, at its deepest level, is not action by contact.

Third. Classical mechanism, a mechanism that was built on a commonsense understanding of causation as pushing or pulling between material bodies, appears as a way to rid science of noncontact forms of causation such as substantial forms and other occult properties. It fails in two respects. First, there were many phenomena such as the orbits of planets and comets and the various phenomena of light and magnetism that could not be satisfactorily explained through causation by push-pull contact. Thus, later scientists had to introduce attractive and repulsive forces that required a new conceptualization of matter. Second, classical mechanism's reductionist tendencies do, in some ways, address the metaphysical problem of causation since the kinds of true causal interactions are reduced to one; that is, all causation is causation by contact among smaller bodies, atoms, or corpuscles having only the properties of size, weight, impenetrability, and motion or rest. For example, the transfer of heat from an oven to the bread, a classic example of a causal connection, becomes simply a story about the rapid movement of atoms or corpuscles. Thus, classical mechanism, while it reduces the number of purported causal connections to one basic kind, never successfully addresses the metaphysics of causation at that level. What happens, metaphysically, when one body moves another, stops another, changes its direction? At this level, classical mechanists resort to metaphor. Descartes talks about the quantity of motion that is not the cause of motion but a measure of the motive force. And which turns out not to be preserved in any case. Hobbes talks about stronger and weaker endeavors; Gassendi talks about more or less active atoms. Thus, the irony is that one of the earliest views of causation, one that promises the greatest simplification and clarification of the nature of causation, ultimately has nothing to say about the metaphysical problem of causation. And because so many cases cannot be explained through simplistic push-pull mechanisms, classical mechanism actually provides an impetus toward noncontact causal explanations.

Fourth. From the earliest stages of the debate there is a contest between those, like Descartes, who seem to want to describe causes as real entities subject to fairly rigid metaphysical conditions, and those like Gassendi, who prefer to talk about causes as entities that may or may not be real but which provide the best explanation of known phenomena. Descartes's strategy and goal take one toward realism and metaphysics; Gassendi's take one toward antirealism and epistemology. Descartes's answer for many of his followers leads to the denial that the causes in scientific explanations are true or proper causes. Gassendi's path can never separate true or proper causation from the causes that occur in scientific explanations, and he offers a largely circular account of "cause," noted in our discussion of (9) above, that ignores the metaphysics of causation completely. The irony is that although the debate is heavily focused on the metaphysical nature of causation, the outcome of the debate is that such an inquiry is unnecessary, unproductive, and should yield to the more antimetaphysical project launched by Gassendi. Thus, the failure of metaphysical discussions became a major motive in a turn to the approach taken by Gassendi.

Fifth. The removal, however, of metaphysical considerations comes with a price. Hume's account of causation does not succeed in bringing philosophy into alignment with science. Hume's definition is too generous; too many pairs of events qualify as cause and effect, specifically it includes pairs that are related as symptoms or stages of growth and that come together because of an underlying common cause. Ironically, what some contemporary philosophers would add is a new version of (3) that insists that in all true causal processes there is a metaphysical connection. Thus, Salmon argues that we need to distinguish between true causal processes and pseudocausal processes; the former but not the latter can convey information (1990, 108-10). The irony is that the metaphysical problem of causation must be addressed at some level in order to correct the generosity of Hume's definitions. The early participants in the debate lost explanatory power by insisting upon a set of metaphysical conditions that effectively precluded the usual candidates for causes from being proper causes. The later participants in the debate lost explanatory power by eliminating so many metaphysical conditions that too many things qualify as proper causes. What this final irony suggests is that the modern causation debate is hardly resolved, the debate concerning the metaphysics of causation has been revived with a new generation of realist and antirealist philosophers (see van Fraassen 1980; Miller 1987).

NOTES

CHAPTER 1

1. The exception being Louis Loeb's excellent *From Descartes to Hume, Continental Metaphysics and the Development of Modern Philosophy* (1981), which offers a discussion of the debate, especially with respect to the rationalists—Descartes, Spinoza, Malebranche, and Leibniz—with a brief foray into Berkeley and Hume. Recently, Steven Nadler's *Causation in Early Modern Philosopy* (1993b) has helped to bring out the importance of examining theories of causation in this period.

CHAPTER 2

1. Clatterbaugh 1980, 383. I have updated the textual references in this quote.
2. Compare CSM I, 211; Antoine Le Grand, *An Entire Body of Philosophy According to Principles of the Famous Renate de Cartes* (London, 1694, 1, 1, vi, 14–15).
3. Anthony Kenny notes that Descartes equivocates on the notion of dependence. Finite substances are *causally* dependent on God, whereas properties are logically dependent on their subjects (Kenny 1968, 134; compare Woolhouse 1993, 14–27). To a contemporary philosopher like Kenny, there seems to be a clear ambiguity in the notion of dependence. However, I shall show in the next chapter that logical and causal dependence are not as sharply drawn by Descartes as they are in contemporary philosophical writing.
4. But such a principle surely allows too much? If we are substances and God's perfections are attributes and if substance has greater reality than properties, then why cannot I be the cause of my ideas of

God's attributes—his perfections such as infinitude, goodness, power, wisdom, etc. Descartes seems to hold that we only know a substance through its properties, qualities, or attributes (CSM II, 31, 34, 114). If so, then Version III needs to be understood to mean that created substances can only be the efficient cause of other created substances, their finite properties, or the ideas thereof. Or Descartes needs to argue that God's properties are not properties in the same sense as the properties of created things. Descartes does not speculate on this concern. I suspect he would opt for the first possibility, if so confronted (compare CSM III, 214).

5. It should be noted here that this justification of the causal likeness principle is what makes the *Meditations* look circular. When Descartes first introduces the causal principle in the "Third Meditation," he has not yet removed the evil deceiver hypothesis by proving that God exists and is not a deceiver. Thus, he seems to beg the question by using a clear and distinctly known principle to prove that God exists in order to be able to trust his clear and distinct ideas.

6. For a defense of Leibniz's doctrine at individual accidents, see Clatterbaugh 1973.

7. I am indebted to Robert Sleigh's paper "Leibniz on Malebranche on Causality" for suggesting these possibilities (1990, 172).

CHAPTER 3

1. Descartes's use of "a priori" and "a posteriori" is idiosyncratic. By "a priori" he seems to mean "prior in the order of knowing." "a posteriori" he seems to mean "posterior in the order of knowing." (Compare CSM II, 110–11).

2. And as Garber has noted, that inspiration is fairly direct. When Gassendi, for example, challenges Descartes on his idea of a conserving God, Descartes's appeal is "to his copy of St. Thomas" (Garber 1992, 265).

CHAPTER 4

1. I owe this point to Nick Serafimidis.

CHAPTER 6

1. Wilson has argued forcefully that it is a mistake to read Axiom 4—"the knowledge of an effect depends on, and involves, the knowledge of its cause" (EMC, 410)—as supporting the inferential interpretation. In her

argument Wilson looks carefully at Axiom 4 and its uses in the *Ethics*. She notes that Spinoza tends to use Axiom 4 to mean that knowledge (not simply adequate knowledge) of an effect involves knowledge of its cause (1991, 141). Specifically, the mode-attribute relationship is said to satisfy Axiom 4—for example, we cannot know the mode of being square without knowing the attribute of extension (Wilson 1991, 146). Thus, if there is an inference to be made, it is from effect (mode) back to cause (attribute), since knowledge of the effect is sufficient for knowledge of the cause, but not conversely. Wilson's discussion, thus, challenges the inferential view of causation; she also brings out the epistemological, rather than metaphysical, content of many of Spinoza's claims about causation. Wilson's view need not be read as denying that sometimes Spinoza speaks of premises as causes, only that that exhausts his notion of causation.

2. Curley's use of "partial" cause is unfortunate since in Definition I of Part III Spinoza makes it clear that God is an adequate cause, that is, not a partial cause. Still, the point Curley makes is clear. From God's nature alone one cannot infer the existence of a finite mode.

3. Curley admits as much when he notes that his view is not a perfect fit, especially with respect to particular things (1969, 64 ff.).

4. My version of the principle differs from that of Sleigh who states it as: "Each state of a substance is a consequence of its preceding state" (1990a, 11).

5. "However, two ways remain for us to know contingent truths, one through experience and the other through reason—by experience when we perceive a thing sufficiently distinctly through the senses, and by reason when something is known from the general principle that nothing is without a reason, or that there is always some reason why the predicate is in the subject" (AG 96).

CHAPTER 7

1. This point was made by Nick Serafimidis in an unpublished paper, "God, Causality, and Explanation in the Thought of Robert Boyle."

CHAPTER 8

1. Apparently Locke did not see the need to publish this work: occasionalism was on the wane. But he did not forbid its publication (McCracken 1983, 121).

2. McCracken's clear and insightful chapter in *Malebranche and British Philosophy* (1983) is the very best and most useful discussion to date of how the causation debate influenced Hume through the works of Malebranche.

3. Kant responded to Hume by making all causal laws, at least at the higher levels synthetic a priori. See Friedman's "Causal Laws and the Foundations of Natural Science" in Guyer 1992.

BIBLIOGRAPHY

Acton, H.B. 1967. George Berkeley in *The Encyclopedia of Philosophy*, edited by Paul Edwards, 8 vols. New York: Macmillan and Free Press.

Adams, Robert M. 1977. Leibniz's theories of contingency, in Kulstad, ed. (1990): 1–41.

———. 1994. *Leibniz: Determinist, Theist, Idealist*. Oxford: Oxford University Press.

Alexander, Peter, 1974. Boyle and Locke on primary and secondary qualities, in Tipton, ed. (1977): 62–76.

———. 1985. *Ideas, Qualities, and Corpuscles: Locke and Boyle on the External World*. Cambridge/New York: Cambridge University Press.

Allison, Henry E. 1975. *Benedict de Spinoza*. Boston: Twayne.

Anderson, Wallace E. 1976. *Cartesian motion*, in Machamer and Turnbull, eds. (1976): 200–23.

Anscombe, Elizabeth, and Peter Thomas Geach. 1971. *Descartes: Philosophical Writings*. Indianapolis: Bobbs-Merrill.

Ariew, Roger, 1983. Mind-body interaction in Cartesian philosophy: A reply to Garber's "Understanding interaction: what Descartes should have told Elisabeth," *Social Journal of Philosophy*, supplementary 21: 33–38.

———. 1992. Descartes and scholasticism: The intellectual background to Descartes's thought, in Cottingham, ed. (1992): 58-90.

Arthur, Richard T.W. 1988. Continuous creation, continuous time: a refutation of the alleged discontinuity of Cartesian time, *Journal of the History of Philosophy* 26: 349–75.

Ashcraft, Richard, Richard Kroll, and Perez Zagorin, eds. 1991. *Philosophy, Science, and Religion, 1640–1700*. Cambridge: Cambridge University Press.

Atherton, Margaret. 1984. The inessentiality of Locke's essences, *Canadian Journal of Philosophy* 14: 277–94

Ayers, Michael. 1991. *Locke.* 2 vols. London and New York: Routledge.

Bacon, Francis. 1620. *Novam Organum*, edited by Thomas Fowler. Oxford: University Press, 1889.

Bacon, Roger. 1983. *Roger Bacon's Philosophy of Nature, A Critical Edition, with English Translation, Introduction, and Notes, of De multiplicatione specierum and De speculis comburentibus*, edited and translated by David C. Lindbrg. Oxford: Clarendon Press.

Barber, Kenneth F., and Jorge J. E. Garcia, eds. 1994. *Individuation and Identity in Early Modern Philosophy.* Buffalo: State University of New York Press.

Barker, Peter, and Roger Ariew, eds. 1991. *Revolution and Continuity: Essays in the History and Philosophy of Modern Science.* Washington, D.C.: Catholic University of America Press.

Basson, A. H. 1958. *David Hume.* Harmondsworth: Penguin Books.

———. 1966. *Hume's First Principles.* Lincoln: University of Nebraska Press.

Bayle, Pierre. 1967. *Pierre Bayle: Historical and Critical Dictionary: Selections*, translated by Richard H. Popkin. Indianapolis: Bobbs-Merrissl, 1965.

Beauchamp, Tom L., and Alexander Rosenberg, eds. 1981. *Hume and the Problem of Causation.* New York: Oxford University Press.

Beck, L. J. 1952. *The Method of Descartes: A Study of the Regulae.* Oxford: Clarendon Press.

Bedau, Mark. 1986. Cartesian interaction, *Midwest Studies in Philosophy* 10: 143–502.

Bennett, Jonathan. 1987. Substratum, *History of Philosophy Quarterly* 4: 197–215.

———. 1996. Spinoza's metaphysics, in Garrett, ed. (1996): 61–88.

Boas, Marie. 1952. The establishment of the mechanical philosophy, *Osiris* 10: 412–541.

Bobro, Marc, and Kenneth Clatterbaugh. 1996. Unpacking the monad: Leibniz's theory of causality, *The Monist* 79: 3, 408–25.

Bolton, M. B. 1976. The origins of Locke's doctrine of primary and secondary qualities, *Philosophical Quarterly* 26: 305–16.

Boyle, Robert. 1772. *The Works of the Honourable Robert Boyle*, edited by Thomas Birch, new edition, 6 vols. London; reprinted, Hildesheim: Georg Olms, 1965–95.

Brand, Myles, ed. 1976. *The Nature of Causation.* Urbana, Chicago, and London: University of Illinois Press.

Brandt, Frithiof, 1927. *Thomas Hobbes' Mechanical Conception of Nature.* Copenhagen: Levin & Munksgaard.

Brett, G. S. 1908. *The Philosophy of Gassendi*. London; Macmillan.

Broad, C. D. 1981. *Leibniz's last controversy with the Newtonians*, in Woolhouse, ed. (1981): 157–74.

Broughton, Janet. 1970. Reinterpreting Descartes on the notion of union of mind and body, *Journal of History of Philosophy* 16: 23–32.

———. 1986. Adequate causes and natural change in Descartes' philosophy, in Donagan, Perovich Jr., and Wedin, eds. (1987): 107–27.

Brown, J. R. and Okruhlik, K., eds. 1985. *The Natural Philosophy of Leibniz*. Dordrecht and Boston: D. Reidel.

Brown, Stuart, ed. 1991. *Nicolas Malebranche: His Philosophical Critics and Successors*. The Netherlands: van Gorcum.

Brundell, Barry. 1987. *Pierre Gassendi: From Aristotelianism to a New Philosophy*, Dordrecht: D. Reidel.

Burns, R. M. 1981. *The Great Debate on Miracles: From Joseph Glanville to David Hume*. Lewisburg: Bucknell University Press.

Burtt, Edwin Arthur. 1925. *The Metaphysical Foundations of Modern Physical Science*. London: Kegan Paul, Trench, Trubner.

Carre, Meyrick H. 1958. Pierre Gassendi and the new philosophy, *Philosophy* 33: 112–20.

Centore, F. F. 1972. Mechanism, teleology, and 17th century English science, *International Philosophical Quarterly* 12: 553–71.

Chappell, Vere, ed. 1966. *Hume: A Collection of Critical Essays*. Garden City, N.Y.: Doubleday Anchor.

———, ed. 1992. Volume 7, *Seventeenth-Century Natural Scientists*. New York and London: Garland.

Charleton, Walter. 1654. *Physiologia epicuro-Gassendo-Charletoniana, Or a Fabricke of Science Natural, Upon the Hypothesis of Atoms, Founded by Epicurus, Repaired by Petrus Gassendus, Augemented by Walter Charleton*. London, New York, and London: Johnson Reprint, 1966.

Clarke, Desmond M. 1977. The impact rules of Descartes' physics, *Isis* 68: 55–66.

———. 1979. Physics and metaphysics in Descartes' Principles, *Studies in History and Philosophy of Science* 10: 89–110.

———. 1982. *Descartes' Philosophy of Science*. Manchester: Manchester University Press.

———. 1995. Malebranche and occasionalism: A reply to Steven Nadler, *Journal of the History of Philosophy* 33: 3, 499–504.

Clapp, James Cordon. 1967. John Locke in *The Encyclopedia of Philosophy*, edited by Paul Edwards, 8 vols. New York: Macmillan Free Press.

Clatterbaugh, Kenneth, C. 1973. *Leibniz's Doctrine of Individual Accidents*,

Sudia Leibnitiana. Sonderheft 4, Wiesbaden: Franz Steiner Verlag.

————. 1980. Descartes's causal likeness principle, *Philosophical Review* 89: 3, 379-402.

————. 1995. Cartesian causality, explanation, and divine concurrence, *History of Philosophical Quarterly* 12: 2, 195–207.

————. 1996. Review of Causation in Early Modern Philosophy, *Leibniz Society Review* (December): 132–140.

Clericuzio, Antonio. 1990. A redefining of Boyle's chemistry and corpuscular philosophy, *Annals of Science* 47: 561–89.

Collins, James. 1960. *God in Modern Philosophy*, London: Routlege & Kegan Paul.

————. 1971. *Descartes's Philosophy of Nature, American Philosophical Quarterly*, Monograph 5. Oxford: Basil Blackwell.

Cope, Jackson I. 1956. *Joseph Glanville, Anglican Apologist.* St. Louis: Washington University Studies.

Copenhaver, Brian P. 1992. Did science have a renaissance? *Isis* 83: 387–407.

Cottingham, John, ed. 1992. *The Cambridge Companion to Descartes.* Cambridge: Cambridge University Press.

Cover, J. A. and Mark Kulstad, eds. 1990. *Central Themes in Early Modern Philosophy*, Indianapolis and Cambridge: Cambridge: Hackett.

Cummins, Philip D. 1966. Berkeley's likeness pnnciple, *Journal of the History of Philosophy* 4: 1, 63–69

Curley, Edwin. 1969. *Spinoza's Metaphysics: An Essay in Interpretation.* Cambridge, MA: Harvard Univesity Press.

————. 1978. *Descartes against the Skeptics.* Oxford: Basil Blackwell.

Delahunty, R. J. 1985. *Spinoza.* London and Boston: Routledge & Kegan Paul.

Des Chene, Dennis. 1996. *Physiologla: Natural Philosophy in Late Aristotelian and Cartesian Thought.* Ithaca and London: Cornell University Press.

Dijksterhuis, E. J. *The Mechanization of the World Picture*, translated by C. Dikshoorn. Oxford: Oxford University Press.

Dobbs, Betty Jo Teeter. 1971. Studies in the natural philosophy of Sir Kenelm Digby, *Ambix* 18: 1–25.

————. 1973. Studies in the natural philosophy of Sir Kenelm Digby, *Ambix* 20: 143–63.

————. 1974. Studies in the natural philosophy of Sir Kenelm Digby, *Ambix* 21: 1–28.

————. 1991. Stoic and Epicurean doctrines in Newton's system of the world, in Ostler, ed. (1991): 221–38.

Donagan, Alan. 1973. Essence and the distinction of attributes in Spinoza's metaphysics in Grene, ed. (1973): 164–81.

————. 1980. Spinoza's dualism, in Kennington, ed. (1980): 89–102.

————. 1996. Spinoza's theology, in Garrett, ed. (1996): 343–82.

Donagen, Alan, Anthony N. Provich, Jr., and Michael V. Wedin, eds. 1986. *Human Nature and Natural Knowledge, Essays Presented to Marjorie Grene on the Occasion of Her Seventy-Fifth Birthday*, Dordrecht: D. Reidel.

Doney, Willis, ed. 1967a. *Descartes: A Collection of Critical Essays*. Garden City, N.Y.: Anchor Books.

————. 1967b. Cartesianism in *The Encyclopedia of Philosophy*, 8 vols., edited by Paul Edwards, New York: Macmillan and Free Press.

————. 1967c. Nicholas Malebranche in *The Encyclopedia of Philosophy*, 8 vols., edited by Paul Edwards, New York: Macmillan and Free Press.

————. 1973. Causation in the seventeenth century, in Wiener, ed. (1973): I, 294–300.

Ducasse, C. J. 1976. Causality: critique of Hume's Analysis, in Brand, ed. (1976): 65–76.

Dugas, R., and P. Costabel. 1958. The birth of a new science: mechanics, *Taton*: 236–67.

Dugas, Rene. 1958. *Mechanics in the Seventeenth Century*, translated by Freda Jacquet. New York: Central Books.

Duhem, Pierre. 1908. *To Save the Phenomena: An Essay on the Idea of Physical Theory from Plato to Galileo*, translated by Edmund Doland and Chaninah Maschler. Chicago: University of Chicago Press, 1969.

Edwards, Paul, ed. 1967. *The Encyclopedia of Philosophy*, 8 vols. New York: Macmillan and Free Press.

Egan, Howard T. 1984. *Gassendi's View of Knowledge: A Study of the Epistemological Basis of His Knowledge*. Lanham, Md.: University Press of America.

Fogelin, R. 1985. *Hume's Skepticism in the Treatise of Human Nature*. London: Routledge & Kegan Paul.

Force, James, and Richard H. Popkin, eds. 1990. *Essays on the Context, Nature, and Influence of Isaac Newton's Theology*. Dordrecht: Kluwer.

Fouke, Daniel C. 1989. Mechanical and "organical" models in seventeenth-century explanations of biological reproduction, *Science in Context* 3: 2, 365–81.

Frankel, Lois. 1986. From a metaphysical point of view: Leibniz and the principle of sufficient reason, *Southern Journal of Philosophy* 24: 3, 321–34.

———— 1989. Causation, harmoney, and analogy, in Rescher, ed. (1989): 57–70.

———— 1993. The value of harmoney, in Nadler, ed. (1993): 197–216.

Freudenthal, Gideon. 1986. *Atom and Individual in the Age of Newton: On the*

Genesis of the Mechanistic World View. Dordrecht: Reidel.

Friedman, Michael. 1992. Causal laws and the foundations of natural science, in Guyer, ed. 1992): 161-99.

Gabbey, Alan. 1980. Force and inertia in the seventeenth century: Descartes and Newton, in Gaukroger, ed. (1980): 230–320.

———. 1985. The mechanical philosophy and its problems: Mechanical explanations, impenetrabiity, and perpetual motion, in Pitt, ed. (1985): 9–84.

———. 1990a. The case of mechanics: One revolution or many: in Lindberg and Westman, eds. (199): 493–528.

———. 1990b. Henry More and the limits of mechanism, in Hutton, ed. (1990): 20–35.

———. 1993. Descartes's physics and Descartes's mechanics: Chicken and egg? in Voss, ed. (1993): 311–23.

———. 1996. Spinoza's natural science and methodology, in Garrett, ed. (1996): 142–91.

Gale, George. 1983. Mind, body, and the laws of nature in Descartes and Leibniz, *Midwest Studies in Philosophy* 8: 105–134.

Garber, Daniel. 1985. Leibniz and the foundations of physics: the middle years, in Brown and Okruhlik, eds. (1985): 27–130.

———. 1987. How God causes motion: Descartes, divine substance, and occasinalism, *Journal of Philosophy* 84: 567–80.

———. 1987. Understanding interaction: what Descartes should have told Elizabeth, *Social Journal of Philosophy supplementary* 21: 15–32.

———. 1988. Descarters and the Aristotelians, and the revolution that did not happen in 1637, in *The Monist* 71: 471–87.

———. 1989. Physics, metaphysics and natures: Leibniz' Later Aristotelianism, in Rescher, ed. (1989): 95–169.

———. 1992. *Descartes' Metaphysical Physics.* Chicago: University of Chicago Press.

———. 1993a. Descartes and experiment in the Discourse and Essays, in Voss, ed. (1983): 288–310.

———. 1993b. Descartes and occasionalism, in Nadler, ed.: 9–26.

———. 1995. Leibniz: Physics and philosophy, in Jolley, ed. (1995): 270–352.

Garrett, Don. 1993. the representation of causation and Hume's two definitions of "cause," *Nous* 27: 167–90.

———. ed. 1996. *The Cambridge Companion to Spinoza.* New York: Cambridge University Press.

Gaukroger, Stephen, ed. 1980. *Descartes: Philosophy, Mathematics and Physics,* Sussex: Harvester Press.

————. 1989. *Cartesian Logic: An Essay on Descartes's Conception of Inference.* Oxford: Calendon Press.

Gilson, Etienne. 1937. *The Unity of Philosophical Experience.* New York: Scribner.

Glanville, Joseph. 1661. *The Vanity of Dogmatizing.* London: Henry Eversden.

Goddu, Andre. 1996. William of Ockham's distinction between "real" efficient causes and strictly sine qua non causes, *The Monist* 79: 3, 357–67.

Goodman, David C., and John Hedley Brooke, eds. 1974. *Towards a Mechanistic Philosophy.* Milton Keynes: Open University Press.

Grant, Edward. 1978. Aristotelianism and the longevity of the medieval world view, *History of Science* 16: 93–106.

Grene, Marjorie. 1963. Causes, *Philosophy* 38: 149–159.

————, ed. 1973. *Spinoza: A Collection of Critical Essays.* Modern Studies in Philosophy. Garden City, N.Y.: Doubleday/Anchor Press.

————. 1985. *Descartes.* Brighton: Harvester Press.

————. 1991. *Descartes among the Scholastics.* Milwaukee: Marquette University Press.

Grener, Marjorie, and Debra Nails, eds. 1986. *Spinoza and the Sciences.* Dordrecht and Boston: Reidel.

Grosholz, Emily R. 1991. *Cartesian Method and the Problem of Reduction.* Oxford: Clarendon Press.

Gueroult, Martial. 1980. The metaphysics and physics of force in Descartes, in Goukroger, ed. (1980): 196–229.

————. 1984. *Descartes' Philosophy Interpreted according to the Order of Reasons,* 2 vols., translated by Roger Ariew. Minneapolis: University of Minnesota Press.

Guyer, Paul, ed. 1992. *The Cambridge Companion to Kant.* Cambridge/ New York: Cambridge University Press.

Hall, Marie Boas. 1952. The establishment of the mechanical philosophy, *Osiris* 10: 412–541.

————. 1965. *Robert Boyle on Natural Philosophy.* Bloomington: Indiana University Press.

————. 1967. Kenelm Digby in *The Encyclopedia of Philosophy,* 8 vols., edited by Paul Edwards. New York: Macmillan and Free Press.

Hankins, Thomas L. 1967. The influence of Malebranche on the science of mechanics during the eighteenth century, *Journal of the History of Ideas* 28: 193–209.

Hatfield, Gary C. 1979. Force (God) in Descartes' physics, *Studies in History and Philosophy of Science* 10: 2, 113–40.

————. 1990. Metaphysics and the new science, in Lindberg and Westman, eds. (1990): 93–166.

———. 1993. Reason, nature, and God in Descartes, in Voss, ed. (1993): 259–87.

Heimann, P. M., and J. E. McGuire. 1971. Newtonian forces and Lockean powers: Concepts of matter in eighteenth-century thought, *Historical Studies in the Physical Sciences* 3: 233–306.

Henry, John. 1986. Occult qualities and the experimental philosophy: Active principles in pre-Newtonian matter theory, *Journal of the History of Science* 24: 335–81.

———. 1990. Henry More versus Robert Boyle: The Spirit of Nature and the Nature of Providence, in Hutton, ed. (1990): 55–76.

——— 1994. Boyle and the cosmical qualities, in Hunter, ed. (1994): 119-38.

Heyd, M. 1987. The new experiemental philosophy: A manifestation of "enthusiasm" or an antidote to it, *Minerva* 25.

Hobbes, Thomas. 1655–56. *Computatio Sive Logica*. (De Corpore, Part I), translation and commentary by Aloysius Martinich, edited with an introductory essay by Isabel C. Hungerland and George R. Vick. New York: Arabis Books.

Hoenen, P. H. J. 1967. Descartes' mechanism, in Doney, ed. (1967) 353–68.

Hoffman, Jashua, and Gary S. Rosenkrantz. 1994. *Substance among Other Categories*. Cambridge: Cambridge University Press.

Holland, A. J., ed. 1985. *Philosophy: Its History and Historiography*, Dordrecht: Kluwer.

Hooker, Michael, ed. 1982. *Leibniz: Critical and Interpretive Essays*. Minneapolis: University of Minnesota Press.

Hunter, Michael. 1994. *Robert Boyle Reconsidered*. Cambridge: Cambridge University Press.

Hutchinson, Keith. 1982. What happened to occult qualities in the scientific revolution? Isis 73: 233–53.

———. 1983. Supernaturalism and the mechanical philosophy, *Journal of the History of Science* 21: 297–329.

———. 1991. Dormitive virtues, scholastic qualities, and the new philosophies, *Journal of the History of Science* 29: 245–78.

Hutton, Sarah, ed. 1990. *Henry More (1614–1687): Tercentenery Studies*. Dordrecht: Kluwer.

Iltis, C. 1973. The decline of Cartesianism in mechanics: The Leibnizian-Cartesian debates, *Isis* 64: 356–73.

Jacobsen, Anne Jaap. 1984. Does Hume hold a regularity theory? *History of Philosophical Quarterly* 1: 75–92.

Jolley, Nicholas. 1984. *Leibniz and Locke: A Study of the New Essays on Human*

Understanding. Oxford, Clarendon Press.

————.1990. *The Light of the Soul: Theories of Ideas in Leibniz, Malebranche, and Descartes*. Oxford: Oxford University Press.

————. 1993. Leibniz: truth, knowledge and metaphysics, in *Routledge History of Philosophy*, 8 vols., edited by G. H. R. Parkinson. London and New York: Routledge.

————, ed. 1995. *The Cambridge Companion to Leibniz*. Cambridge: Cambridge University Press.

Joy, Lynn Sumida. 1987. *Gassendi the Atomist: Advocate of History in an Age of Science*. Cambridge: Cambridge University Press.

————. 1988. The conflict of mechanisms and its empiricist outcome, *Monist* 7: 498–514.

————. 1992. Epicureanism in renaissance philosophy, *Journal of the History of Ideas* 53: 573–83.

Kargon, R. H. 1966. *Epicurean Atomism in England from Hariot to Newton*. Oxford: Oxford University Press.

————. 1964. Walter Charleton, Robert Boyle and the acceptance of Epicruean atomism in England. *Isis* 55: 184–92.

Keating, Laura. 1993. Un-Locke-ing Boyle: Boyle on primary and secondary qualities, *History of Philosophy Quarterly* 10: 4, 305–23.

Keeling, S. V. 1968. *Descartes*, 2d ed. Oxford University Press.

Kennington, Richard, ed. 1980. *The Philosophy of Baruch Spinoza*. Studies in Philosophy and the History of Philosophy, vol.7. Washington, D.C.: Catholic University of America Press.

Kenny, Anthony. 1968. *Descartes: A Study of His Philosophy*. New York: Random House.

Klever, W. N. A. 1996. Spinoza's life and works, in Garrett, ed. (1996): 13–60.

Kovach, Francis J. 1989. Action at a distance in the cosmology and the metaphysics of Leibniz, in Rescher, ed. (1989): 71–82.

Kroll, Richard W. F. 1984. The question of Locke's relation to Gassendi and some methodological implications, *Journal of the History of Ideas* 45: 339–59.

Kulstad, Mark A., ed. 1977. *Essays on the Philosophy of Leibniz*. Rice University Studies 63: 4.

Kulstad, Mark A. 1993a. Causation and prestablished harmony in the early development of Leibniz's philosophy, in Nadler, ed. (1993): 93–117.

————. 1993b. Two interpretations of the pre-established harmony in the philosophy of Leibniz. *Synthese* 96: 477–504.

Laudan, Laurens. 1966. the clock metaphor and probabilism: The impact of Descartes on English methodological thought, 1650–65, *Annals of Science*

22: 73–104.

Leijenhorst, Cees. 1996. Hobbes's theory of causality and its Aristotelian background, *The Monist* 79: 3, 426–47.

Lennon, Thomas M. 1974. Occasionalism and the Cartesian metaphysic of motion, *Canadian Journal of Philosophy*, supplement I: 29–40.

———. 1980. Philosophical commentary, in Lennon and Olscamp, trans. (1980): 757–848.

———. 1983. Locke's atomism, *Philosophy Research Archives* 9: 1–28.

———. 1991. The Epicurean new way of ideas: Gassendi, Locke, and Berkeley, in Osler, ed. (1191): 259–71.

———. 1993a *The Battle of the Gods and Giants, The Legacies of Descartes and Gassendi, 1655–1715.* Princeton: Princeton University Press.

———. 1993b. Mechanism as a silly mouse: Bayle's defense of occasionalism against the preestablished harmony, in Nadler, ed. (1993b): 179–95.

Lennon, Thomas, M., and Patricia Ann Easton. 1992. *The Cartesian Empiricism of Francois Bayle.* New York: Galand.

Lenoble, R. 1958. The 17th-century scientific revolution, in Taton, ed. (1958): 180–199.

Lesher, James H. 1973. Hume's analysis of "cause" and the "two-definitions" dispute, *Journal of the History of Philosophy* 11: 3: 287–312.

Lindberg, David C., and Robert S. Westman, eds. 1990. *Reappraisals of the Scientific Revolution.* Cambridge: Cambridge University Press.

Lindberg, David C. 1990. Conceptions of the scientific revolution from Bacon to Butterfield: A preliminary sketch, in Lindberg and Westman, eds. (1990): 1-26.

Loeb, Louis E. 1981. *From Descartes to Hume: Continental Metaphysics and the Development of Modern Philosophy.* Ithaca: Cornell University Press.

———. 1985. Is there a problem of Cartesian interaction? *Journal of the History of Philosophy* 23: 35–49.

Machamer, Peter, and Robert G. Turnbull, eds. 1976. *Motion and Time.* Columbus: Ohio State University Press.

Machamer, Peter. 1976. Causality and explanation in Descartes's natural philosophy, in Machamer and Turnbull, eds. (1985): 168–99.

MacIntosh, J. J. 1991. Robert Boyle on Epicurean atheism and atomism, in Ostler, ed. (1991): 197–238.

MacIntyre, Alasdair. 1967. Spinoza in *The Encyclopedia of Philosophy*, 8 vols., edited by Paul Edwards. New York: Macmillan and Free Press.

MacNabb, D. G. C. 1967. David Hume in *The Encyclopedia of Philosophy*, 8 vols., edited by Paul Edwards. New York: Macmillan and Free Press.

———. 1986. Spinoza in the century of science, in Grene and Nails, eds.

(1986): 3–13.

McCann, Edwin. 1985. Lockean mechanism, in Holland, ed. (1985): 213–236.

McCracken, Charles. 1983. *Malebranche and British Philosophy*. Oxford: Oxford University Press.

McGuire, J. E. 1968. Force, active principles, and Newton's invisible realm, *Ambix*, XV: 154–208

———. 1972. Boyle's conception of nature. *Journal of the History of Ideas* 33: 523–41.

———. 1983. *Certain Philosophical Questions: Newton's Trinity Notebook*. Cambridge: Cambridge University Press.

McMullin, Ernan. 1978. *Newton on Matter and Activity*. Notre Dame: University of Notre Dame Press.

———. 1990. Conceptions of science in the scientific revolution, in Lindberg and Westman, eds. (1990): 27–92.

Mates, Benson. 1986. *The Philosophy of Leibniz*. Oxford/New York: Oxford University Press.

Mattern, Ruth. 1980. Locke on active power and the obscure ideas of active power from bodies, *Studies in the History and Philosophy of Science* 11: 39–77.

Maull, Nancy. 1978. Cartesian optics and the geometrization of nature. *Review of Metaphysics* 32: 253–73.

Michael, Emily, and Fred S. Michael. 1988. Gassendi on sensation and reflection: A non-Cartesian dualism, *History of European Ideas* 9: 583–95.

Miles, Murray Lewis. 1988. Descartes' mechanism and the medieval doctrine of causes, qualities, and forms, *Modern Schoolman* 65: 97–117.

Miller, Richard W. 1987. *Fact and Method: Explanation, Confirmation and Reality in the Natural and the Social Sciences*. Princeton: Princeton University Press.

Nadler, Steven. 1990. Deduction, confirmation, and the laws of nature in Descartes, *Principia philosophiae, Journal of the History of Philosophy* 28: 359–83.

———. 1993. Occasionalism and general will in Malebranche, *Journal of the History of Philosophy* 31: 1: 31–47.

———. 1993b. *Causation in Early Modern Philosophy*. University Park, Pennsylvania State University Press.

———. 1993c. The occasionalism of Louis de la Forge, in Nadler, ed. (1993b): 57–73.

———. 1995. Malebranche's occasionalism: A Reply to Clarke, *Journal of the History of Philosophy* 33: 505–8.

———. 1996. "No necessary connection": The medieval roots of the occasionalist roots of Hume, *The Monist* 79: 3, 448–66.

Norton, David Fate. 1981. The myth of "British Empiricism," *American Philosophical Quarterly* I: 331–44.

————, ed. 1993. *The Cambridge Companion to Hume.* Cambridge: Cambridge University Press.

Oakley, Francis. 1961. Christian theology and the Newtonian science: The rise of the concept of laws of nature, *Church History* 30: 433–57.

O'Neill, Eileen. 1983. "Mind and Mechanism: An Examination of Some Mind-Body Problems in Descartes' Philosophy" (Ph. D. diss., Princton University).

————. 1987. Mind-body interaction and metaphysical consistency: A defence of Descartes, *Journal of the History of Philosophy* 25: 2, 227–45.

————. 1993. Influxus Physicus, in Nadler, ed. (1993b): 27–55.

Osler, Margaret J. 1970. John Locke and the changing ideal of scientific knowledge, *Journal of the History of Ideas* 31: 1–16.

————. 1979. Descartes and Charleton on Nature and God, *Journal of the History of Ideas* 40: 445–56.

————. 1983. Providence and divine will in Gassendi's views on scientific knowledge, *Journal of the History of Ideas* 44: 549–60.

————, ed. 1991a. *Atoms, Pneuma, and Tranquillity: Epicurean and Stoic Themes in European Thought.* New York and Cambridge: Cambridge University Press.

————. 1991b. The intellectual sources of Robert Boyle's Philosophy of Nature, Gassendi's voluntarism, and Boyle's Phyico-Theological Project, in Ashcraft, Kroll, and Zagorin, eds. (1991): 178–98.

———— 1994. *Divine Will and the Mechanical Philosophy: Gassendi and Descartes on Contingency and Necessity in the Created World.* New York and Cambridge: Cambridge University Press.

———— 1996. From immanent natures to nature as artifice: The reinterpretation of final causes in seventeenth-century natural Philosophy, *The Monist* 79:3, 388–407.

Osler, M., and P. L. Farber, eds. 1985. *Religion, Science and Worldview.* Cambridge: Cambridge University Press.

O'Toole, Frederick J. 1974. Qualities and powers in the corpuscular philosophy of Robert Boyle, *Journal of the History of Philosophy* 12: 4, 295–315.

Papineau, David. 1981. The vis viva controversy, in Woolhouse, ed. (1981): 139–56.

Parkinson, George Henry Radcliffe. 1954. *Spinoza's Theory of Knowledge.* Oxford: Clarendon.

————. 1969. Science and metaphysics in the Leibniz-Newton controversy, *Studia Leibnitiana supplementa* 2: 79–112.

————, ed. 1993a. *Routledge History of Philosophy*, 8 vols. London and New York: Routledge.

————. 1993b. Spinoza: Metaphysics and knowledge in *Routledge History of Philosophy*. 8 vols., edited by G. H. R. Parkinson. London and New York: Routledge.

Passmore, John. 1967. Robert Boyle in *The Encyclopedia of Philosophy*, 8 vols., edited by Paul Edwards. New York: Macmillan and Free Press.

Penelhum, Terence. 1992. *David Hume: An Introduction to his Philosophical System*. West Lafayette, Indiana: Purdue University Press.

Peters, R. S. 1967. Thomas Hobbes in *The Encyclopedia of Philosophy*, 8 vols., edited by Paul Edwards. New York: Macmillan and Free Press.

Pitt, Joseph C., ed. 1985. *Change and Progress in Modern Science*. Dordrecht: Reidel.

Popkin, Richard H. 1964. So, Hume did read Berkeley, *Journal of Philosophy* 61: 774–75.

————. 1967. Pierre Gassendi in *The Encyclopedia of Philosophy*, 8 vols., edited by Paul Edwards. New York: Macmillan and Free Press.

Radner, Daisie. 1971. Descartes' notion of the union of mind and body, *Journal of the History of Philosophy* 9: 2, 159–70.

————. 1978. *Malebranche*. Amsterdam: Van Gorcum.

————. 1993. Occasionalism in *Routledge History of Philosophy*, 8 vols., edited by G. H. R. Parkinson. London and New York: Routledge.

————. 1985. Is there a problem of Cartesian interaction? *Journal of the History of Philosophy* 23: 227–31.

Reid, Thomas. 1880. *Works*, 8th ed., edited by W. Hamilton. Edinburgh.

Rescher, Nicholas. 1981. *Leibniz's Metaphysics of Nature*. Dordrecht: Reidel.

————, ed. 1989. *Leibnizian Inquiries*. New York: University Press of America.

Richards, Thomas J. 1966. Hume's two definitions of cause, in Chappell, ed. (1966): 148–61.

Richardson, Robert. 1985. Replies to Daisie Radner's "is there a problem of Cartesian interaction?" *Journal of the History of Philosophy* 23: 221–26.

Richmond, Samuel A. 1994. Newton and Hume on causation: Alternative strategies of simplification, *History of Philosophy Quarterly* 11: 12, 37–52.

Riker, Stephen. 1996. Al-Ghazali on necessary causality in The Incoherence of the Philosophers, *The Monist* 79: 3, 315–24.

Robinson, J. A. 1966. Hume's two definitions of "cause," in Chappell, ed. (1966): 129–47.

Rodis-Lewis, Genevierve. 1993. From metaphysics to physics, in Voss, ed. (1993): 242–258.

Romanell, Patrick. 1984. *John Locke and Medicine: A New Key to Locke*. Buffalo:

Prometheus.

Rome, Beatrice K. 1963. *The Philosophy of Malebranche.* Chicago: Regnery.

Rosenberg, Alexander. 1993. Hume and the philosophy of science, in Norton, ed. (1993): 64–89.

Russell, L. J. 1967. Gottfried Wilhelm Leibniz in *The Encyclopedia of Philosophy,* 8 vols., edited by Paul Edwards. New York: Macmillan and Free Press.

――――. 1980. The correspondence between Leibniz and De Volder, in Woolhouse, ed. (1981): 105–18.

Rutherford, Donald P. 1993. Natures, laws, and miracles: The roots of Leibniz's critique of occasionalism, in Nadleer, ed. (1993b): 145–58.

――――. 1995. Metaphysics: The late period, in Jolley, ed. (1995): 124–75.

Salmon, Wesley C. 1990. *Four Decades of Scientific Explanation.* Minneapolis: University of Minnesota Press.

Sanchez-Gonzalez, M. A. 1990. Medicine in John Locke's philosophy. *The Journal of Medicine and Philosophy* 15: 675–95.

Sarasohn, Lisa T. 1985. Motion and morality: Pierre Gassendi, Thomas Hobbes, and the mechanical world-view, *Journal of the History of Ideas* 46: 363–79.

Sargent, Rose-Mary. 1986. Robert Boyle's Baconian inheritance: A response to Laudan's Cartesian thesis, *Studies in History and Philosophy of Science* 17: 469–86.

――――― 1995. *The Difffident Naturalist: Robert Boyle and the Philosophy of Experiment.* Chicago and London: University of Chicago Press.

Savan, David. 1986. Spinoza: scientist and theorist of scientific method, in Grene and Nails, eds. (1986): 95–123.

Schouls, Peter A. 1970. Cartesian certainty and the "natural light," *Australiasian Journal of Philosophy* 50: 30–39.

Schuster, John A. 1993. Whatever should we do with Cartesian method? Reclaiming Descartes for the history of science, in Voss, ed. (1933): 195–223.

Shannahan, Timothy. 1988. God and nature in the thought of Robert Boyle, *Journal of the History of Philosophy* (October): 547–69.

Shoemaker, Sydney. 1986. *Identity, properties, and causality, in identity, Causality, and Mind.* Ithaca: Cornell University Press.

Sleigh, R. C., Jr. 1990a. *Leibniz and Arnauld: A Commentary on Their Correspondence.* New Haven: Yale University Press.

――――. 1990b. Leibniz on Malebranche on causality, Cover and Kulstad, eds. (1990): 161–93.

Soles, D. 1985. Locke's empiricism and the postulaton of unobservables,

Journal of the History of Philosophy 23: 339–70.

Sorrell, Tom. 1986. *Hobbes*. London and New York: Routledge & Kegan Paul.

———. 1988 Descartes, Hobbes, and the body of natural science. *The Monist* 7: 515–25.

———. 1993. Seventeenth-century materialism: Gassendi and Hobbes in *Routledge History of Philosophy*, 8 vols., edited by G. H. R. Parkinson. London and New York: Routledge.

Sorley, W. R. 1965. *A History of British Philosophy to 1900*. Cambridge: Cambridge University Press.

Spector, Marshall. 1975. Leibniz vs. Cartesians on motion and force, *Studia Leibnitiana* 7: 135–44.

Strawson, Galen. 1989. *The Secret Connexion: Causation, Realism, and David Hume*. Oxford; Clarendon Press.

Suarez, Francis. 1597a. *Disputationes metaphysicae* as in Norman J. Wells, trans. *On the Essence of Finite Being as Such, On the Existence of That Essence and their Distinction* [Disputation XXXI] (1983). Milwaukee: Marquette University Press.

———. 1597b. *Disputationes metaphysicae* as in Cyril Vollert, trans. *On the Various Kinds of Distinctions* [Disputation VII] (2947). Milwaukee: Marquette University Press.

Taton, Rene, ed. 1958. *The Beginnings of Modern Science: From 1450–1800*. London: Thames and Hudson.

Thomas Aquinas, St. 1970. *Commentary on the Posterior Analytics of Aristotle by St. Thomas Aquinas*, translated by F. R. Larcher. Albany: Magi Books.

Tipston, I. C., ed. 1977. *Locke on Human Understanding*. Oxford: Oxford University Press.

Turbayne, C. M., ed. 1982. *Berkeley: Critical and Interpretive Essays*. Minneapolis: University of Minnesota Press.

van Fraassen, Bas C. 1980. *The Scientific Image*. Oxford; Clarendon Press.

Vienne, J. 1993. Locke on real essence and internal constitution, *Proceedings of the Aristotelian Society* 93: 139–53.

von Leyden, W. 1968. *Seventeenth-Century Metaphysics: An Examination of Some Main Concepts and Theories*. New York: Barnes & Noble.

Voss, Stephen, ed. 1993. *Essays on the Philosophy and Science of René Descartes*. New York and Oxford: Oxford University Press.

Wagner, Stephen. 1993. Mind-body interaction in Descartes, in Voss, ed. (1993): 115–27.

Wallace, William a. 1972. *Causality and Scientific Explanation*, 2 vols. Ann Arbor: University of Michigan Press.

Walton, Craig. 1969. Malebranche's ontology, *Journal of the History of*

Philosophy 7: 2: 143–61.

Watkins, J. W. N. 1975. Metaphysics and the advancement of science, *British Journal for the Philosophy of Science* 26: 91–121.

Watson, Richard A. 1966. *The Downfall of Cartesianism, 1673–1712*. The Hague: Martinus Nijhoff.

———. 1967. Jacque Rohault in *The Encyclopedia of Philosophy*, 8 vols., edited by Paul Edwards, New York: Macmillan and Free Press.

———. 1982. What moves the mind: An excursion in Cartesian metaphysics, *American Philosophical Quarterly* 19: 73–81.

———. 1987a. *The Breakdown of Cartesian Metaphysics*. Atlantic Highlands, N.J.: Humanities Press.

———. 1987b. The Cartesian theology of Louis de La Forge, in Watson, ed. (1987a): 171–77.

———. 1993. Malebranche, models, and causation, in Nadler, ed. (1993b): 75–91.

Watt, A. J. 1972. The causality of God in Spinoza's philosophy, *Canadian Journal of Philosophy* 2: 2, 171–89.

Westfall, R. S. 1958. *Science and Religion in Seventeenth-Century England*. New Haven: Yale University Press.

——— 1962. The foundations of Newton's philosophy of nature, *British Journal of the History of Science* 1: 2, 173–82.

———. 1971a. *The Construction of Modern Science*. New York: Wiley.

———. 1971b. *Force in Newton's Physics: The Science of Dynamics in the Seventeenth Century*. New York: American Elsevier.

Wiener, Philip P., ed. 1959. *Leibniz Selections*. New York: Scribners.

———, ed. 1973. *Dictionary of the History of Ideas*, 5 vols. New York: Scribner.

Williams, Bernard. 1967. René Descartes in *The Encyclopedia of Philosophy*, 8 vols., edited by Paul Edwards. New York: Macmillan and Free Press.

———. 1978. *Descartes: The Project of Pure Inquiry*. Harmondworth: Penguin.

Wilson, Margaret D. 1976. Leibniz's dynamics and contingency in nature, in Machamer and Turnbull, eds. (1976): 264–89.

———. 1978. *Descartes*. London: Routledge & Kegan Paul.

———. 1979. Superadded powers: The limits of mechanism in Locke, *American Philosophical Quarterly* 16: 143–50.

———. 1990. Descartes on the representaionality of sensaton, in Cover and Kulstad, eds. (1990): 1–22.

———. 1991. Spinoza's causal axiom (Ethics I, Axiom 4), in Yovel, ed. (1991), 133–60.

———. 1993. Compossibility and law, in Nadler, ed. (1993b): 119–33.

———. 1996. Spinoza's theory of knowledge, in Garrett, ed. (1996): 89–141.

Wood, Rega, and Robert Andrews. 1996. Causality and demonstration: An early Scholastic Posterior Analytics commentary, *The Monist* 79: 3, 325–56.

Woolhouse, Roger, ed. 1981. *Leibniz: Metaphysics and Philosophy of Science*. Oxford: Oxford University Press.

———. 1982. The nature of an individual substance, in Hooker, ed. (1982): 45–64.

———. 1988. *The Empiricists*. Oxford and New York: Oxford University Press.

———. 1990. Spinoza and Descartes and the existence of extended substance, in Cover and Kulstad, eds. (1990): 23–48.

———. 1993. *Descartes, Spinoza, Leibniz*. London and New York: Routledge.

Wright, John P. 1983. *The Sceptical Realism of David Hume*. Minneapolis: University of Minnesota Press.

Yablo, Stephen. 1990. The real distinction between mind and body, *Canadian Journal of Philosophy Supplementary* 16: 23–32.

Yates, F. 1984. *Thinking Matter: Materialism in Eighteenth-Century Britain*. Oxford: Basil Blackwell.

Yovel, Yirmiyahu. 1991. *God and Nature in Spinoza's Metaphysics*. Leiden and New York: Brill.

INDEX

Salmon, W. C., 210
Sargent, R., 165
Scholastics, the, 12–15, 17, 19,
59, 66, 81–2, 105, 111, 130,
147, 158, 176, 207. *See also*
Aristotle; influx model of, 83
science, 78–80; epistemology of,
48
scientific: explanation, 4, 48, 68,
75, 82, 84, 90, 93, 97, 137,
157, 167, 186, 190, 194–5,
202, 206, 208, 210; inquiry,
188; knowledge, 194; laws,
146, 154, 195; revolution, 159
Seratimidis, N., 213n 1, 214n 1
Sextus Empiricias, 93
signifier, 79
signs, 79, 89–90, 194
Sleigh, R. C. Jr., 3, 42, 116, 122,
147–8, 151, 213n 4
Snell's law, 144
Sorell, T., 80
Spinoza, 7, 17, 48, 57, 129–55,
184, 186, 194–5, 198, 213n
2; concept of causation, 138,
141; *Descartes's Principles*,
129; *Ethics*, 2, 47, 129–30,
133–41, 146; *Theological-
Political Treatise*, 130
Spinozism, 130–1, 147
Stoics, the, 89
Suarez, F., 12–13

substances, 43, 71, 103–4, 108,
114–15, 118–19, 122, 129,
131, 133, 142–3, 146–8,
152–3, 169–70, 184, 187–8,
190, 194, 199, 206, 207;
alteration of, 32; concept of,
2; created, 33–4, 39, 42–3,
48, 149; finite, 32; material,
191–2, 206
suppositions, 56–7
synthesis, 53–4, 76–7, 110

theology, 18, 47
transference model, 29–30, 44,
142
truths, 50, 56, 63–4, 66, 89, 91,
109, 113, 116, 124–5, 133,
137, 151, 167, 176
Tschirnhause, Baron von, 130

vacuum, 167–8, 177–8, 181

Wagner, S., 35
Watson, R., 74–5, 119, 124
Watt, A. J., 136
Westfall, R. S., 93, 159
Whiston, W., 191
Williams, B., 43
Wilson, M. D., 2, 26–7, 29, 38,
43, 213n 1
Woolhouse, R., 150